DIVIDED SOCIETIES

Class Struggle in Contemporary Capitalism

RALPH MILIBAND

CLARENDON PRESS · OXFORD
1989

Oxford University Press, Walton Street, Oxford OX2 6DP
Oxford New York Toronto
Delhi Bombay Calcutta Madras Karachi
Petaling Jaya Singapore Hong Kong Tokyo
Nairobi Dar es Salaam Cape Town
Melbourne Auckland
and associated companies in
Berlin Ibadan

Oxford is a trade mark of Oxford University Press

Published in the United States
by Oxford University Press, New York

© Ralph Miliband 1989

British Library Cataloguing in Publication Data

Miliband, Ralph
Divided societies.
1. Capitalism
I. Title
330.12'2
ISBN 0-19-827535-8

Library of Congress Cataloging in Publication Data
Miliband, Ralph.
Divided societies: class struggle in contemporary capitalism
Ralph Miliband.
Bibliography: p.
Includes index.
(Oxford University Press)
1. Capitalism.   2. Social conflicts.   3. Pressure groups.
4. Elite (Social sciences)   I. Title.
HB501.M655   1989   305.5—dc20   89-15975
ISBN 0-19-827535-8

Set by Oxford Text System
Printed in Great Britain by
Courier International Ltd
Tiptree, Essex

Preface

THIS book has its origins, by now fairly distant, in the Marshall Lectures which I gave at the University of Cambridge in Spring 1982, under the title 'Class Conflict Revisited'. My purpose in the lectures was twofold: first, to discuss the meaning which should nowadays be attached to the notion of class conflict in the context of advanced capitalism; and secondly, to argue that, in the meaning which I attributed to it, and in that context, class conflict remained the most important, indeed the absolutely central, fact in the life of advanced capitalist societies.

The same purpose has also inspired the present work. The lectures were no more than a very preliminary foray into a very complex and controversial field; and I am grateful to the Faculty of Economic and Social Science at Cambridge for giving me the opportunity to present then the ideas I was seeking to develop. It was obviously not possible in the compass of those lectures to explore many of the issues which the subject raised. This is what I have tried to do in this book. Even now, I am very conscious that each of the issues which is discussed here could do with a great deal of further elaboration and discussion. But there is a limit to what can be done in a single book, particularly where, as in the present case, the nature of the subject requires consideration of a large number of seemingly disparate questions. At least, I hope to show that, disparate though the questions may seem to be, they do in fact form part of a total process—namely, the process of class struggle.

I should also say that the work I have done for the book since I gave the lectures has strongly confirmed my belief that class struggle (which is, I think, a better term for my purpose than class conflict, in so far as it conveys more strongly a sense of striving and pressure) is the key phenomenon for the understanding of the societies in question. To say this today is to run the risk of instant dismissal as an unreconstructed fundamentalist, obstinately blind to the vast changes which have occured in these societies, and which have, so it is insistently claimed, rendered the 'old' notions of class struggle irrelevant and obsolete. I will have more to say about such claims later; but I would urge any impatient reader to surmount his or her impatience and at least to consider seriously the argument which I seek to present here.

My point of departure is what I take to be Marx's 'model' of class struggle; and this requires a frequent use of references to the writings of Marx and, to a lesser extent, those of Engels. But I should like to stress that the book is in no sense yet another exegesis of these writings, or an attempt to demonstrate their validity. It is or should be obvious that a theoretical construct elaborated in the mid-nineteenth century cannot be adequate and sufficient for the interpretation of social reality at the end of the twentieth. This, however, does not mean, as is so often suggested, that the 'model' should be discarded. I think that Marx had the essence of the matter; but that a point of departure cannot be taken as a point of arrival, and that the 'model', as will be suggested in the following pages, requires substantial modifications in the light of later developments.

My main frame of reference is advanced capitalist countries—notably Britain and the United States, though I believe that the main argument is applicable to all such countries. They are of course very different in many important respects: but they nevertheless have some crucial characteristics in common, and this, I believe, makes it possible to view them as one kind of economic, social, and political system, without however losing sight of their differences and specificities.

The three main characteristics which these countries have in common are: first, that they are highly developed in industrial and technological terms; second, that the predominant part of their means of economic activity—industrial, commercial, and financial—is under private ownership and control; and third, that all of them have had the same kind of political regime since World War II, namely, what is commonly called 'democracy', but what is more accurately called 'capitalist democracy'—and most of them have in fact had a capitalist–democratic regime a great deal longer than that.

These *combined* characteristics differentiate the countries concerned both from Communist societies on the one hand, and from non-Communist ones in the 'third world' on the other. A few Communist countries—the USSR, Czechoslovakia, the German Democratic Republic—have a highly industrialized and technologically advanced economic base, but the means of economic activity in all Communist states, whatever their level of economic development, are for the most part under public ownership and control (though this may have to be increasingly qualified in the years to come); and their political regimes are also radically different from those of capitalist democracies.

As for the non-Communist countries of the 'third world', they do have private ownership and control of the main part of their means of economic activity, and some of them also have capitalist-democratic regimes, but they are generally at a fairly low level of industrial and technological development—often at a very low level—and this differentiates them very profoundly from advanced capitalist countries.

In Chapter 1, I discuss some of the fundamental propositions of class analysis in relation to class struggle; and I also suggest there some of the modifications which need to be made to the classical Marxist 'model' of such struggle. Furthermore, I note in this chapter some of the main questions and criticisms which I seek to answer in the book.

In Chapter 2, I present a 'social map' of advanced capitalist societies, and identify the main classes which make up their social structure.

Chapter 3 is concerned with class struggle 'from below', mainly with reference to struggles and pressures involving members of the working class, and articulated (in their own way) by such organizations as trade unions and political parties. A major theme of this chapter is the decisive influence which capitalist democracy has had upon the nature and forms which this 'pressure from below' has assumed.

Chapter 4 considers sources of conflict and pressure related to gender, race, and ethnicity, and to such concerns as ecology and peace; and I discuss there the significance of these movements in relation to their own aims and to social change in general.

Chapter 5 deals with class struggle 'from above', with particular emphasis on what I take to be the 'partnership' which links capital and the state in that struggle; and I also discuss there the main ways in which conservative forces seek to maintain the existing structures of power, property, and privilege.

Chapter 6 is concerned with the international dimension of class struggle, and notably with the ways in which external intervention has since the end of World War II affected internal struggles for reform or revolution all over the world. External intervention is in fact a crucial factor in class struggle; and I also argue in this chapter that it is in the attempt to contain and defeat movements of revolution and radical reform that the roots of confrontation between East and West must be sought.

Finally, Chapter 7 discusses the future of class struggle in advanced capitalist societies, and the alternative scenarios which may be proposed in this connection; and I suggest in this chapter why it is illusory to think that class struggle in these societies is coming to an end.

An enormous literature already exists on the issues which are discussed in this book. I have derived great benefit from what I have been able to read of this literature, and (as will be seen from my references) I have made extensive use of other people's empirical findings. My own purpose has not been to add to the empirical material, but rather to 'theorize' class struggle in ways which seem to me appropriate to the understanding of social reality, and which are not on the whole to be found in the relevant literature.

Anthony Giddens, Leo Panitch, John Saville, Andrew Schuller of Oxford University Press, John Westergaard, and an anonymous reader for the Press, read an earlier version of the book, and I am grateful for their comments and suggestions. A great deal that appears in the book was at one time or another presented to graduate seminars, notably at York University, Toronto, and at the Graduate School of the City University of New York. I found the sharp controversies which were often generated in these seminars extremely useful in clarifying my thoughts, and I am grateful to the students who were involved in the controversies. I also acknowledge with much pleasure the benefits I have derived from my many discussions with David and Edward Miliband. My greatest debt, as usual, is to Marion Kozak for her acute criticisms and unfailing support. Of course, I alone am responsible for what follows.

Marcel Liebman, to whose memory this book is dedicated, allied an intrepid spirit to a questing mind and a great warmth of character. The dedication is a small token of gratitude for a close friendship extending over some thirty years.

August 1988 R.M.

Contents

1

Introduction

In a letter written in 1852 to his friend Wedemeyer in the United
States, Marx said that he made no claim 'to have discovered
either the existence of classes in modern society or the struggle
between them.' 'Long before me', he went on, 'bourgeois his-
torians had described the historical development of this struggle
between the classes, as had bourgeois economists their economic
anatomy.'[1] But notwithstanding this disclaimer, it was undoubtedly Marx (and Engels) who did give to class and class
struggle the theoretical basis for what has come to be known as
class analysis; and it is with the nature and substance of class
analysis, and with its relationship to the notion of class struggle,
that I am mainly concerned in this introductory chapter.[2]

In its classical Marxist form, class analysis embodies a very
large claim: namely, that it provides a uniquely powerful *organizing
principle* of social and political analysis; and that, as such, it offers
the best method available to give theoretical and empirical
coherence to the enormous accumulation of data of every kind
which makes up the historical record and the present life of
society.

Marx himself once sarcastically warned, in another letter—this
time in 1877 to the Editor of the Russian journal *Otechestevennye
Zapiski*—against any attempt to use 'as one's master key a general
historico-philosophical theory, the supreme virtue of which consists in being super-historical'.[3] The warning is well taken, but
class analysis does not, or at least need not, fall under the rubric
'super-historical' or 'historico-philosophical': on the contrary, it
is very firmly grounded in historical and contemporary reality,
and thoroughly testable in relation to it.

For his part, Engels, writing two years after Marx's death,
proclaimed that

it was precisely Marx who had first discovered the great law of motion of history, the law according to which all historical struggles, whether they proceed in the political, religious, philosophical or some other ideological domain, are in fact the more or less clear expression of struggles of social classes.

This 'law', Engels added, in characteristic fashion, had 'the same significance for history as the law of the transformation of energy for natural science'.[4]

This kind of reference to 'laws' in relation to human affairs is now very unfashionable, indeed highly suspect. On the Right, it is readily denounced as doctrinaire arrogance, crass historicism, naïve hubris, and other such sins, all of which inexorably point in the direction of totalitarianism and the Gulag Archipelago. But many people on the Marxist Left have themselves come to be very cautious about the claims which they think it proper to make on behalf of class analysis in the Marxist mode as a tool of historical and contemporary analysis. Very commonly in recent years, such analysis has come to be criticized from within the Marxist Left (or the 'post-Marxist' Left) as fatally flawed by a simplistic and obsolete 'class reductionism', which robs it of the capacity to account for crucial aspects of social reality—for instance, the failure of the working class to play the historical role of 'grave-diggers' of capitalism assigned to it by Marx and later Marxists; or the enduring strength of sexism, racism, and nationalism, not least among the working class and in labour movements; or the experience of Communist regimes; and a lot else which, it is alleged, mocks and defies class analysis.[5]

These and other such strictures will be considered presently. But I should perhaps state my own view at the outset that, even though class analysis does run the danger of a simplistic kind of economic reductionism, such a deformation is not inherent in the mode of analysis itself; and that, handled with all due care, it does constitute a uniquely valuable approach to the interpretation of social reality.

II

The fundamental proposition of class analysis in classical Marxism is enshrined in the famous passage in the *Communist Manifesto* in which Marx and Engels declared that 'the history of all hitherto existing society is the history of class struggle':

Freeman and slave, patrician and plebeian, lord and serf, guildmaster and journeyman—in a word, oppressor and oppressed, stood in constant opposition to one another, carried on an uninterrupted, now hidden, now open fight, a fight that each time ended either in a revolutionary re-constitution of society at large or in the common ruin of the contending classes.[6]

Seen in this way, class analysis is largely *class struggle analysis*. It is a mode of analysis which proceeds from the belief that class struggle has constituted the central fact of social life from the remote past to the present day. The subject-matter of class analysis is the nature of this struggle, the identity of the protagonists, the forms which the struggle assumes from one period to another and from one country to another, the reasons for the differences in these forms, and the consequences which flow from these differences; and class analysis is also concerned with the ideological constructs under which the struggle is conducted, and with the ways in which class relations in general affect most if not all aspects of life.

This mode of analysis clearly has a very strong 'economic' theme; but it also has strong political and ideological themes, which are intertwined with the economic one, and all of them come together in an inseparable totality. It is not the 'economic factor' which provides the 'master key' to the understanding of historical or contemporary reality, but class relations and the struggles which they generate. Class analysis, in this sense, could be described, somewhat grandiosely, as the 'science of class struggle'.

In the classical Marxist perspective, the main protagonists of class struggle are the owners of the means of production on the one hand, and the producers on the other; and these protagonists are locked in a conflictual situation which is absolutely ineluctable, 'structurally' determined by their respective location in the process of production itself. This is so because the owners of the means of production are necessarily driven to try and extract the greatest amount of surplus labour which it is possible to extract from the producers in the given historical conditions; whereas the producers, for their part, are driven with the same compelling force to try and minimize that amount, and to work under the least burdensome conditions which it is possible for them to achieve.

According to this view, the relationship between owners and producers is essentially one of exploitation, a term which is quite naturally charged with very strong normative connotations, but which may also be used in a 'technical', descriptive sense to denote the appropriation of surplus labour by people other than the producers, on the basis of property or position.

This appropriation of surplus labour is not of course peculiar to capitalism. As Marx noted in the first volume of *Capital*,

capital did not invent surplus labour. Wherever a part of society possesses the monopoly of the means of production, the worker, free or unfree, must add to the labour-time necessary for his own maintenance an extra quantity of labour-time in order to produce the means of subsistence for the owner of the means of production.[7]

The intensity of exploitation has varied enormously over the ages; and its degree clearly depends on many different factors and circumstances—the nature of the mode of production and its class relations, material and cultural conditions, the degree of resistance which exploitation encounters, and so on. Children may be put to work at a very early age, or not; and the conditions under which production is carried on are subject to great variations over time and place. But the specific circumstances in which exploitation occurs—crucial though this is for the workers themselves—can only affect its character and intensity: exploitation itself remains. Its existence is inscribed in the very nature of the process of appropriation, whatever the conditions under which it occurs.

Marx noted on more than one occasion that all societies, whatever their mode of production and character, need to appropriate some part of the product from the producers for such purposes as the reproduction and extension of productive capacity, the provision of collective services, the maintenance and welfare of the young, the old, the sick, and the handicapped.[8] In a classless society, however, these purposes would presumably be the *only* ones for which such appropriation would occur: no part of the product would be appropriated on the basis of property rights or privileged position. In such circumstances, the appropriation of surplus labour by some such public agency as the state and the allocation of part of the surplus product to recipients other than the producers might not warrant the label 'exploitation'; or it would, at least, be something like 'socialized exploitation', undertaken for common and agreed purposes.

The antagonism and struggle generated by the opposed interests of owners and producers manifest themselves in very different forms, and the intensity of the struggle between them is by no means necessarily commensurate with the intensity of exploitation. There may indeed be extended periods in which the struggle assumes very weak collective forms, or even no collective form at all, and is confined to covert acts of individual resistance or revenge (the slave spitting in the soup he has prepared for the masters, or a worker engaging in a small piece of sabotage), because those subject to exploitation are unable or unwilling, for whatever reason, to struggle against it in organized fashion.

Nor are conflict and co-operation between owners and producers necessarily incompatible: the two do in fact regularly coexist, even though they may do so very uneasily. It would be impossible for production and economic activity in general to proceed—at least, in the conditions of capitalist democracy, where there are limits to the degree of coercion which may be employed towards labour—if a certain level of co-operation could not be elicited from the producers; and most employers are well aware of the fact. A host of different factors clearly intervene to determine the precise attitude of employers towards their workers; but it is only a very stupid employer who would want to use a strategy of unremitting warfare against his or her employees. Where repressive legislation is readily available, employers in dispute with their workers may well want to invoke it, resort to the courts, seek injunctions, and so forth. But many employers prefer less abrasive strategies so as to safeguard future relations. In other words, class struggle at the point of production does not rage permanently and is not red in tooth and claw. Nevertheless, the antagonism is there, and precludes effective pacification: such co-operation as is achieved is always fraught and unstable, and frequently collapses into confrontation and conflict.

Another point, of great importance for the whole discussion of class struggle, is that the protagonists may not themselves have any notion that it is 'class struggle' in which they are engaged, even though they are well aware that they are engaged in some

kind of conflict. Geoffrey de Ste Croix is right to defend the use
of the term 'class struggle' even in situations 'in which there may
be *no explicit common awareness* of class on either side, *no specifically
political struggle* at all, and perhaps even *little* consciousness of
struggle . . .'.[9] Similarly, Louise and Charles Tilly, referring to
a variety of struggles, note that their image of class conflict

> opens us to the objection that the people involved did not cast their
> actions in terms of class, were not truly aware of their class interests or
> defined their enemies accurately. To these hypothetical objections, we
> can only reply that such demanding standards for class conflict nearly
> banish class conflict from history; however engaging the vision of workers
> speaking in class terms and acting decisively on the basis of an accurate
> perception of their interests and enemies, the event itself has been rare
> indeed. We settle for a less demanding and wider ranging conception of
> class conflict.[10] .

I shall return presently to the question of class consciousness;
but I note here that it seems perfectly reasonable to say that the
nature of the struggles in which people are engaged is not
determined by the perception which they have of it. That
perception is extremely important in many different ways, and
may well determine the *form* and the *outcome* of the struggle; but
this does not all the same determine its *nature*. Workers (and
employers) may not define struggles in which they are engaged
in class terms at all; but that does not mean that these struggles
cannot be described in such terms. The same, incidentally, is true
for other struggles, for instance, war. Soldiers in war may well
believe that they are fighting for Queen and Country, or for the
defence of their homeland and their families, or for the greater
glory of God, or whatever; but the war may nevertheless he
fought for entirely different reasons—as in the case of colonialist
or imperialist wars.

III

The Marxist emphasis on the extraction of surplus labour as of
paramount importance is, I believe, altogether justified. But the
focus on the exploitation of workers by employers which this
entails is nevertheless too narrow, on a number of counts. For

one thing, it tends to occlude or cast into shadow struggles which are not directly related to the process of exploitation at the point of production, for instance, over social welfare and benefits, collective services, the incidence of taxation, trade union and civic rights, and many more, all of which are clearly part of class struggle.

Relatedly, these struggles may involve many people who, though members of the working class, are not workers, at the point of production—unemployed or retired workers for instance, and other workers who are not 'direct producers', and a great many other people as well. In the same vein, the focus on employers leaves out of account a major protagonist in class struggle: the state.

Also, the emphasis on exploitation at the point of production tends to ignore struggles by various movements based on gender, race, or ethnicity, or on causes such as ecological protection or disarmament. These 'new social movements', which are discussed in Chapter 4, are not 'class struggles' in the general meaning of the term, but they are nevertheless important forms of protest and pressure, and require consideration in the analysis of conflict in the countries of advanced capitalism.

Finally, the focus on exploitation also occludes the general phenomenon of domination. Exploitation and domination are closely linked, in so far as the latter is indispensable for the achievement of the former. But domination also encompasses aspects of human relations which do not come within the meaning ascribed to exploitation in the Marxist sense of the world. The most obvious example is provided by the many aspects of the domination of women by men which are 'exploitative' in ways other than, or additional to, their exploitation at the point of production.

The emphasis on domination, it may be added, does not in the least conflict with Marx's own perspectives. On the contrary, the issue of domination was at the very core of his thought, and is inextricably linked with that of exploitation. Marx's whole purpose might indeed be summed up as being the achievement of a social order in which all relations of domination and exploitation had been abolished. It is the concern with domination, and with the process of exploitation which it makes possible, which informs every page of *Capital*, and which makes the work a treatise on domination, with particular reference to the forms of exploitation which it makes possible under capitalism.

Class domination means the capacity of a particular class to create and maintain conditions under which it is able to appropriate surplus labour. In this connection, a sharp distinction has often been drawn between capitalism and earlier modes of production in regard to the role of coercion in the extraction of surplus labour. Thus Perry Anderson writes that

capitalism is the first mode of production in history in which the means whereby the surplus which is pumped out of the direct producers is 'purely economic' in form—the wage contract: the equal exchange between free agents reproduces, hourly and daily, inequality and oppression. All the previous modes of exploitation operate through *extra-economic* sanctions—kin, customary, religious, legal and political.[11]

There is an important element of truth in such formulations. But they also tend to obscure the degree of coercion which is present in the extraction of surplus labour under the capitalist mode of production. No doubt there are major differences in the ways in which coercion is exercised in that mode of production as compared with earlier ones. Most notably, capitalist employers do not have anything like the power to coerce and punish that was available to owners and controllers of the means of production in earlier times. Nevertheless, coercion and the threat of coercion have remained an intrinsic part of the capitalist mode of production: and this has been a crucial issue of class struggle, at the point of production and beyond it. It is only by dint of pressure and struggle, by workers and others, that the degree of coercive power which employers were able to deploy against their workers was eroded. Thus many of the weapons which were available to employers in the early stages of the Industrial Revolution, such as the beating of children and apprentices, or the imposition of fines for indiscipline, are no longer readily available;[12] and the use of such other weapons as dismissal, demotion, discrimination, and harassment is, to a greater or lesser extent, depending on the country, somewhat circumscribed, particularly where trade unionism is strong and militant. But these weapons are by no means obsolete anywhere, and remain an important part of the coercive power of employers.

The really important difference in this respect between the

capitalist and earlier modes of production is not that capitalism does not rely on coercion or the threat of coercion, but that the control and management of coercion have very largely passed into the hands of the state. It is the state which assumes prime responsibility for the protection of owners' rights and managerial authority, which enforces contracts and punishes transgressions by workers, which regulates and curtails the rights of workers in the labour process, and which limits the ways in which employers can be resisted—for instance, by imposing legal constraints on the right to strike or to picket; and it is also the state which, conversely, is required to impose limits upon the exercise of managerial power in relation to workers.

Seen thus, the relations of production of capitalism are far from being purely 'economic': they are governed by custom, convention, past struggles, class successes and class defeats, 'conjunctural' circumstances, and ultimately by the coercive power of employers and the state. In this sense, there are similarities as well as differences between the capitalist and earlier modes of production: just as the extraction of surplus labour under capitalism is not purely 'economic', so was its extraction under earlier modes of production not purely coercive. As Rodney Hilton notes in regard to feudalism, 'the peasantry was sufficiently cohesive, at least at the local level, to place definite limits on seigneurial exploitation.'[13]

A major reason why coercion, in one form or another, must necessarily be part of the capitalist mode of production is that capitalism is peculiarly prone to resistance and struggle. This is not because capitalism is necessarily more oppressive than earlier systems of exploitation, but precisely because producers under capitalism, as formally free agents, are better able to struggle against their employers than was ever previously the case. Not only are they better able to do so individually, but also collectively: the notion of a trade union or party of slaves or of serfs is absurd, whereas trade unions of wage-earners are the 'natural' product of the capitalist mode of production.

The very nature of the wage contract is itself productive of conflict. Marx refers in *Capital* to the 'peculiar nature of labour as a commodity'; and he explains that this 'peculiarity' resides in the fact that labour power, as a commodity, 'does not in reality pass straightforward into the hands of the buyer on the conclusion of the contract between buyer and seller . . . the alienation of labour-power and its real manifestation, i.e. the period of its existence as a use-value, do not coincide in time.'[14] Samuel Bowles and Herbert Gintis aptly make the same point as follows:

This 'peculiarity' is so critical that it renders labour-power conceptually different from any other commodity . . . the enjoyment of the use-value of any other commodity is non-problematic: the bread does not resist being eaten. The use-value of labour-power, however, depends not only on the technical attributes of the worker, but also on the ability of the capitalist to induce the worker to perform . . . Authority at the point of production must be used to evince worker behaviour not guaranteed by the labour contract.[15]

The 'peculiarity' of labour as a commodity has had immense consequences for the development of capitalism. It has been one of the main reasons (another is competition between firms) for the capitalist drive to substitute machines for workers: here, in class struggle at the point of production, is an essential cause of the tremendous modernizing, innovative dynamic of capitalism. Workers need to be coaxed, persuaded, threatened, and coerced; machines do not—they only need tending, which is a very different matter. Human labour, in a context of domination and subordination, is always a problem; 'dead' labour, in the form of machinery, is not nearly so troublesome.

However, human labour cannot be dispensed with; and this also accounts for the growth within advanced capitalism of a vast 'industrial relations' enterprise, whose purpose is to elicit from wage-earners the 'positive' attitudes, the 'loyalty' and co-operative spirit which the collective, 'socialized' process of production requires, but which the dynamic of capitalism serves to undermine.

Zygmunt Bauman captures well the conflictual essence of the labour contract:

A labour contract creates an inherently equivocal, under-determined relationship; it cannot be implemented without affecting aspects of the workers' life which, on the face of it, were not the subject of negotiation and argument. Hence the 'buying of labour' inevitably leads to a permanent power struggle in which the 'glossed over' issues of autocracy and control are resolved. The conflict between employees and their employers is, therefore, a permanent and irremediable feature of 'contractual' labour relations. Its inevitability results from the very ambiguity of the power situation which the labour contract cannot help creating.[16]

This conflict is not confined to the 'direct producers' and their employers; it is also present in the relations which bind *all* wage-earners to their employers, whether they are industrial, white-collar, service, or distributive workers. Nor indeed is the conflictual nature of the labour contract peculiar to capitalism. It also governs the relations of production in a 'collectivist' system where the means of production are under public ownership, but where workers are deprived of any effective say in the work process, or beyond it. Overt conflict in such a system may be ruthlessly suppressed; but it nevertheless occurs, in forms which render managerial control somewhat problematic.[17]

Even in a mode of production that was truly 'socialized' and was based on the 'free association of the producers', conflicts would no doubt arise at the point of production. But it is reasonable to assume that such conflicts would be drastically reduced and made much more easily amenable to conciliation and resolution because of the essentially non-conflictual nature of the system itself. Conflict would then be a deviation from the norm, rather than an inherent aspect of it.

IV

It was noted earlier that the main protagonists of class struggle, in the classical Marxist perspective, were the owners of the means of production on the one hand, and the direct producers on the other. Of course, Marx and Engels knew perfectly well that there were many other participants and protagonists in the class struggle; but the primary emphasis in classical Marxism—and for that matter in post-classical Marxism as well—is nevertheless firmly focused on the encounter between employers and workers. Such direct encounter is indeed crucial: but an equally crucial fact about class struggle is that it involves *other* protagonists, speaking for—or purporting to speak for—capital or labour, or claiming to speak and act in the general interest. It is in fact a matter of paramount importance in the nature of class struggle in the conditions of contemporary capitalism that much of it is conducted by other protagonists than capital and labour: much of the present work is concerned with what this has meant for the character and outcomes of class struggle in the twentieth century.

A subsidiary issue, which must nevertheless be noted because so much has been made of it, is the divorce between the ownership and control of capital and capitalist firms. It has long been the case that the class of employers is made up not only of the people who actually own 'their' firms, but also of people who control firms, without owning more than a relatively small part of the stocks and shares that make up their capital. In fact, a great many of the largest industrial, commercial, and financial firms in the advanced capitalist world are now controlled on the basis of appointment rather than ownership.

More will be said about this in a later chapter, but what is important about it in the present context is that the people who control capitalist firms without owning them are (contrary to a vast apologetic literature) at least as resolute in the pursuit of profit for their firms as owner capitalists ever were, and that this involves them in the same conflictual relationship with their employees. Their importance lies in the fact, not that they constitute a new breed of employers, moved by an entirely different set of motives than the old ones, but that they control gigantic resources, and represent a kind of 'vanguard' of capitalist employers.

There is, it might be added, nothing very remarkable or new about non-owners playing a major role in economic life or class struggle. The Church was the largest landowner in the Middle Ages, but the fact that those who controlled the land which the Church owned were not themselves its owners did not prevent them from engaging with the same zeal as actual landowners in the extraction of surplus labour. The point, in a contemporary context, not only applies to controllers of large private corporations, but also to the controllers of state corporations, who act as extractors of surplus labour, but have no ownership at all in the enterprises which they control. Here as elsewhere, the critical element is effective control.

A much more substantial aspect of class struggle, which has already been alluded to, is that the state is involved in it in absolutely crucial ways—so much so that the antagonism of capital and labour has to be seen as involving in reality the state and capital on the one hand, and labour on the other. This obviously raises some large questions about the exact relationship of the state to capital (and to labour), and this too will be discussed in subsequent chapters. But it is at any rate beyond question that the state does have a unique, indispensable, and pre-eminent role in the conduct of class struggle, and in the defence of the prevailing social order. It is, incidentally, the discharge of that role which must be taken to be a major contributory factor in the expansion of state power and the growth of 'statism': the dynamic of that development is, at least in part, to be found in the various functions which the state is called upon to perform, and which it alone is able to perform, in order to contain or repress class struggle.

Even to speak of the state and capital as both involved in class struggle from above leaves out of account the many people, grouped in associations of many different kinds, who are neither part of the state nor of capital but who are deeply involved in that struggle: conservatism, which is here taken to mean the defence of the existing structures of power, property, and privilege (in whatever name that defence is conducted), has many prot-agonists, not to speak of supporters, who have themselves very little power, property, and privilege. The defence of the social order in the countries concerned could not have been so relatively successful had this not been the case.

Nor are capital and the state to be taken as each constituting a monolithic bloc, with both of them linked in an equally monolithic partnership. Capital is made up of many distinct (and often conflicting) elements, interests, and 'fractions', and different parts of the state system are always at odds with each other. So, too, the 'partnership' between capital and the state is far from perfectly harmonious. However, I will argue that, in relation to class struggle and the social order, these differences, however important they may otherwise be, have not *normally* prevented capital and the state, separately and together, from achieving an adequate degree of cohesion. The emphasis is intended to suggest that cases are to be found where differences in the upper levels of the social structure *have* prevented the achievement of such a degree of cohesion; and the regime then enters upon a very dangerous crisis.[18]

In the classical Marxist perspective, the struggle of workers at the point of production, which is the primary cell of class struggle, its essential starting-point, is a difficult and painful process, whose development is likely to be full of disappointments, setbacks, and defeats; yet it is also bound, in that perspective, to turn wage-earners into a revolutionary class. Of the inevitability of such an outcome, Marx and Engels never had any doubt. As early as 1844, they had written that

it is not a question of what this or that proletarian, or even the whole proletariat at the moment *regards* as its aim: it is a question of *what the proletariat is*, and what, in accordance with this *being*, it will historically be compelled to do. Its aim and historical action is visible and irrevocably foreshadowed in its own life situation as well as in the whole organisation of bourgeois society today.[19]

Both men held to this conviction throughout their lives. But nowhere in the advanced capitalist world, of course, has the working class made a revolution of the kind which Marx and Engels had in mind, or even attempted any such revolution. The working class has indeed been 'historically compelled' to engage in class struggle—at times at a very high level of intensity. But experience has clearly shown that such a struggle—even at a high level of intensity—does not necessarily produce what Marx meant by revolutionary consciousness, namely, the will to overthrow the existing system and replace it by an altogether different one. This raises two questions: why such a development has effectively been blocked in the countries of advanced capitalism; and what the working class *has* actually done over the hundred years or so in which the modern labour movement, properly speaking, has been in existence in these countries.

Both questions involve consideration of a development which is of massive importance in the history of labour movements and in the history of class struggle, but to which Marx and Engels did not pay much attention, and to which they could not have been expected, in their own epoch, to pay much attention: this is the fact that the working class, in waging class struggle, requires representative agencies, and that such agencies, notably in the form of trade unions and political parties, have come to occupy a crucial place in the history and politics of the working class. It would be impossible to exaggerate the importance of that development.

The first lines of the Rules which Marx had drafted for the First International in 1864 had expressed succinctly one of his (and Engels's) most fundamental convictions: namely, that 'the emancipation of the working classes must be conquered by the working classes themselves.'[20] Neither Marx nor Engels opposed the formation of working-class parties; and they were in fact much involved, from London, in the affairs of the German Social Democratic Party in the 1870s—usually, it should be said, in a highly critical vein. Engels himself had after Marx's death in 1883 a close personal relationship with the leading figures of the German Social Democratic Party, and with leaders of other socialist parties as well in Europe and North America. But the focus of both men, particularly Marx, was the working class itself: for them, here and nowhere else was the authentic 'subject' of revolutionary struggle. In the crucial matter of the relationship between class and party, it was for them the class which was paramount, with the party as an ancillary organization. Marx could not have had any real sense of the importance which parties, in a number of different ways, were to acquire in the conduct (or avoidance) of class struggle in capitalist-democratic regimes. In the twelve years by which he survived Marx, and which witnessed the rapid development of socialist and labour parties in many countries, Engels acquired a better perception of the place which these parties were destined to occupy in the politics of labour; but he could not then have fully realized the many implications this would have. That aspect of class struggle belongs to the history of the twentieth century; and it will receive extensive attention in the following pages.

V

It may be useful briefly to list here the main objections which have been raised in recent years—though some of them are much older—against the notion that the antagonism between labour on the one hand and capital (and the state) on the other remains the 'primary contradiction' in advanced capitalist societies and the fundamental source of conflict in these societies. Such a list cannot do full justice to the arguments which have been advanced against the 'traditional' view of class struggle, not only on the Right but also on the Left; but it does, I believe, at least encompass the main items of the case. Not all the critics subscribe to all the objections noted below; but all of them subscribe to at least some of these objections.

To begin with, there is the view, reiterated on the Right in many different versions, that the very notion of the 'working class' has itself been rendered very dubious by virtue of the relentless levelling, egalitarian, and democratizing tendencies which have, so it is claimed, been at work in the societies of advanced capitalism. Allied to this, it is further said, there is the vast range of improvements which have occurred in the condition of the working class, on a scale that could not have been imagined fifty, let alone a hundred, years ago. No doubt, it is conceded, the process of improvement regrettably leaves in existence areas of deprivation, notably among racial and ethnic minorities; but this should not be allowed to obscure the gains achieved by the vast majority.

In the light of these gains, it is also said, it is hardly surprising that the great majority of wage-earners should have quite decisively refused to play the revolutionary role which Marx and later Marxists assigned to them; and that they should have been unwilling even to adopt the militant industrial postures and the confrontational politics urged upon them by left activists.

In any case, many of the critics on the Left say, the working class is itself being rapidly transformed by technological developments, by new patterns of work, and by a new international division of labour. Marx and his disciples conceived of the working class as made up of white, male, industrial workers. But that working class is in sharp decline everywhere in the advanced capitalist world, so much so that much the larger part of the working class is increasingly made up of an agglomeration of workers in white-collar, service, and distributive occupations, and forming sectors divided by the work they do, by gender, race, ethnicity, nationality, religion, conditions of work, organization (or the lack of it), and so on.

It is in these sectors, the argument proceeds, that are to be found the most exploited and oppressed workers; and the source of their oppression is their gender, their race or ethnicity or sexual preference. Indeed, while male workers themselves play a significant part in the fostering of this exploitation and oppression, by supporting policies of discrimination and exclusion, and by a racism and sexism which is widespread in the working class. This, it is added, gives the lie to the notion of the working class as a 'universal class', whose emancipation was both a condition and a guarantee of the general liberation of society from the shackles clamped upon it by class domination. Such claims, the critics maintain, have again and again been shown to be spurious. Even if a white and male-dominated working class, or the agencies which purport to speak for it, did achieve the overthrow of capitalism, there is no reason to believe, so we are told, that the new social order would be free from the hierarchical, oppressive, and discriminatory features of the old, or that those features would not be replaced—or even supplemented—by new, conceivably worse ones.

All notions of the working class as a 'universal class', it is said, are part of a 'labour metaphysic', which ought to have no place in serious social analysis, or for that matter in socialist strategy. Organized labour, in so far as it is possible to speak of it as an entity at all, is just one 'interest' among many others, and in no way a 'privileged' subject, charged with some kind of historical mission of redemption.

Nor, according to this view, is there any substance in the claim that the conflicts in which labour engages with capital or the state must be allocated a special, central or primary place in the configuration of pressure and struggle in advanced capitalist societies. Conflicts based on gender, race, ethnicity, or sexual preference, or on such issues as the protection of the environment or disarmament, are at least as important and significant, it is claimed, as labour conflicts; and they have, it is further claimed, in fact proved in the last few decades to be much more radical, innovative, and challenging than the limited, traditional, and 'corporatist' struggles of organized labour.

In a rather different perspective, the point is often also made that class struggle in the countries of advanced capitalism pales into insignificance in comparison with the reality and the struggles of the 'third world'. The really important conflict in the modern world, we are told, is not that which occurs inside the rich countries of the West, or even the conflict between East and West, but that between North and South—that is, between the rich, industrialized world on the one hand, and the under-industrialized, poor, super-exploited 'third world' on the other.

This too, in its own way, relegates class struggle in advanced capitalist countries to a question of subsidiary importance.

All this constitutes a familiar—and seemingly formidable—indictment of the Marxist or Marxist-derived 'model' of class struggle. I hope to show in what follows that most of the items in that indictment are to one degree or another misconceived. But this obviously needs detailed argument. It should, however, be noted here that two rather different questions are at issue. The first concerns the nature of class and class struggle in contemporary capitalism; and this is a question which is susceptible to rigorous analysis. The other, related but distinct, question is whether there is any likelihood that class struggle from below can bring about a new society, radically different from (and radically better than) the existing social order.

About this second question, there is bound to be surmise, hope, and aspiration, rather than unqualified assurance. At the same time, much depends, in considering this question, on what is meant by a 'new society'. There was a time when that notion was invested on the Left with strong salvationist overtones, and interpreted to mean the creation, by way of instant social engineering, of a society wholly free from strife, in which power itself would soon be banished from all human relations. In any serious perspective, this cannot be what the notion of a 'new society' must be taken to mean. What it does mean, I suggest, is the creation of a social order whose economic, social, political, and moral mode of being makes possible the drastic reduction of domination, exploitation, and discrimination, to the point where, in a process which is bound to be arduous and prolonged, these evils may be eliminated altogether.

Any such enterprise, however soberly it is conceived, can readily be dismissed as 'utopian'. But I hope that the analysis which is presented here may, on the contrary, help to show that this notion of a new society, far from a being a *vision*, spun from idle dreams, is in fact a *project*, solidly grounded in material conditions, human will, and historical experience.

2

Class and Power in Contemporary Capitalism

An extraordinary degree of confusion and obfuscation attends the discussion of class in relation to advanced capitalist societies. Yet the discussion of class struggle clearly requires a precise identification of the nature and composition of classes in these societies. This, and some of the main questions which it raises, is the subject of the present chapter.

A 'class map' of advanced capitalist societies may be drawn in the shape of a pear-shaped pyramid, as follows:

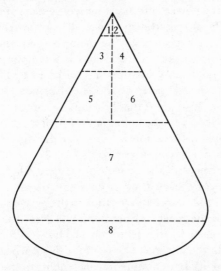

The space at the apex of the pyramid with the numbers 1, 2, 3, and 4 denotes what will here be called *the dominant class*. The broken line which separates 1 and 2 from 3 and 4 is intended to mark an important distinction between a *power elite*, to use C. Wright Mills's term, and the rest of the dominant class. Mills used the term in relation to the United States, and saw the power elite as having three distinct components: the 'chief executives' of the 'hundred or so corporations which, measured by sales and capital, are the largest';[1] the 'political directorate'—meaning in effect the people in charge of the main 'command posts' of the state; and the top people in the military. The term 'power elite' is used here to denote the first and second of these groups (numbers 1 and 2): the people who wield corporate power by virtue of their control of major industrial, commercial, and financial firms; and the people who wield state power. The military occupy a distinct place in the system, but their power is not such as to give them a co-equal place with the other two groups. This is not to deny them a great deal of influence, authority, and power, particularly in crisis situations and in wartime. For the most part, however, the political regimes of advanced capitalism have tended to be civilian-oriented, with the military kept fairly effectively in a subordinate position.

The important point in the present context concerns the power which makes the power elite a distinctive element of the dominant class. As Mills put it, the members of the power elite 'are in positions to make decisions having major consequences. Whether they do or do not make such decisions is less important than the fact that they do occupy such pivotal positions . . . They occupy the *strategic command posts* of the social structure';[2] and Mills also made the crucial point that 'no one . . . can be truly powerful unless he has access to the command of major institutions, for it is over these institutional means of power that the truly powerful are, in the first instance, powerful.'[3]

The state element of the power elite is here taken to be part of the dominant *class*, even though its members are not located in the process of production. But location in the process of production and relation to the means of production are not the only criteria that must be used in the definition of class. More will be said presently about the criteria to be used for this purpose. But power (or the lack of it) is undoubtedly one such criterion, of crucial importance; and those wielding state power at the uppermost levels of the state system undoubtedly qualify for membership of the dominant class on this criterion.

Numbers 3 and 4 on the pyramid denote the part of the dominant class which is not in the power elite; and it is of course much larger than the power elite. On the one hand (number 3), there are the people who control, and who may also own, a large number of medium-sized firms, which constitute a vast scatter of very diverse enterprises, dwarfed by the corporate giants, yet forming a substantial part of total economic activity. On the other hand (number 4), there is a large professional class of lawyers, accountants, middle-rank civil servants and military personnel, men and women in senior posts in higher education and in other spheres of professional life—in short, the people who occupy the upper levels of the 'credentialized' part of the population of these countries. Many such people are employed, full-time or part-time, by corporate enterprise, or by the state, or work independently of either.

Both the business and professional members of the dominant class who are not part of the power elite represent in effect the bourgeoisie of today's advanced capitalist societies—what is often called the upper middle class, or the middle class. The people concerned need to be clearly distinguished from the power elite by virtue of the fact that they do not have anything like its power. Even so, it is appropriate to speak of them as members of a dominant class, in so far as they exercise a substantial amount of power in society, individually and collectively, and wield a great deal of influence in economic, social, political, and ideological or cultural terms. They are 'notables', 'influentials', 'opinion leaders'; and they are also at the upper levels of the income and ownership scale. It is from their ranks, so to speak, that are mainly recruited the members of the power elite; and it is to their ranks that return those who have ceased, by virtue of retirement, resignation, or demotion, to be members of the power elite.

Numbers 5 and 6 on the pyramid refer to two parts of a substantial petty bourgeoisie or 'lower middle class' which is to be found in all advanced capitalist societies. The part represented by number 5 is made up of a large number of people who own and run small businesses—small factories and workshops, garages, building firms, shops, offices offering a variety of services, and so on. These enterprises employ a small number of workers; and this part of the petty bourgeoisie also includes a wide range of self-employed craftsmen, artisans, and petty traders. These are the minnows of capitalist enterprise—minor entrepreneurs of every sort. Their social and political importance, however, not to speak of the contribution they make to the daily life of society by the services they render, must be taken to be very substantial.

The other part of the petty bourgeoisie, denoted by the number 6, is formed by a semi-professional, sub-managerial, supervisory element, comprising schoolteachers, social workers, journalists, designers, laboratory technicians, computer analysts, civil servants, and local government officers at the lower levels of the administrative structure—in short, men and women who have some degree of power and responsibility in the operation of the mechanisms of production, administration, supervision, control, and repression which help in the daily reproduction of the whole social order. Marx had already noted in *Capital* that 'an industrial army of workers under the command of a capitalist requires, like a real army, officers (managers) and N.C.O.'s (foremen, overseers), who command during the labour process in the name of capital. The work of supervision becomes their established and exclusive function.'[4]

The growth of corporate capitalism has meant a vast increase in the army of 'foremen' and 'overseers' of every description; and the equally vast inflation in the role of the state has also entailed an enormous increase in the number of people whom it employs in the fulfilment of its administrative, welfare, supervisory, regulative, and repressive functions.

There is much that separates the business element of the petty bourgeoisie from its sub-professional element. But they do have in common the fact that they are quite distinct from the bourgeoisie on the one hand, and from the working class on the other. Its members do form an authentic 'intermediate' class, a term which is in no way intended to convey any suggestion that it is unimportant: on the contrary, the petty bourgeoisie has often played an important role in political life, and more will be said presently about this.

Number 7 on the pyramid denotes that vast aggregate of people in advanced capitalist societies, amounting to something like two-thirds to three-quarters of their population, who constitute the working class: industrial workers, clerical, distributive, and service workers, skilled and unskilled, young and old, white and black and brown, men and women. Moreover, the working class must also be taken to include a host of people who are not 'workers', in the sense that they are not wage-earners. This is the case, pre-eminently, for women who are not 'employed' but who, as the wives or partners of wage-earners, do make a crucial contribution to the production of surplus value by meeting the various domestic and other requirements which make it possible for wage-earners to resume work each day in reasonable physical and mental shape. Also, women who are not 'employed' make a crucial contribution to the continued viability of the system in a different way as well: namely, by the reproduction and the nurturing of future wage-earners.

Furthermore, the working class also includes many other people than the wives and partners of wage-earners—unemployed workers, children and other dependants of wage-earners, sick and retired workers; and note must also be taken on a sizeable 'under-class', which is in some ways part of the working class and is mostly recruited from it, yet which is distinct from the bulk of wage-earners, in so far as it is made up of the poorest and most deprived members of the working class, people at the margin of society, the permanently unemployed, disabled, and chronically sick people very largely or entirely dependent on transfer payments from public funds, help from relatives, or charity. This 'under-class' is indicated on the pyramid by the number 8.

Here too, it may be noted, the notion of class is being extended far beyond the process of production. For it is surely unreasonable to argue that unemployed workers do not belong to the working class; or that wives or partners of wage-earners, who are not themselves wage-earners (though so many of them now are) do not belong to it.

In effect, the working class of advanced capitalist countries must be taken to be made up of all those people whose main, and usually exclusive, *source of income* is the sale of their labour power, or transfer payments by the state, or both; whose *level of income* places them in the lower and lowest income groups; and whose individual *power* at work and in society at large is low or virtually non-existent. It is the combination of these factors which defines membership of the working class, and it is on the basis of these combined factors that the vast majority of people in these countries may be said to belong to the working class.

The same combination of factors also determines the location of other classes in the social structure. They too may be grouped on the basis of their source of income, the level of that income, and the degree of power, responsibility, and influence they wield at work and in society. As in any such classification, the separation between the classes becomes problematic at the edges; and there are always individuals in one occupation or another who defy classification by the stipulated criteria. But this does not significantly affect the separation itself: taken as a whole, the classes in question are quite distinct.

It may be noted that the business bourgeoisie derives the main part of its income from profit, interest, rent, and speculation; whereas the bulk of the professional bourgeoisie derives the larger part of its income from salaries. The difference, such as it is, is of no great consequence for the specific purpose of placing the people concerned in the social structure. In any case, the business bourgeoisie also draws salaries; and the professional bourgeoisie owns stocks, shares, and other property. Similarly, the level of their income places them in the same upper income groups; and the degree of power, influence, and responsibility they exercise is roughly comparable, whether the reference is to the corporate and state elite or to the rest of the bourgeoisie.

Differences are more marked in the case of the petty bourgeoisie. Its business part derives its income from profit, rent, the rendering of services, and so on; whereas the sub-professional part of the petty bourgeoisie mainly derives its income from employment in the private and public sectors. But the level of that income (though by no means identical) places both parts in income groups far below the bourgeoisie, yet, generally speaking, above the working class. So too the individual power which members of the petty bourgeoisie exercise is far inferior to that of members of the bourgeoisie, but a good deal greater than that wielded by members of the working class.

The bare enumeration of the classes which fill the 'empty spaces' of the social pyramid is open to the objection that it is far too static, and that class relations, on the contrary, are part of a dynamic process, in which consciousness, for instance, plays a crucial role. The objection is well taken and will be met in the remainder of this chapter and in later chapters. It is clear that the present enumeration is no more than a first step, intended as a preliminary exploration of the terrain.

It may also be said, in the same vein, that to locate classes as is done here is to imply that people are frozen in their location, in other words that no account is taken of social mobility. Social mobility is of course a matter of great importance in shaping class relations, since the possibility or likelihood of movement upward (or downward) which is presented to members of given classes and to their children is also likely to have a considerable influence on the ways in which they view the social order. But while social mobility *is* important, classes themselves do nevertheless remain stable over long periods of time, in fact over whole epochs. The dominant class in capitalist societies has undergone many changes in terms of its composition; and so has the subordinate class in these societies. But a dominant class, based upon the control of economic and political power, and a subordinate class, mainly made up of wage-earners and their dependants, have nevertheless remained the main classes throughout the history of industrial capitalism. Neither social mobility nor blurred boundaries between classes annul this division, even though they may, together with many other factors, affect its sharpness.

The division, it may be added, finds expression in terms of power, income, wealth, responsibility, 'life chances', style and quality of life, and everything else that makes up the texture of existence. People may approve of such differences and divisions, or deplore them, or declare them to be regrettable but inevitable, or view them in some other way. But what cannot or rather should not be done is to deny or ignore the existence of the divisions, or to underestimate the central importance which they have for the life of the society in which they occur. In fact, serious politics is essentially about these divisions—whether to maintain them, or enhance them, or reduce them, or abolish them. One of the most notable features of political theory in its prevailing mode (or of much recent socialist writing for that matter) is precisely the neglect, in the discussion of conservatism, liberalism, democracy, equality, justice, and so forth, of any serious consideration of class structure and class divisions in the societies under consideration. In the face of the constant tendency to ignore this context, it is first of all necessary to insist on the reality and the

centrality in advanced capitalist societies of a class structure based
upon relations of domination and subordination.

II

There are of course many people who find the very notion of a
'dominant class' unacceptable, even outrageous, in relation to
Western societies. Indeed, the bulk of the apologetic literature
devoted to the issue of power in the post-war decades was precisely
concerned to demonstrate—or often simply took it for granted—
that no dominant class or power elite could possibly exist in the
democratic, pluralist, open societies of advanced capitalism (now
renamed 'mixed economies' or 'post-capitalist' or 'post-industrial'
or, most recently, 'post-Fordist' societies). Power in these societies,
it was claimed, was not concentrated but divided, fragmented,
and there were mechanisms in plenty to ensure that even if power
did come to be concentrated at any point, 'countervailing' forces
would soon come to challenge and reduce it. At most, it was
conceded that there might be found many *different* pyramids of
power, representing many different, divergent, and competing
interests, in a system of 'elite pluralism', which was the very
negation of a 'power elite' or 'dominant class'. In fact, many
power elites guaranteed that there could be no power elite.[5]

This view of power in advanced capitalist societies remains
very strongly entrenched, both in academic thought and in
political discourse. Nor is this really surprising, given how much
hinges on the issue. For acknowledgement of the existence of a
formidable concentration of power at the top of the social structure,
with that power exercised with considerable independence by
a very small number of people, greatly hinders, to say the least,
the advancement of the claim that these are truly democratic
societies, in which power is effectively dispersed, and where the
people are the real rulers.

Classes in power in earlier epochs had no need to try and
dissimulate their power: they merely affirmed it, and legitimated
it by the invocation of divine or natural arrangements, backed by
force. In the secular, sceptical context of advanced capitalist
societies, permeated by strong democratic currents of thought
and rhetoric, there is a much greater need to dissemble the reality

of power, and this is done by denying the existence of a dominant class. That denial, however, flies in the face of reality.

In any class society, of whatever kind, a dominant class may be so designated by virtue of the effectiveness and cohesion it possesses in the control of *the three main sources of domination*: control over the main means of economic activity—and this may involve (and usually has involved) the ownership of these means, but need not do so; control over the means of state administration and coercion; and control over what may broadly be called the means of communication and persuasion. The dominant class of advanced capitalist societies, and notably their power elites, do have the requisite effectiveness and cohesion.

The notion of control is here of paramount importance; but this is in no way intended to devalue the importance of ownership. Ownership remains of fundamental importance in the life of these societies, and pervades every aspect of it. In middle-sized and small firms, it also remains the basis on which are built relations of domination and exploitation. Also, ownership remains the primary source of the vast disparities of income and wealth which continue to prevail in these societies, notwithstanding the proclamations that class differences, in these and other terms, have all but disappeared, or are at least well on the way to disappearance.[6]

But important though ownership may be in many different respects, it is not an essential prerequisite, either in economic or in political terms, for the power wielded by members of the power elite and others in the dominant class, and it may not even be allied with much power at all. Control does mean power. Wealth, particularly great wealth, may do so too, if those who have it choose to use it for the purpose—for instance, by funding political causes, movements, and institutions. Conservative foundations, in the United States and elsewhere, and other conservative enterprises of various kinds do rely on rich people to help them by way of large donations to help save the world from 'communism'; and these people may thereby be said to exercise a measure of power. But wealthy people may choose, on the other hand, to confine themselves to the enjoyment of the ease and privileges which their wealth affords them, and to be content with the limited power they are able to wield over those whom they employ in their personal service.

I have already noted that many of the largest firms in the capitalist system are controlled by people who do not own them. This 'managerial revolution' has not proceeded everywhere at the same pace; and many very large firms remain owner-controlled and directed. 'Even in the late 1960s and early 1970s,' it has been observed, 'of the two hundred biggest French industrial companies, half were family controlled and of these, thirty-six had absolute family majority control . . . Of the twenty biggest firms, six were controlled by single families.'[7] In Britain, slightly more than half of the largest 250 manufacturing firms in 1975 were still under proprietary control.[8] In the United States, on the other hand, a recent study found that 'more than four-fifths of the largest two hundred nonfinancial corporations were under management control by 1974 (up from 24 per cent of a comparable set of firms under management control in 1900 and 41 per cent in 1929).'[9]

Nor in any case is the divorce between ownership and control usually total. The top managers of large firms generally hold substantial amounts of stock in these firms. In 1974, for instance, 'the median value of company shares held by officer-directors of the 100 largest U.S. manufacturing companies exceeded $900,000. Most managers own only a tiny fraction of their company's shares, but in terms of the individual manager's portfolio the investment is very large.'[10]

This, however, does not affect the very strong trend towards control without what might be called old-fashioned ownership; and it is a trend which is very likely to accelerate as a result of the equally strong trend towards concentration, which is so prominent a feature of advanced capitalism; and the people who control these vast economic concentrations do form an authentic corporate elite.

Their control—and hence their power—extends beyond the means of production, distribution, and exchange: it includes control over a major weapon in the struggle for domination, namely, the 'mental means of production', in the phrase Marx and Engels used in *The German Ideology* in 1846. At least, the corporate elite has control over a very large part of the 'means of mental production' in the private sector of the economy, with the state in control of most of the rest. Communication in all its forms is now very big business. Newspapers, magazines, books, the cinema, theatre, radio, television, videos, and all other means of communication are an important part of capitalist enterprise; and the trend in the last decade towards the privatization of parts of the communications industry that were under public ownership and control has increased still further the share of capitalist control over the industry.

Of course, the power wielded by the corporate elite is not absolute, undivided, or unconstrained. I will discuss in a moment the power wielded by the other part of the power elite, namely, that part of it which controls state power; but it is obviously the case that other forces in society do exercise a certain amount of influence and power, and do sometimes place corporate power on the defensive. This is usually taken to validate the notion of 'pluralism', as in 'pluralist societies'. But pluralism means a lot more than the existence and recognition of a plurality of groups, interests, and associations in society; it also means, and is intended to mean, the existence of a rough *equilibrium of power* between contending interests and social forces. This is precisely what is *not* present in the configuration of power in advanced capitalist societies. In all 'normal' circumstances, capital wields incomparably greater power and influence than any other 'interest' in society. The only force in society—the state is a different matter—which may occasionally match the power of capital, by way of the collective deployment of its collective strength, is organized labour—for instance, in a general strike, or in a revolutionary upheaval. But these are naturally very rare occurrences, and they can hardly be taken to invalidate the general point that, in terms of its control of resources vital to the whole of society, capital is incomparably more powerful than labour or any other interest or force in society.

Nor is this power confined within the boundaries of any given society. On the contrary, its reach, to use Richard Barnet's phrase, is now truly global;[11] and this is notably, but not exclusively, true of so-called multi-national corporations.[12] The enormous concentration of power which these organizations represent constitutes a major factor in the countries where they operate; and they are a crucial point of reference for the governments of these countries, particularly in the poorer countries of the world, where their decisions can have a vital impact on the countries' economies.

It is ultimately the state which is responsible for the imposition of constraints upon corporate power; and the relation of the state to corporate power is therefore, on this and on many other counts, of the greatest importance in the analysis of the distribution of power in advanced capitalism.

State power is controlled by the people who occupy the command posts of the state system—presidents, prime ministers, and their immediate ministerial and other colleagues and advisors; top civil servants; senior officers in the armed forces, the police, and the surveillance and intelligence agencies; senior judges; and the people in charge of state enterprises, regulatory commissions, and similar agencies. In some political systems (such as that of the United States), the list would also include senior members of the legislative branch. In some strong federal systems (such as the Canadian), provincial prime ministers and their colleagues and advisers might also be taken to be part of the state elite. Generally speaking, however, the senior people in weak federal systems, and in local or regional government everywhere, would not qualify for inclusion as members of that elite. Their power, in many instances, may not be negligible; but it is not of the same kind as the power exercised by the controllers of state power at the centre of affairs.

I noted earlier that different parts of the state system are often at odds with each other; and this is certainly the case in regard to the dealings which governments, legislators, judges, and regulatory agencies have with this or that capitalist interest. It is not uncommon, for instance, for legislatures to pass laws relating to one aspect or other of business, only to find them invalidated by the courts. Even so, the state system does, in this as in other respects, usually function with a reasonable degree of coherence (which is not the same as competence); and we may therefore leave aside for the moment the constant frictions which attend the relationship between different parts of the system.

What, then, is the relationship between state power and corporate power?

In the model of the social pyramid presented at the beginning of this chapter, the corporate elite and the state elite stand on a par with each other: both dwell on the same level of the commanding heights of the social order.

This is not how capital and the state are viewed in the traditional Marxist perspective. In that perspective, the state, however great its importance and power, is taken to be ultimately subordinate to the capitalist class, or to the impersonal but inexorably compelling power and logic of capital, or to a combination of both. The 'relative autonomy of the state' may be invoked to qualify this subordinate position, but does not negate it: the power of capital and capitalists, in Marxist terms, is ultimately decisive in regard to what the state does, and also, which is scarcely less important, in what it does not do.

It is right to stress that the state is indeed located in a given economic context which is decisively shaped by the capitalist mode of production; and that what the state does or does not do is crucially affected by the imperative requirements of capital and by the power of those who own and control capital.

However, the danger which this emphasis presents is that it tends to devalue the power of the state, and the fact that its power has often been used for purposes and policies which were not only pursued without reference to the capitalist class, but also at times against the wishes of many parts of that class, or even the whole of it. It is because the state has had, and still has, this power that it has been able to make itself the architect of the reforms which have been such a conspicuous part of the history of capitalism in the last hundred and fifty years or so.

It may well be said that this reforming activity of the state has never gone so far as to create a root and branch challenge to the interests of capital; and that even in its most reforming guise, the state remains the protector of the social order which gives capital its preponderance. Reform, according to this view, is taken to be a means of strengthening the social order, not a means of weakening it. But however this may be (and the impact of reform is rather more complex than this), the implication is that unless the state actually engineers revolutionary change, it has to be seen as subordinate to capital. This is too restrictive, in so far as it focuses on the extreme ends of a spectrum, whereas the state usually operates within the spectrum.

The point is of importance in relation to class struggle. The state does not, normally and of its own volition, intervene in class struggle on the side of labour. But this does not mean that it is necessarily subservient to the purposes and strategies of capital. It is in fact often compelled, by virtue of its concern for the defence and stability of the social order, to seek some intermediate position, and to act upon it, however much that position may differ from the position of capital.

Nothing of this must be taken to mean that the state is not the ultimate protector of a capitalist-dominated social order. But it is to suggest that the state provides such protection as those who control it think fit, and, in many different spheres, with a high degree of independence—even at times with complete independence, though always, of course, within a determinate economic, social, political, and cultural context.

In one of his early writings, Marx refers to the question of the relationship between the state and 'property' as follows:

We are . . . faced with two kinds of power, on the one hand the power of property, in other words, of property-owners, on the other hand, political power, the power of the state. 'Power also controls property' means: property does not control the political power but is harassed by it, for example by arbitrary taxes, by confiscations, by privileges, by the disruptive interference of the bureaucracy in industry and trade and the like. In other words: the bourgeoisie has not yet taken political shape as a class. The power of the state is not yet its own power.[13]

However, Marx goes on to say, the assertion that 'power rules property' loses its meaning 'in countries where the bourgeoisie has already conquered political power and political rule is none other than the rule, not of the individual bourgeois over his workers, but of the bourgeois class over the whole of society'.[14]

But the 'domination of the bourgeois class over the whole of society' has never been complete in the countries of advanced capitalism, and neither has its domination of the state. In an earlier epoch, the bourgeoisie had to contend for effective power with a well-entrenched aristocratic order; and in a later one, it had to contend with the pressures exercised by organized labour and other forces. Its success in establishing its predominance was very considerable. But that success was nevertheless far from total; and this was also reflected in the state itself.

It is to take account of the independence and power of the state that I have advanced the notion of a *partnership* between corporate power and state power—a partnership between 'two different, separate forces, linked to each other by many threads, yet each having its own separate sphere of concerns'.[15]

The terms of this partnership are not firmly fixed; and the

relations between the partners, though close, are far from smooth. There are in fact many bones of contention between them, and a good deal of suspicion and even contempt. This arises from the fact that each partner does have its own sphere of concerns, and that this tends to produce tension and conflict between them. 'The true meaning of freedom for the American bourgeoisie', it has been said—but the point does not only apply to the American bourgeoisie—'is the ability of those who own or control economic resources to allocate or appropriate them as they see fit—without interference from labour unions or government officials';[16] and capital does indeed have an extraordinary degree of freedom from 'interference', even though the decisions which flow from its exercise have direct and major consequences for workers, towns, regions, and countries. But there are nevertheless *some* constraints upon that freedom, most of them imposed by the state; and imposed, it may be added, for the sake of the health and stability of the capitalist social order itself.

The state's interventionist propensities and its imposition of constraints on business are particularly marked in periods of crisis and unrest. It is notable, for instance, that even in the United States, where the capitalist class is more powerful than its equivalent in any other advanced capitalist country, 'between 1965 and 1975, more than twenty-five major pieces of federal regulatory legislation in the area of consumer and environmental protection, occupational health and safety and personnel policy were enacted by the Federal Government.'[17] Those were of course years of great turmoil in the United States; and some of the measures in question, it may also be noted, were taken by the Nixon Administration, which no one could suspect of radical tendencies. It is also relevant, however, to note that many of the same measures were grievously undermined by the Reagan Administration after 1981, in a period of political stagnation and conservatism. Similar instances of constraint upon business by way of state intervention, and of the erosion of such constraints, are to be found in all advanced capitalist countries.

These differences, tensions, and conflicts between corporate power and state power are real and important; but they do not for the most part greatly impair the underlying cohesion which binds capital and the state. It is in this respect a perverse and obfuscating methodology which postulates that, because the power elite and the rest of the dominant class are not perfectly united in regard to the policies to be pursued, they cannot be said to be cohesive at all.

The cohesion which is to be found in power elites and dominant classes is based on a number of distinct but related factors. The most important of these, it seems reasonable to assume, is the very basic material set of interests which the members of these classes have in common, in terms of property, privilege, position, and power. Here, by definition, are the people who have done very well out of the existing social order and who, quite naturally, have every intention of continuing to do very well out of it, for themselves and their offspring.

Nor is this simply a matter of mere cynical self-interest. On the contrary, there is also the very strong conviction that the system in which these people have themselves done very well is also the best possible for others who have not been so fortunate. Ideological dispositions, in other words, constitute a crucial bond between members of power elites and dominant classes in general.

At the very heart of these dispositions, there is the profound belief that 'free enterprise' is the essential foundation of prosperity, progress, freedom, democracy, and so forth, and that it is also therefore synonymous with the 'national interest'. People who take this view may admit that 'free enterprise' occasionally produces unwelcome results; but these, they also believe, must be taken to be blemishes which do not in the least bring the system itself into question. Viewed in this way, the notion that capitalism (or whatever else it may be called) is not the best possible system in an imperfect world is readily taken to be an absurd aberration, concocted by dreamers and propagated by agitators and demagogues.

The ideological differences which do nevertheless exist among the people in question in regard to capitalism are mostly concerned with the degree of state intervention and regulation which it requires. Also, there are of course innumerable differences and disputes over specific items of policy and strategy which arise between members of dominant classes. But however sharp these may be, they do not seriously impair an underlying consensus about the essential goodness and validity of the system itself.

This consensus is enormously strengthened by its ideological corollary: namely, a common hostility towards 'socialism', not to speak of 'communism'. Members of power elites and dominant classes may differ on many things; but they are at least united on *this* score. Differences here only arise in relation to the policies and strategies to be adopted in order to contain, repel, and defeat challenge from the Left.

This hardly exhausts the ideological repertoire of the people at the upper and uppermost levels of the social pyramid, but a fervent belief in 'free enterprise' and a detestation of any kind of alternative to it are more than sufficient to provide a very powerful bond. Moreover, these and related sentiments provide an excellent set of criteria by which to judge whether candidates for membership of the power elite are suitable. Membership largely depends on 'sponsored mobility'; but the sponsorship is unlikely to be forthcoming for people unwise enough to hold heterodox views on crucial matters. Even where there occurs 'contest mobility', the contest is likely to be restricted to those who can be relied on, by virtue of the views they hold, to play the game.

Membership of the dominant class, apart from the power elite, is less subject to such tests; and there have been quite a number of 'class traitors' in the bourgeoisie ever since labour movements have come to be established, and there have been more and more of them as the twentieth century has progressed—people, that is, who have in one way or another rejected the main planks of the dominant ideology and who have gone over, so to speak, to the other side. As Lenin observed in *What is to Be Done?* (1902), it was from the ranks of the bourgeoisie that originated most socialist intellectuals and theorists in the early days of the socialist movement; and it is from these ranks too—and from the ranks of the sub-professional petty bourgeoisie—that have been recruited many of the leading figures of labour and socialist parties.

Nevertheless, the vast majority of the bourgeoisie has shared to the full the ideological and political dispositions of the power elite: in the things that ultimately matter most, that majority has stood solidly behind the power elite.

It is not, incidentally, their ideological and political dispositions which *distinguish* the power elite and the rest of the dominant class from the population at large: vast numbers of people in other classes, including the working class, also share these dispositions. What distinguishes members of the power elite and the dominant class from the rest, in this context, is their power and influence, not their views.

Mention should also be made here of another factor of cohesion, closely related to the previous ones: this is the common patterns of life shared by members of the dominant class, either by virtue of social provenance, or by absorption. This also produces networks of kinship and friendship, old school associations, intermarriage, club membership, business and political ties, common pastimes and leisure pursuits, rituals of enjoyment and formal celebrations, all of which are based on and reinforce a common view of the world, of what is right and, even more important, of what is wrong.[18] There was a time when a sharp distinction could be drawn between the landowning aristocracy and the bourgeoisie; and the aristocracy may still serve in some countries (for instance, England) as a 'role model' for the bourgeoisie. But aristocrats have long come to be 'bourgeoisified' in economic terms and absorbed into the world of capitalist activity. For all practical purposes, the distinction may now be ignored.

There is one quite common occurrence in the political life of advanced capitalist countries which appears to create a breach in the ideological cohesion of the power elite: namely, the arrival in office of social democratic governments, sometimes backed by parliamentary majorities, and involving the entry of social democratic officials, advisers, and other appointees into various parts of the state system. The extreme case is that of Scandinavia, where state power has for decade after decade since the early thirties been penetrated by social democrats, in government and in other 'strategic' parts of the state. 'Social Democrats and their sympathisers', it has been said, 'are integrated into the institutional machinery at all levels. They constitute a sizeable proportion of the higher state bureaucracy, the provincial administration, the judiciary and, indeed, every major political instrumentality in Scandinavia. Exactly the same is true at the local and intermediate levels.'[19] Social democratic parties elsewhere have been rather less successful; but they have nevertheless carved out an important presence for themselves in political life and, quite often, in the state system.

The presence of social democrats in government undoubtedly

produces a certain ideological dissonance in the power elite; and it has repercussions in some areas of policy, notably in economic and social policy. At the same time, the ideological distance which separates most social democratic leaders and ministers from their conservative opponents must not be exaggerated. Social democrats in government do tend to favour a much greater degree of state intervention in economic life than is wanted by the corporate elite and traditional power-holders in the state; and they have at times significantly extended the public sector by way of nationalization, which is generally abhorrent to their opponents. On the other hand, they have never, *in practice*, given any indication that they wished to turn the public sector into the predominant part of the 'mixed economy';[20] and agreement between them and other members of the power elite, both in the corporate sector and the state system, has in fact been much greater than the rhetoric of either side would often suggest. This is not, it should be said, because conservatives have moved over to the social democratic camp; but rather because social democratic ministers have regularly made the reverse journey. This consensus has been particularly marked in the realm of foreign and defence policy, but it has been present—give or take minor differences—in the realm of economic and social policy as well. Political exigencies may require that left socialists, even Communists, should be admitted to ministerial positions, or other positions of power and influence, as has occasionally happened with left socialists in Britain, and with Communist in Italy, France, and other Western countries. But all such people were carefully kept out of positions of real power. The role of social democracy in advanced capitalist countries will be further discussed in Chapter 3, but it is at any rate the case that the presence of social democrats in the state system has not been nearly as damaging to the cohesion of the power elite as rhetoric might suggest.

III

The bourgeoisie is one of the two 'fundamental' classes in advanced capitalist societies; the working class is the other. It was said at the beginning of this chapter that the working class makes up the vast majority of the people in these societies; and this requires further discussion.

The attempt has sometimes been made on the Left to restrict the working class to 'productive' workers.[21] It was Marx who had made the distinction between 'productive' and 'unproductive' labour. In the context in which he had used the terms, they did not possess the connotation that might at first sight be attributed to them: for they merely referred to the production of surplus value. Thus Marx noted in *Capital* that 'the only worker who is productive is one who produces surplus-value for the capitalist, or in other words contributes to the self-valorization of capital'; and he illustrated the point with an example 'outside the sphere of material production':

A schoolmaster, is a productive worker where, in addition to belabouring the heads of his pupils, he works himself into the ground to enrich the owner of the school. That the latter has laid out his capital in a teaching factory, instead of a sausage factory, makes no difference to the relation.[22]

The distinction between productive and unproductive workers is therefore 'not derived from the material characteristics of labour (neither from the nature of the product nor from the particular character of the labour as concrete labour) but from the definite social form, the social relations of production, within which the labour is realised'.[23] On this basis, 'a writer is a productive labourer not in so far as he produces ideas, but in so far as he enriches the publisher who publishes his works, or if he is a wage-labourer for a capitalist.'[24]

Whatever significance the distinction between 'productive' and 'unproductive' workers may have in other respects, it cannot serve to define who does or does not belong to the working class. An important reason for this is that it is in reality impossible to differentiate between workers in relation to the production of surplus value. This may be illustrated by reference to the discussion of the distinction by two Marxist economists, Laurence Harris and Ben Fine, who are concerned to stress its importance, but who then say the following:

The issue at stake in the categorisation of state employees is not whether they perform a useful function for capital. There can be no doubt that they do, and so, of course, do commercial workers. The point is that they do not directly produce surplus value, they therefore constitute unproductive labour and their usefulness for capital stems solely from their 'indirect' role, their role in the processes which support but are ultimately dependent upon the production of surplus value by productive labour.[25]

These formulations suggest how doubtful the distinction is. For the acknowledgement that 'unproductive' workers 'support' the production of surplus value concedes the point that they do play a role—and it is in fact an indispensable one—in its production; and the notion that these workers are 'ultimately dependent' upon the production of surplus value by 'productive' labour, though true, fails to acknowledge the fact that 'productive' workers are themselves just as 'ultimately dependent' on 'unproductive' workers.

Marx himself, it should be recalled, spoke of the increasingly 'social' nature of production, and saw it as performed by the 'collective worker', a formulation which must obviously be taken to encompass both 'productive' and 'unproductive' workers. Thus Marx wrote that 'in order to work productively, it is no longer necessary for the individual himself to put his hand to the object; it is sufficient for him to be an organ of the collective labourer, and to perform any of its subordinate functions.'[26]

Marx nevertheless excluded 'clerks' and 'commercial employees' employed by 'merchant capitalists' from the category of 'productive' workers. But he also said that, even though their 'unpaid labour' does not create surplus value, it 'does create his [the merchant capitalist's] ability to appropriate surplus-value, which as far as this capital is concerned, gives exactly the same result; i.e. it is its source of profit'.[27] This too very clearly suggests that the distinction between 'productive' and 'unproductive' workers is too flimsy to be of real significance in determining who belongs to the working class and who does not.

The subordinate position of the working class in advanced capitalist societies is most directly manifested in the work process; but it is reflected in all other areas of life as well. In so far as these societies correspond to Max Weber's image of an 'iron cage', it is above all the working class which is most securely imprisoned in it: to abstract class from that image is to ignore an essential aspect of the phenomenon it seeks to depict, namely, the fact that bureaucratization, rules, regulations, controls, the 'officialization' of more and more aspects of life constrain the working class much more effectively than other classes.

Subordination is not experienced equally by all members of the working class. Just as women workers and black workers experience super-exploitation, so too do they experience super-subordination; and one additional aspect of this, for women, is subordination in the home, and in the experience of domination by male members of the working class as well as others. The home is in fact the only sphere in which working class men may successfully seek to exercise domination—which is hardly, needless to say, a reason for excusing it.

But even though distinctions have to be made in regard to the degree of subordination experienced by different sections of the working class, it is nevertheless the working class as a whole which is subordinate; and one major expression of that fact is of course its conditions of life. One must no doubt avoid in this connection what has in France sometimes been called 'misérabilisme', or the painting of all working-class life as unredeemed deprivation. It would obviously be wrong to ignore the many improvements which have occurred in the condition of the working class in the twentieth century. But the fashion is in fact all the other way, in the sense that the stress is most commonly on the 'affluence' in which the working class, or most of the working class, is now supposed to be basking. It used to be said that 'we are all working class now': the much more common current cry is that 'we are all middle class now', or almost all. On any criterion, this is nonsense, so much so that the people who really are 'middle class', in other words the people who belong to the bourgeoisie, would—quite rightly—think themselves catastrophically impoverished and intolerably impaired if they had to share the condition of the working class, even if it was the condition of the 'aristocracy of labour'; and they would, it may be added, feel much the same way if they were reduced to the condition of the petty bourgeoisie.

The assertion made earlier in this chapter that the working class constitutes the vast majority of the population of the countries of advanced capitalism runs counter to the familiar notion that this class is in steep decline. I have already suggested why this is misconceived, in so far as the working class must be taken to include clerical workers, service and distributive workers, and public and state employees. The manufacturing part of the working class is declining in these countries, though not as rapidly as is often claimed. But the working class as a whole, on the criteria set out earlier, is actually growing in numbers, given the decline of independent and self-employed artisans.

The point needs to be made in this connection that the working class is in a constant process of 'recomposition' as a result of the changes which are always occurring in the development of capitalism and the labour process. The most dramatic instance of this 'recomposition' in the twentieth century is probably the reduction of the number of workers on the land, to the point where they have come to form a minute percentage of the 'labour force'; the other major instance of 'recomposition' in this period is the extraordinary growth in the number of clerical workers, and the 'feminization' of that occupational category.

I have taken throughout a rigorously 'objective' view of class, and this too now requires further discussion.

Marx himself said some confusing things on the subject. In *The Poverty of Philosophy* (1846), he spoke of a class which was not 'class conscious' as constituting a 'class-in-itself' rather than a 'class-for-itself'; and he went further in *The Eighteenth Brumaire of Louis Bonaparte* (1852) where, speaking of small-holding French peasants, he said that 'in so far as there is merely a local interconnection' among them, so that 'the identity of their interests begets no community, no national bond and no political organisation among them', 'they do not form a class'.[28] Similarly, Marx sometimes speaks of the working class 'forming itself into a class' as it becomes organized and is involved in struggle.

This would seem to suggest that the existence of a class depends upon the awareness of its members that they are part of a class, and upon their will to struggle against other classes for their perceived common interests. On this view of class, another term would have to be found to denote a specific social aggregate which did not possess this consciousness and will. But no such word is required: 'class' will do very well, because the existence of a class does not in fact depend upon the consciousness, organization, and struggles of its members.

The contrary view of class has been much in favour in recent

times: that view is well summarized in an influential formulation
of E. P. Thompson at the beginning of *The Making of the English
Working Class*:

Class happens when some men, as a result of common experiences
(inherited or shared) feel and articulate the identity of their interests as
between themselves, and against those whose interests are different from
(and usually opposed) to theirs.[29]

Thompson also suggests that 'classes arise because men and
women, in determinative productive relations, identify their
antagonistic interests, and come to struggle, to think and to value
in class ways.[30]

Class, however, does not 'happen' because people feel and
articulate interests opposed to other interests; it exists quite
independently of their feelings and the articulation of these
feelings. As Perry Anderson notes,

classes have frequently existed whose members did not 'identify their
antagonistic interests' in any process of common clarification or struggle.
Indeed, it is probable that for most of historical time this was the rule
rather than the exception.[31]

This does not of course mean that how men and women think
through and act out their class position is unimportant; it is, on
the contrary, crucial. The point is rather that class remains a
social fact, however men and women think through and act out
their class position, and even when they do not.

What is the point, it may be asked, of an identification of class
in 'objective' terms, without the 'subjective' element which gives
life to class relations? The answer must surely be that such an
identification of classes in a given society is indispensable for the
understanding of the fundamental relations prevalent in it. The
'social map' which it provides is no substitute for the analysis of
these relations; but it is an essential point of departure for that
analysis.

This 'objective' identification of classes does involve the at-
tribution 'from outside' of an identity to people who may well
reject it; and in the case of the working class, it also leads to the
insistence that it 'ought' to have the particular consciousness
which is deemed, from outside, to be appropriate to it. Thus
Thompson also writes, with evident disapproval, that if the

working class 'is assumed to have a real existence', 'it becomes possible to deduce the class consciousness which "it" ought to have (but seldom does have) if "it" was properly aware of its own position and real interests'.[32]

Some important issues need to be disentangled here. In one of his most famous pronouncements, Marx said that 'it is not the consciousness of men that determines their being, but on the contrary their social being that determines their consciousness.'[33] 'Social being' is a useful concept, which cannot be taken to refer exclusively to an individual's class position; Other factors undoubtedly enter into its constitution—gender, race, ethnicity, personal history, and a multitude of other factors which together form an exceedingly complex totality, a kind of social DNA.[34] The Marxist claim, which I believe to be wholly justified, is that class is the decisive factor in this combination. Other factors in 'social being' do have an influence on the ways in which class itself is experienced; but class nevertheless crucially shapes the whole of 'social being'.

The complex totality represented in 'social being' produces or 'determines' a consciousness which is correspondingly complex, and often contradictory, with a great variety of sentiments, feelings, ideas, opinions, prejudices, attitudes, and emotions which coexist more or less easily and coherently with each other (or more or less uneasily); and the closer the analysis of consciousness gets to particular individuals, the more complex and varied and often contradictory that consciousness will reveal itself to be. An obvious example would be that of a male socialist who deeply believes in the emancipation of the working class, but is also the prisoner of deeply racist or sexist attitudes and sentiments.

Nevertheless, there does exist a much greater correlation between class position and political consciousness than is often suggested. This is obviously so for dominant classes: the members of these classes do for the most part quite naturally favour the social order which affords them their power and privileges, and will therefore generally be found on various points of the conservative side of the political spectrum. As for the working class, there have also been large segments of it which have always dwelt on the same conservative side of the spectrum; and this shows well enough that the subordinate position of the working class in the social structure does not necessarily produce a transformative and emancipatory class consciousness in its members. But it is also in the working class that has been generated the basis of support for the main agencies of social change and of challenge to the existing social order in advanced capitalist societies.

Also, it is difficult to see what is wrong with the notion that the working class 'ought' to be aware of the nature of its subordination and exploitation; that it has an interest in the creation of a society in which it would no longer be subject to them; and that it 'ought' therefore to struggle towards that goal. These propositions may be opposed on the grounds that the working class is not in fact exploited and subordinate; or that a society free from exploitation and subordination is impossible; or that struggle can only make matters worse; and so forth. But this does not affect the core issue, which is that it is perfectly proper to believe that individuals and groups 'ought' to think and act in certain ways, and not in others. The particular stipulation may be mistaken, but that is not the point; and stipulations of this sort are in fact always and inevitably made. To refuse to make them is to opt for a wholly unrealistic and quite immoral relativism, according to which there is, for instance, no ground for saying that it was not in the interest of German workers to support the Nazis, and that, for this and other reasons, they should not have supported them.

The danger to which critics of the notion of 'false consciousness' allude lies elsewhere: namely, in the attempt to *force* upon the working class (and everybody else) the 'consciousness' which people in power choose to 'impute' to it, to use George Lukács's famous formulation, and to require subscription to all notions, ideas, and positions which such people stipulate to be part of what they define as true or class or revolutionary consciousness. With such imputation, class consciousness turns into another version of the people's 'real will', or the will that they really do will, even if they are not aware of it, and which it is therefore incumbent upon their rulers and guides to will for them. This kind of imputation and imposition has frequently occurred in the twentieth century, not least in the name of Marxism, but it cannot reasonably be taken to be the inevitable consequence of the view that the working class does have certain interests and that it ought to support certain ideas and causes rather than others.

A rather different objection to this view is that the divisions within the working class (even if one agrees on what the working class is) are so great as to render illusory any notion of even potential class homogeneity or common consciousness. Thus Professor Skidelsky, for instance, writes that

the further progress of the division of labour produces not a Marxist simplification into proletarians and capitalists, but increasing occupational diversity leading to growing conflicts of interests, values, understandings and life-styles . . . Trade unionism becomes not an army organised for battle under capitalism but an arena, where group conflicts are fought out.[35]

On this view, the working class all but becomes a figure of speech, and can hardly be said to exist at all; and Professor Skidelsky does indeed see it as 'subject to dissolution'.[36] Not only is it not a 'class-for-itself', but it is not even, properly speaking, a 'class-in-itself'. It is rent by division, fragmentation, occupational diversity, sectionalism, huge differences between an organized sector—in which are mostly to be found white male workers— and a largely unorganized one—predominantly made up of women workers, blacks, and members of other, super-exploited minorities and others in vulnerable positions and occupations.

As if this were not enough, there is also the fact, so it is said, that massive technological change is steadily replacing workers by machines, and 'deskilling' the workers who remain. Thus, in a book which has had considerable resonance, André Gorz has argued that

automation and computerisation have eliminated most skills and pos-sibilities for initiative and are in the process of replacing what remains of the skilled labour force (whether blue or white collar) by a new type of unskilled worker. The age of the skilled workers, with their power in the factory and their anarcho-syndicalist [*sic*] projects, has now to be seen as an interlude which taylorism, scientific work organisation, and, finally, computers, and robots have brought to a close.[37]

Similarly, another book which has been accorded much attention argues that the 'increasing replacement of men by machines' means that by the end of the century the 'entire area of blue-collar work may have diminished so greatly that the term will lose its sociological meaning as new categories, more appropriate to the divisions of the new labor force, are established'.[38]

Given these vast changes, it naturally follows that the working class, or rather, the 'working class', cannot realistically be viewed as an agency of radical transformations in advanced capitalist societies (assuming of course that such transformations are at all desirable).

The two major questions at issue concern the divisions within the working class, and the technological changes which have occurred in recent decades. With regard to the first of these questions, it may be worth recalling, in no spirit of complacency, that division, fragmentation, sectionalism, and so forth, have *always* been present in the working class, and that while some of these features (for instance, occupational diversity) are more marked now than in the past, others (notably divisions among different layers of the working class) do not seem more profound than they were in earlier epochs. The working class has never been a homogeneous, united, and 'class conscious' class. Nor of course did Marx believe that it was: what he did believe was that the divisions and differences which existed in the working class would in due course be drastically reduced by the development of capitalism and subdued and overcome by a common revolutionary consciousness. This 'homogenization', either in economic or in political terms, or in any other, has not in fact occurred; but this does not resolve the question whether different sectors of the working class are capable of achieving a *sufficient* degree of ideological and political unity to be an effective force for radical change in capitalist society. To return a firmly negative answer to that question is very rash.

Much of the discussion of what the working class may or may not be expected to do politically is based on the usually unspoken assumption that it is industrial workers, the 'direct producers', who must be expected to be the most 'class conscious', combative, and radical, whereas workers in other occupations cannot be expected to exhibit these qualities. This should not be taken for granted. Industrial workers, notably in skilled occupations, are usually much better *organized* than workers in other occupations; but their class consciousness may be quite limited and far from conducive to militancy; and such militancy as they evince may be directed at quite narrowly 'economistic' targets, and may have very little or no radical and transformative charge. Very often in the past, the vaunted militancy and class consciousness of workers in 'traditional' occupations has largely been confined to the vigorous and stubborn assertion of a 'labourism' which was very limited in scope and free for the most part from any kind of revolutionary purpose. This is not to say that their resistance to the oppression of employers was not admirable, only that it should not be invested, in contrast to what is occurring in present times, with qualities which it did not necessarily possess. Much of the class struggle in which American workers in 'traditional' occupations have engaged exhibits this restricted character.

On the other hand, workers in non-industrial occupations have often displayed a high degree of militancy. Again and again, service and distributive workers, municipal and state employees, and many others who are not industrial workers, have shown a high degree of combativity and determination in pressing and struggling for a wide range of demands. The traditional image of the 'typical' proletarian class fighter—white, male, skilled—stands in the way of an appreciation of the potential for pressure and struggle of all other sections of the working class.

Nor is there any good reason for accepting the notion that occupational and other divisions in the working class create an unbridgeable gulf between different groups of workers. Frank Parkin puts the point well when he writes that 'it is less than convincing to claim that there is a fundamental antagonism between dockers, railwaymen, miners and so forth on the one hand, and nurses, teachers, social workers and so forth, on the other.'[39] It is notable in this connection that trade unionism has grown tremendously in occupational sectors where it had previously been very weak; and that many people in these sectors have not hesitated to engage in forms of struggle—strikes, for instance—which they had previously shunned. Some of them, like teachers, are part of the sub-professional petty bourgeoisie, and the fact that they are now much more willing than in the past to engage in forms of pressure which they had previously considered to be beneath them and reserved for mere 'workers' suggests at least a potential for joint action much greater than is allowed by the prophets of 'post-industrial' society.

In no way is this intended to belittle the reality of the many divisions that do exist in the working class, and of the lack of solidarity, to say the least, which they generate. Yet it also does need to be said that these divisions have not prevented workers deeply divided on many counts from coming together in industrial and political struggles, and from sustaining industrial and political organizations in which these divisions and antagonisms have been sufficiently subdued to permit common action against what were perceived to be common enemies. Again and again, large groups of workers have displayed solidarity in struggle; and the fact that this solidarity has often proved brittle and vulnerable, and has regularly been followed by relapse into division, does not alter its reality as a part of the history of class struggle. The point is that what inhibits lasting solidarity is not some atavistic and ineradicable trait, but specific economic, social, political, and cultural factors which enhance and encourage division. The problems this poses for effective and coherent action are formidable; but they are not beyond resolution.

What, then, of the technological developments which have been held to be transforming the working class to the point of virtually destroying it as a class?

A great deal here hinges on what these developments have meant in relation to the work process. On this, there has been a sharp division between those writers who, following Harry Braverman's classic *Labour and Monopoly Capital: The Degradation of Work in the Twentieth Century* (1974), have argued that workers are being progressively 'deskilled'; and those who have denied that this is the case—with, of course, many intermediate positions.

What seems to be occurring, however, is a simultaneous process of 'deskilling' at one level, and of 'reskilling' at another. Automation and computerization greatly simplify the labour process; but they also demand from workers the acquisition of new skills for the tending, control, repair, and general management of the new machines. However complex and sophisticated these may be—and indeed, because of their sophistication and complexity—they require the most careful tending. Without this, and without all the sensitivity and knowledge which such tending requires, the machines will soon fail to perform the tasks assigned to them, with more or less catastrophic results. As one writer puts it, 'it is as unproductive for radical critics as it is unprofitable for capitalist managers to underestimate the scope of the knowledge required of the operator to know when to hit that STOP button'.[40]

For all the efforts of managers to reduce their dependence on workers by breaking down the tasks at hand into their simplest component parts, and by reducing to the greatest possible extent the skill and initiative required of workers, these efforts are defeated on the shop floor itself. As J. Zeitlin observes,

the more bureaucratic the administration of production the more dependent management becomes on ordinary workers' initiatives to avoid costly breakdowns and on small groups of highly skilled craftsmen to repair them; and the more interdependent the production process, the more vulnerable it becomes to disruption at the hands of strategically placed work groups.[41]

The argument, however, is not only that workers are being 'deskilled' by machines, but that they are being replaced by them altogether, so that what is occurring, in Gorz's phrase, is the emergence of a 'non-class of non-workers'.

Two things may be said about this. The first is that, as Ernest Mandel puts it,

the short- and medium term impact of full-scale automation or robotisation on total employment (the number of wage-labourers employed) has been virtually nil till the beginning of the seventies (taking into account shifts of employment between branches, which are of course very real), and remains modest today and for the foreseeable future.[42]

The same author also notes that 'recent OECD studies predict that between now and the nineties, robotisation will cut somewhere between 4% and 8% of all existing jobs *in the West* (and between 2% and 5% of all existing jobs on a world scale.'[43] What this means is that the working population in advanced capitalist countries will not be significantly reduced in the relevant future, but that occupational patterns will be greatly altered, and that the 'recomposition' of the working class will proceed at an even faster pace.

The second point is that technological change is not, in the words of David Noble, 'an irreducible first cause; its social effects follow from the social causes that brought it into being: behind the technology that affects social relations lie the very same social relations. Little wonder, then, that the technology usually tends to reinforce rather than subvert those relations.'[44] In this perspective, new labour processes are just as much terrains of class struggle as the old ones. As another author puts it, in relation to earlier attempts by management to 'rationalise' production, 'the bureaucratic reorganisation of the labor process developed . . . not through some technological imperative, but through a historically specific process of class struggle which was understood and articulated as such by the contending parties.'[45]

André Gorz himself, it may be noted, stresses the fact that technology is not simply an 'objective' constraint: on the contrary, it is, he writes,

the stake of a struggle for power. Employers demand of technology the elimination of the human factor from the process of production and everything in that process to be capable of being forecast, programmed, controlled and calculated. The deskilling of the labour force is not only sought for economic reasons but because skill is, in its essence, a power which the worker applies in his work, and therefore a source of uncertainties for the employer.[46]

This is a rather far cry from the picture of workers 'deskilled' in an inexorable process. It is not in fact 'technology' which does anything, but men and women seeking to serve given purposes, which technology may help or hinder. It is employers who are driven to seek technological change out of the imperative need to maximize their profits; and the system of which they are a part does not require them to take individual or social cost into account—indeed, it requires them to take as little account of any such cost as possible. It is, on the other hand, workers, seeking to protect jobs, wages, and their conditions of work, who are driven to resist changes which threaten them. A system impelled by a different dynamic would heed the human cost of technological change, and seek to minimize it.

Nothing that has happened in recent years to the working class warrants the view that workers will not continue to wage class struggle and exercise pressure upon employers and the state for the satisfaction of their grievances and demands. But there is nothing, either, in recent developments which affords any automatic assurance that the struggle will be waged effectively, or that the working class will inevitably acquire the kind of class consciousness that would drive it to seek radical change. Everything in this realm, now as always before, depends on the many different factors which determine the nature, terms, purposes, and outcomes of the struggle. It is these factors which require investigation.

IV

Reference was made earlier to the 'intermediate' location of the petty bourgeoisie in the social structure of advanced capitalist countries. This 'intermediate' location precludes the petty bourgeoisie from constructing a distinct, autonomous vision of society. The dominant class does have such a vision, which is roughly defined in terms of the existing social order, no doubt with suitable modifications designed to strengthen its position; and working-class movements for their part have generally been pledged, at one level of commitment or another, to the creation of an alternative society. The petty bourgeoisie, on the other hand, has no such comprehensive project; its most distinctive demand, as a class, has tended to be for a capitalism freed from the domination of 'big business' and 'finance capital', and from the greedy demands of trade unions.

Also, the 'intermediate' location of the petty bourgeoisie finds expression in respect of subordination. As I noted earlier, it clearly constitutes a subordinate class in relation to the bourgeoisie, and its position on this score is not qualitatively different from that of the working class. In relation to the working class, however, it occupies positions of command and supervision, and mediates power 'from above'.

In political terms, the petty bourgeoisie has commonly been assigned a reactionary role. Professor A. J. Mayer thus expresses a familiar view when he writes that 'although it may waver along the way, in the final analysis the lower middle class resolves its ambiguous and strained class, status and power relations to the power elite above and the underclass below in favour of the ruling class'; and he also speaks of an 'inner core of conservatism' in the petty bourgeoisie, which is 'ultimately revealed in moments of acute social and political conflict . . .'.[47]

This echoes some of the things which Marx and Engels said about the petty bourgeoisie in the *Communist Manifesto*, even though their remarks on the subject are not free from ambiguity; [48] and J. M. Wiener has rightly recalled that Marx in many of his writings took a much more positive view of the political potential of the petty bourgeoisie.[49] Even Lenin, who used the term 'petty bourgeois' as a form of abuse, sometimes acknowledged that the political positions of the petty bourgeoisie were not irrevocably fixed by its 'intermediate' economic and social position, but were to a considerable extent shaped by external pulls and pressures, and notably by the skill and determination displayed by the main contending forces in society.[50]

A distinction needs to be made here between the two main parts of the petty bourgeoisie. As far as the small-business, entrepreneurial, shopkeeping element of the class is concerned, the pull towards positions on the right, even the far right, of the political spectrum is generally strong. British shopkeepers, it has been said, subscribe to the Conservative Party's slogan of a 'property-owning democracy', believe in a free market, are solidly Conservative voters, and are hostile to labour, trade unions, socialism, and the Left, and have ambivalent attitudes towards big business.[51] British shopkeepers have their counterparts everywhere else in the capitalist world. Even so, it is worth noting that this business petty bourgeoisie is not a monolithic bloc, and that parties of the Left—for instance, the Italian Communist Party—have had a measure of success in attracting support among artisans, shopkeepers, and small entrepreneurs.[52]

This attraction, however, is much more marked in the sub-professional part of the petty bourgeoisie. Large sections of it have historically voted for and supported parties of the Left; and many activists and people in leading positions have indeed been drawn from that class. So too have many such people joined and played an active role in the 'new social movements' which have emerged in recent decades.

This trend is likely to be accentuated by the growth in advanced capitalist countries of an often mis-employed (or unemployed) petty bourgeois *intelligentsia*, unable to find a place in the occupational structure commensurate with its ability, training, skills, and expectations. It is also these people who feel most keenly the assault by government on social and collective services in which many of them are employed. That assault inevitably fosters among them a militant concern with salaries, conditions of work, and indeed employment itself. This makes them at least potential allies of industrial, service, and other workers in struggle, and creates new possibilities of joint pressure and alliance.

This brings us back to class struggle; and it is to this struggle that we may now turn.

A Note on the Distribution of Wealth and Income

The following are no more than some general observations on a subject which is a minefield for the non-expert.

It may first be noted that alongside the distribution of power, the distribution of wealth and income is clearly crucial in the determination of the nature and texture of a society. Yet, all analysts, whatever their other differences, agree that, even for the relatively few countries where a reasonable amount of data is available, the evidence is very partial and highly ambiguous. The effort to compile really reliable and up-to-date information on the subject is clearly not a high priority with governments; and this is in marked contrast with their concern to accumulate all possible information on other subjects relating to their populations.

As a matter of common sense, it must also be presumed that the data available grossly underestimates both the wealth and the income of most sections of the population; but this is most obviously true for the better-off parts of it. The great majority do not have much room for tax avoidance (legal) or tax evasion (illegal), whereas the rich and the super-rich do have a great deal of room for the purpose, and expert advice as well. This means that the wealth of the rich and the super-rich is a lot greater than the actual figures suggest; and this (to a lesser extent, given the greater risk attached to understated returns) is most probably true of income as well.

Moreover, the evidence lends itself to considerable manipulation. This is particularly true in regard to the decline in the inequality of wealth. In gauging how much decline has occurred in recent decades, different results will be obtained if 'wealth' is taken to include owner-occupied housing, consumer durables and other household goods, cash, current bank accounts, public and private insurance schemes, as well as stocks and shares, land, and other forms of marketable property.

Even if the latter alone are taken into account—which is much the more reasonable way to proceed—two features regarding the distribution of wealth seem to stand out. The first is that the share of wealth owned by the richest 10 per cent of the population of these countries appears to have declined in the last fifty years; but the second is that the inequality of wealth between the richest 20 per cent and the remaining 80 per cent has remained enormous, with the latter owning little, or very little, or nothing. Even the degree of redistribution which this may be taken to signify must be treated with some caution. Thus one author, writing about Britain, notes what seems to be an impressive decline from the 1920s to the 1970s in the share of wealth owned by the top 1, 5, and 10 per cent of wealth-holders; but he then goes on to say the following:

Intra-family changes in the pattern of asset ownership could account for much of the movement in wealth shares. Assuming that the wealth of families, rather than individuals, is the more relevant variable for social policy, this line of reasoning suggests that the observed decline in wealth concentration is exaggerated, *and possibly completely spurious*.[53]

Vast disparities of income similarly prevail in the countries concerned, and are in part related to the disparities in the distribution of wealth, since wealth itself is a major source of income.

Much has been made of the vast increase which has occurred in institutional shareholding by way of pension funds, insurance companies, and investment trusts. But important though this may be in other ways, it has no marked bearing on the distribution of disposable wealth in the form of stocks, shares, land, and other forms of property.

Nor, it must also be said, does 'privatization' have such an effect. The purchase by workers of shares in newly privatized enterprises has given a new lease of life in Britain and other countries to the cry of 'people's capitalism' which was current in the United States in the post-war years. But such purchase will make no substantial— indeed, not any—difference to the prevalent concentration of share ownership. The fact that millions of people own a few hundred shares, and that many such people are workers, may well have *political* consequences which are important. But it is of no real consequence in the general pattern of the distribution of wealth and income (*and* power) in these societies. The same, incidentally, is true of the spectacular appreciation of house values in many urban centres. A substantial number of working-class families (and of course others) have come as a result into possession of sizeable sums of money— assuming they can find cheaper accommodation elsewhere, or leave their houses to their descendants. But this too cannot seriously affect the general pattern of wealth ownership. The system itself constantly reproduces great—at the extremes staggering, monstrous— inequalities of wealth, income, and power. A radical transformation in this situation can only be achieved by a radical transformation of the system itself.

Instead, the regressive policies of conservative administrations in such countries as Britain and the United States in the eighties have greatly reinforced inequalities of wealth and income, and have given added force to the injunction that 'to him who hath shall be given'. More will be said on this score presently.

3

The Politics of Class Struggle, I

I

'Class struggle from below' refers to the struggles waged by workers and the organizations which speak, or which purport to speak, for them—trade unions and political parties, but also a variety of other groupings and people that form part of the labour movement.

Class struggle from below cannot of course be separated from the class struggle which is waged 'from above': the two form part of a total process and constantly react upon one another. The demands and pressures which emanate from below encounter resistance from above, and become objects of contestation and struggle; and vice versa. Also, the forms of struggle chosen by one of the protagonists are influenced by the forms of struggle chosen by the other. In short, the two processes are closely interwoven.

But even though class struggle is one process, usually involving protagonists from above and from below, the contending forces do nevertheless have their own agencies, politics, history, traditions, modes of action and adaptation. So, too, do they have their own demands and interests. I shall therefore discuss class struggle from below in this chapter, and leave class struggle from above to a later one. Some overlap is inevitable, but the separation is nevertheless worth making.

An initial question which arises in relation to class struggle from below concerns *who* engages in it. To speak of 'the working class' in this connection is plainly inaccurate on more than one count. It is quite likely that most workers will, at one point or another of their working lives, be involved in some form of struggle with their employers; and there are occasions when great numbers are involved in struggle simultaneously, for instance, in a great wave of strikes or in a general strike. But such episodes are almost by definition quite rare; and it is for the most part a minority, even a small minority, of workers who are involved at any one time in active, concerted, collective 'industrial' action.

As for political action, it needs to be said first of all that a substantial part of the working class has historically supported bourgeois and conservative parties rather than ones on the Left. Indeed, this has traditionally been true of a majority of the working class—nowhere more so than in the United States, but in other advanced capitalist countries as well. It is only since World War II that this pattern has been less pronounced; and the support which members of the working class give to parties of the Left is for the most part confined to the act of voting. Having voted, the great majority of the working class tends to relapse into political passivity.

In other words, it is only a minority of the working class which is involved in class struggle from below in a sustained and committed fashion, whether in the industrial or political sphere. This minority has always constituted the *activist* ingredient of the labour movement (a term to be defined in a moment), those whom R. H. Tawney once called its 'energumens' and 'zealots', the people who work at the grassroots, the hewers of wood and the drawers of water in trade unions, political parties, and other organizations of the labour movement. Their willingness to take on the chores associated with organizational work, on a mainly voluntary and amateur basis, usually without much (or any) expectation of tangible reward, has played an immensely important role in sustaining these organizations.

By no means all activists are more radical and militant than their leaders: many of them are perfectly content to be faithful servants of their organization and its leaders, and are in fact quite hostile to activists on their left. It is these left activists who have always formed the major radical ingredient of their organizations and the main opposition to their 'moderate' leaders. This division between left activists and their leaders has been a phenomenon of great importance in the life of trade unions and social democratic parties, and more will be said about it presently.

In the light of the minority character of sustained activism in the working class, it is clearly by way of a figure of speech that one speaks of 'the working class' as thinking, or wanting, or doing this or that: this is a kind of inflation to which the Right is at least as prone as the Left—witness the claim of conservative politicians after an election which has given them victory on a minority of votes that 'the American people' or 'the British people' have spoken and shown what policies they preferred.

Even 'organized labour', which may be taken to denote that part of the working class which belongs to trade unions, is a term that must be used with great reservations, since what is usually attributed to 'organized labour' is what its leaders say and do on its behalf, in a representation of what their members think and want which may or may not be particularly accurate.

As for the 'labour movement', in the common usage of the term, and as I use it here, it encompasses a wide range of people and institutions: trade unions and organized labour in general; labour and socialist parties; activists in unions, parties, groupings, and sects of the Left; newspapers, journals, magazines which support the labour movement; the men and women who professionally staff the movement's organizations; trade union and party leaders and parliamentarians; intellectuals, journalists, writers, and artists who present, defend, and propagate the ideas and perspectives of the labour movement, in all their diversity and frequent contradictoriness.

The members of the labour movement have never been drawn from the working class alone; but the great majority of activists, in trade unions and political parties, *have* been of the working class. It is above all the support of workers—including the financial and electoral support of largely passive workers—which has sustained the main agencies of the labour movement. Without that support, trade unions could not have survived, and labour and socialist parties would have been reduced to small sects and groupings with little or no influence on the life of their societies. The building of labour movements in the last hundred years in all advanced capitalist countries is an extraordinary *working class* achievement, whose magnitude has not received the acknowledgement, even on the Left, which it deserves—particularly if account is taken of the difficulties and obstacles of every kind which stood in the way of the people who built these movements, from the poverty of resources at their disposal to the opposition and repression which they faced from employers and the state.

It is all the more fitting that the achievement should be acknowledged, because the extension of citizenship and democratic rights which has occurred in these countries is in large part due to the struggles and the pressures of labour movements—indeed, to the very fact of their existence. The pressure for reform did not come from labour movements alone; other forces in capitalist society, of bourgeois and petty bourgeois provenance, were also involved in the advancement of many demands, from the enlargement of civic rights to struggles over issues of foreign and imperial policy—sometimes in alliance with labour movements, sometimes independently. But the fact nevertheless remains that the direct and indirect pressure of labour movements played a considerable, even a decisive, part in the achievement of the social and political advances of the last hundred years in these countries. 'Indirect' pressure here simply means the awareness of middle-class and petty-bourgeois reformers, and of quite conservative governments, that, if dangerous socialist ideas and revolutionary promptings were to be contained and (it might be hoped) neutralized, concessions would have to be made to the working class and labour movements. In this perspective, the fact that advanced capitalist societies are more civilized today, or less uncivilized, than they were, let us say, fifty years ago (not to speak of a hundred years ago) is in large part due to the pressure which the existence and the struggles of labour movements exerted upon structures of domination and exploitation. Nowhere in the countries in question have the reforms which have been achieved brought about the disappearance of exploitation and domination. But they have, at different levels for different parts of the working class, served to improve the conditions in which domination and exploitation are experienced.

II

The labour movement has always been exceedingly diverse and divided; but there have been some fundamental ideological and political divisions within it which must be noted here, since they have so deeply af;ected the conduct of class struggle. One of them was the division between those people in labour movements who were essentially social reformers, and whose horizons, as distinct from their rhetoric, were in practice confined to the improvement of existing society, without much (or any) commitment to its radical transformation; and those for whom such a transformation was precisely the paramount aim. A further line of division, which assumed crucial importance after 1914, lay between socialists who believed that electoral and parliamentary struggle, led by a mass party of the working class and oriented towards every kind of reform, including 'structural' reforms, was an essential, even a primary means of socialist advance; and those who stressed the imperative need for extra-parliamentary struggle, and the inevitability of revolutionary upheaval, to be prepared for by a vanguard party.

No doubt, people who were mentally and politically very firmly installed in bourgeois society, and who sought nothing more than limited social reform, were perfectly willing, even eager, when occasion demanded it, to proclaim their own vision of an altogether different kind of society; but they envisaged its coming in very general and vague terms, and as an exceedingly distant eventuality, which must not be allowed to interfere with immediate pre-occupations. For their part, vanguard revolutionaries generally accepted the need to struggle for immediate reforms, and for electoral and parliamentary activity, even though they viewed it, at best, as a second-level business, fraught with great dangers of opportunism and compromise.[1] As for socialists concerned with advance within the framework of bourgeois democracy, and by way of electoral and parliamentary gains, they too very often agreed on the need for extra-parliamentary struggles. Yet despite the many qualifications and refinements which these lines of division require, they do indicate a definite line of demarcation between distinct and alternative positions.

These divisions had existed in labour movements long before 1914. But they did not before then produce an unbridgeable gulf between the protagonists of different positions. The degree of 'co-habitation' that was then possible between them is perhaps best indicated by the fact that the Second International, whose affiliated parties harboured most left tendencies, managed to hold its congresses and remain in one piece from 1889 to the eve of the war. At no time in those years was the international labour movement irrevocably split into absolutely opposed and warring camps.

This was fundamentally changed by the sundering produced by the outbreak of World War I, and by the Bolshevik Revolution in 1917. A split in the ranks of the major working-class parties, of great dimension, was almost certainly inevitable as a result of the war. The bitterness, radicalism, and militancy produced by the war would, in all likelihood, have brought into existence socialist parties determined to distance themselves from the traditional leaders of social democratic parties, now fully engaged in what their socialist opponents saw as class collaboration in support of the war. Such a split is precisely what occurred in the German Social Democratic Party, with the coming into being of the Independent Socialist Party in 1915, which included some of the most prestigious figures of German social democracy, for instance, Karl Kautsky and Rudolf Hilferding.

Nevertheless, the divisions in labour movements assumed an immeasurably more virulent and irremediable character as a result of the Bolshevik Revolution; or, more accurately, as a result of the determination of Lenin and the Bolshevik leaders to bring about a total split between what they took to be true revolutionaries on the one hand, and all other tendencies and positions on the other. This was a decision of the greatest consequence for labour movements everywhere; and it deeply influenced their history and the history of class struggle in subsequent decades.

At its second Congress in Moscow in July—August 1920, the Third International adopted Lenin's famous Twenty-one Conditions for membership of the organization. These Conditions were calculated to split all labour movements from top to bottom. They included subscription to the 'dictatorship of the proletariat'; the 'merciless and systematic' denunciation not only of the bourgeoisie, 'but also its assistants, the reformists of every shade'; the removal from all responsible posts throughout the labour movements of all reformists and 'followers of the "centre" '; the creation in acknowledgement of the coming of civil war in 'almost all of the countries of Europe and America', of a parallel illegal apparatus; the acceptance of strict 'democratic centralism', 'iron discipline bordering on military discipline', with the party centre as 'a powerful, authoritative organ with wide powers'; the changing of the names of the parties wishing to join the International to that of Communist Party; and, of crucial importance, the acceptance of all decisions of the Congress of the International as binding upon all member parties.[2]

The Twenty-one Conditions were certain to be rejected by

most leaders of the existing labour and socialist parties, and by large numbers of their members as well—in many cases by the vast majority of their members. Lenin and his colleagues had expected that there would be some shedding and splitting: one of the Conditions insisted that the split with 'reformism' and 'reformists' should be brought about 'with the least delay'. 'The Communist International', its leaders had said, 'cannot reconcile itself to the fact that such avowed reformists as Turati, Kautsky, Hilferding, Hillquit, Longuet, McDonald, Modigliani, and others, should be entitled to consider themselves members of the Third International.'[3] But the Bolsheviks had confidently expected that the parties of the Second Intenational would rapidly dwindle and that Communist parties would replace them in the leadership of labour movements: this was a grave miscalculation. In France, the new Communist Party was, as a result of the Congress of Tours in 1920, initially larger than the Socialist Party from which it had split; and the Communist Party of Germany, though smaller than the Social Democratic Party, was a substantial force in German political life until the Nazi assumption of power in 1933. But the predominance of the old social democratic parties over their labour movements was soon re-established everywhere: in some cases—for instance, in Britain—it had never been seriously challenged.

However, the division was now institutionalized and ever more firmly cemented by the hatred which each side felt for the other.

One of the main grounds for the division, on the social democratic side, was proclaimed to be the Communists' rejection of parliamentary democracy. This was undoubtedly true in the first fifteen years or so of the Third International. In that period, Communist parties remained wholly faithful to Lenin's view that bourgeois democracy was a sham and a fraud, which Communists could only use to hasten the day when an altogether different form of political regime, 'a million times more democratic than bourgeois democracy', would be brought into being.[4]

Nor was this simply a matter of proclamations. From their foundation in the immediate post-war years until the turn to the Popular Front Strategy in 1934/5, Communist parties in advanced capitalist countries, under the direction of the Comintern, were self-consciously revolutionary parties. In some cases, notably in Germany, they made insurrectionary bids for power which were doomed to dismal failure, at the cost of many lives. With this naturally went extreme hostility towards social democracy and all its works. The sectarianism which marked those early years reached new heights in the so-called Third Period,[5] from the late twenties until 1934/5, in which period the Comintern decreed that the main enemy of the working class, against whom the main thrust of Communist opposition must be directed, was social democracy, whose description by Stalin himself as 'social fascism' thereby acquired unquestioned status in Communist ranks.

This was allied with pleas for 'unity' of the labour movement at the grassroots; but the combination of vehement denunciation of the leaders of social democracy with appeals to the rank and file to 'unite' with the Communists made the strategy seem like no more than clumsy manœuvres designed to disrupt and wreck hated rival organizations.

The country where these policies had the most disastrous results was Germany, where it left the labour movement utterly divided, with social democrats and Communists more than ever separated by an insuperable wall of mutual hatred which made any united action against the Nazis quite impossible. Reconciliation and united action in the face of the common Nazi threat would in any case have been difficult enough, given the history of bitter hostility which had existed ever since the formation of the KPD: but the policies of the Comintern, unswervingly supported by the KPD, made rejection of any form of co-operation with the Communists that much easier.

What made this all the more tragic was that the KPD enjoyed substantial growth in those years, with an increase in membership from 125,000 in the late twenties to 170,000 in 1930, 240,000 in 1931, and 360,000 at the end of 1932.[6] As the threat of Nazism grew, there was a reluctant acknowledgement on the part of the Communist Party that there were differences between social democracy and fascism, to which Communists could not remain indifferent, but the acknowledgement was very grudging, and mixed with the same vociferous attacks as hitherto. Nor, it should be added, were these attacks groundless: there was plenty to criticize in social democratic policies and actions.[7]

The policies of the Third Period were not abandoned until well after Hitler had come to power. Even after the Left in Germany— Social Democrats and Communists—had been crushed, the

Executive Committee of the Comintern was still saying that 'the establishment of an open fascist dictatorship, by dissipating the illusions of the masses, by liberating them from the influence of social democracy, accelerates the march of Germany towards revolution.'[8]

The turn finally came in 1934/5, with the movement towards Popular Fronts. In the present context, the crucial significance of that turn lies in the fact that it also betokened the reconciliation with bourgeois democracy of the Communist parties in capitalist-democratic regimes. This will be discussed below. But the reconciliation, which was in any case hinged with various qualifications, did not bring Communists and social democrats closer together. For there were other weighty grounds for the division between them.

One of these was the peculiar relationship of Communist parties to the Soviet Union. It was suggested earlier that revolutionary parties, under one name or another, were almost certain to come into being as a result of World War I. But the fact that it was Communist parties which did come into being, at the behest of the Comintern, is a fact of cardinal importance in the history of class struggle in the twentieth century. For the character and life of these parties was decisively shaped by their adherence to the Comintern and to a Soviet leadership enjoying unique prestige by virtue of the Bolshevik Revolution. Given the origin of these parties, and their acceptance of the Twenty-one Conditions demanded by the Comintern, it was all but inevitable that they should have come under Soviet domination. That domination, however, was far from complete in the first years of the International; but it became total with Stalin's ascendancy in the late twenties and the Stalinization of the Communist parties which went with it everywhere. As a result, Communist parties acquired a crucial characteristic, which also served to draw a profound line of division between them and social democratic parties: namely, their unqualified acceptance of every word and deed of Soviet leaders, and above all of Stalin. It was Stalin who set out very clearly as early as 1927 what was demanded of Communists everywhere:

A revolutionary is one who is ready to protect, to defend the USSR without reservation, without qualification, openly and honestly . . . An internationalist is one who is ready to defend the USSR without reservation, without wavering, unconditionally; for the USSR is the base of the world revolutionary movement and this revolutionary movement cannot be defended and promoted unless the USSR is defended. For whoever thinks of defending the world revolutionary movement apart from, or against, the USSR, goes against the revolution and must inevitably slide into the camp of the enemies of the revolution.[9]

This typically Stalinist, 'either/or' view carried immense weight for the next thirty years. It was only with Khrushchev's 'secret speech' at the Twentieth Party Congress of the CPSU that qualifications began to be accepted to the demand for unconditional support of everything Soviet. The harm this unconditional support did to labour movements everywhere is incalculable.

Had the Soviet regime not degenerated into Stalinism, it would have been possible for revolutionaries in capitalist countries to defend the USSR against the vilification and attacks to which it was subjected by western media and governments, while at the same time distancing themselves from some of the things that might be done by Soviet leaders. This, however, was not acceptable to Stalin. What was required was, as he had said, unqualified defence of every twist and turn of Soviet home and foreign policy, and for every pronouncement and action of the Soviet government and party. Communists were thus turned into the unswerving apologists of the Soviet regime, whatever it might do, and however much anything that it might do or say at one point contradicted what had been done or said earlier. This required an abdication of critical thought on the part of many of the best, ablest, and most dedicated activists in labour movements; and it also required them to close their eyes and their minds to the terrible deeds committed in the name of socialism and revolution under Stalin's rule.

Acquiescence and unqualified support, it should be stressed, were imperatively required and imposed, with any deviation from the path of obedience, however slight, instantly visited with denunciation and likely excommunication and, in the case of some Communist parties, with the physical 'liquidation' of deviant leaders and others, or for that matter of people merely suspected of deviance or even of *future* deviance.

That all this was so readily accepted, and most often not even perceived as an abdication of critical thought, is one of the most extraordinary episodes in the history of the twentieth century. Of all the many reasons for it the most important was no doubt the fervent conviction that the USSR, the first workers' state, alone and beleaguered, was building a 'new civilization' under the most arduous circumstances; and that any criticism of it, in any field, was to give help to its capitalist enemies. The rise of Nazi Germany, with its declared aim to destroy 'communism', gave to the argument a sharper and more compelling edge: to criticize the Soviet Union, on any count, was 'objectively' to help fascism, indeed, to side with it. This proved to be an effective form of political blackmail, well in tune with Stalinist modes of thought.

The image of the Soviet Union was gravely damaged for many communists by the Nazi–Soviet Pact of August 1939. But that image was soon redeemed by the decisive Soviet contribution to the defeat of Germany; and the new conflicts which broke out at the end of the war between the western powers and a new Communist 'bloc' led by the Soviet Union served to keep Communist parties in the Stalinist fold.

There was, however, yet another major reason for the enduring division between social democracy and Communist parties; and this is a reason which in many ways goes deeper than the Communists' attitude to bourgeois democracy, or even their allegiance to the Soviet Union. This was the fact that Communist parties were also the most vocal and persistent advocates of programmes of reform much more radical than was acceptable to 'moderate' social democratic leaders, in trade unions and political parties. How deep this went is suggested by the fact that social democratic leaders remained bitterly opposed to Communists long after the latter had given up their revolutionary ambitions, and long after they had detached themselves from their allegiance to the Soviet Union. The point also finds confirmation in the hostility which these leaders showed to left socialists within their own ranks, precisely because they too advocated programmes and policies which were deemed, for reasons that I will discuss later, to be too radical or 'extreme' by social democratic leaders.

In other words, it was by no means the Communists' allegiances or their rhetoric alone which divided them from social democratic leaders in trade unions as well as parties: what these allegiances and Communist rhetoric did was to strengthen hostility which was *in any case* strong on other grounds, and they also greatly facilitated the struggle of social democratic leaders to isolate the Communists and to defeat the radical policies advocated by them and by many other socialists in the labour movement as well.

There were some few occasions when the split between social democratic and Communist parties was partially and temporarily overcome in some countries, notably in the years of the Popular Front in Spain and France in the thirties, and again in France, Italy, and other western countries in the years 1944-7, when it was politically impossible to deny the Communists the representation in government which they demanded. Even so, the division endured, and never ceased to constitute a debilitating weakness for the Left and its struggles.

In this perspective, and particularly nowadays, when much that divided Communists from other socialists has faded into history, the fundamental line of division on the Left is the first one: namely, the division between social reformers on the one hand, and the advocates of what may be called 'classical reformism' on the other, among whom the Communists must now certainly be counted. We shall encounter that line of division again and again in the following pages. The second line of division is that noted earlier between 'classical reformists' on one side, and on the other the various Marxist-Leninist groupings and sects, many of them of Trotskyist inspiration, who are well entitled to claim that they are the rightful heirs of the Leninist version of Marxism.

The ideological and political line of division between social democratic reformers and socialists seeking more radical change also places in its proper perspective the conflict between leaders and rank-and-file members of working-class parties which Robert Michels depicted in his 'Political Parties'.

In that book, written before World War I, Michels attributed the conflict to an 'iron law of oligarchy' which, he believed, was bound to create a gulf between leaders and led. This notion of an 'iron law of oligarchy', relentlessly and ineluctably undermining and destroying democratic forms of organization, may be dismissed as a misconceived hyperbole; but Michels was undoubtedly pointing to a very real and powerful *tendency* at work in any organization towards an appropriation of undue power by those in charge of it, and towards a disjunction going well beyond a mere division of labour between representatives and those they were supposed to represent.

Michels attributed the working of his 'law' to a series of political, organizational, and personal factors affecting working-class parties; but he placed far too little emphasis on the division, in social democratic parties, between 'moderate' leaders on the one hand, concerned, at best, with reform at the edges, and *left activists* in the rank and file, concerned with the advancement of radical programmes and policies. Given this division, which has always run very deep, it is easy to see why leaders want and need more power: that power is required in order to contain and defeat the pressure exercised by left activists and others of similar disposition. It is not, in this perspective, an 'iron law of oligarchy' which creates the division between leaders and rank and file; it is on the contrary the division between leaders and left activists, *based on quite concrete ideological grounds*, which imperatively requires leaders to preserve and enlarge their room for manœuvre, so that they may pursue the moderate policies they favour, against the wishes, promptings, and pressures of radical critics in their organizations. 'Oligarchy' in this context is largely the product of a Right–Left struggle, and has a strongly 'functional' basis.

This is not to say that the tendency to 'oligarchy' disappears where such a struggle is not being waged: it clearly exists in any system of power. The point is rather that, in the case of social democratic parties, the struggle between Right and Left has always been a crucial factor in the efforts of leaders to achieve the greatest possible amount of independence from their left activists. The same is true of trade union leaders as well. In this endeavour, they have on the whole been quite successful, even though the battle is never finally won; and their success has been of massive importance in the politics of labour in advanced capitalist countries, given the predominance of social democracy in the labour movements of these countries.

There is, in this connection, a notable difference between dominant classes and subordinate ones. A dominant class has, by definition, ample resources to affirm its power, and there are many authoritarian regimes where the lack of representative agencies such as parties is not particularly injurious to its interests, given the reliance that the dominant class may safely place on the state's defence of these interests. In capitalist democratic regimes, on the other hand, dominant classes do need such agencies; but they also have plenty of other means at their disposal for the purpose of wielding influence and achieving desired purposes.

The working class has far fewer such means. No doubt, workers can and do act spontaneously, lay down tools, go on strike, engage in many different forms of action without the benefit (or hindrance) of organization. Also, revolutionary upheavals have often been sparked off by spontaneous and quite unpremeditated action from below, as was the case in the February Revolution which toppled the Czarist regime in 1917 and opened the way for the Bolshevik Revolution in October.

On the other hand, the Bolshevik Revolution could not have happened had not a party been in existence for Lenin to lead—in fact to bludgeon—into revolution. Spontaneous action from below can do many things, most notably in revolutionary situations, but also in any situation of crisis and conflict. In 'normal' conditions of class struggle, however, spontaneous action cannot take the place of trade unions and parties, however much it may supplement them.

This imperative need for agencies formally empowered to advance working-class interests and demands is not an unmixed blessing: on the contrary, it is in many ways a curse, because of its many negative consequences. But however this may be, the fact remains that agencies have played an absolutely determinant role in the politics of labour and in the prosecution (or avoidance) of class struggle.

Let us therefore turn to role of these agencies.

III

In relation to social democracy, that role may be summarized in terms of a deep ambiguity, which has marked social democratic organizations throughout their existence. The ambiguity consists in the fact that social democratic organizations have been *both* major agencies for the advancement of demands from below, and *also* major agencies for the containment of these demands. On the one hand, they have served to articulate grievances and mobilize discontent; on the other, they have striven to curb and defeat militancy within their own ranks. They have been agencies of pressure and reform, and also of demobilization and accommodation.

By their very nature, trade unions exhibit this duality very clearly. They are essentially the product of the conflictual nature of the relations which govern the encounter between employers and wage-earners. At the core of these relations, there are the permanent issues of 'wages, hours, and conditions'; and beyond or linked to them, there are such issues as the struggle for control of the work process, for the curbing of managerial—and sub-managerial, supervisory—authority, struggles over dismissal, promotion, demotion, the classification of jobs, work schedules, grievances, lay-offs, training, work rules, time and motion study, bonus plans and so on.

These struggles do not only involve 'industrial' workers. On the contrary, they are waged by all workers—in industry, in white-collar, distributive, and service occupations, in public service and state enterprises at all levels; and also by men and women who are part of the sub-professional petty bourgeoisie, in schools, central and local government, supervisory and welfare occupations and services. It is here that the similarity of grievances of workers at all levels is most clearly manifested; and it is this that forms the basis (which does not mean that it provides the guarantee) of alliance for common purposes.

One of the most notable features of all such struggles is that they very often occur outside 'official' or regular trade union channels—indeed, in opposition to official union leaderships. 'An overwhelming majority of British stoppages', Richard Hyman noted in a book first published in 1977, 'are . . . unconstitutional' (i.e. not sanctioned by the union); 'disputes', he added, 'have traditionally stemmed principally from the initiative of union rank and file'.[10] Alternatively, strikes may be 'official'; but a struggle then often occurs between union leaders and strikers over strategy and action. This is particularly the case in periods of intense conflict and grassroots militancy. In Italy in the period of the 'hot autumn' at the end of the sixties, one writer observes,

the actions of the rank and file quickly outstripped the unions' tactics. The workers prolonged strikes beyond the time period set by the unions, and they broadened the demands. They occupied plants, organised slow-downs, and set up militant picket lines and roadblocks. They marched through cites and held demonstrations. There were many sharp, even violent confrontations with employers and the police.[11]

This is not to suggest that workers are hell-bent on permanent struggle, and that unions are forever seeking to contain their ardour. 'Industrial relations' under capitalist conditions *are* a battlefield; but the battlefield is relatively quiescent over much if not most of its area for long stretches of time, particularly when economic political conditions are unfavourable to militant action, as has been the case in the eighties. Moreover, prolonged strike action, even in 'good' times, is certain to bring hardship to strikers and their families: the loss of income, the exhaustion of such savings as there are, the difficulty of meeting mortgage and hire purchase payments, the curtailment of all but the most essential expenditure, the worries and the strain and the danger which picketing presents to activists. It is only in bourgeois mythology that workers go on strike at the drop of a hat, without thought for themselves, their families, and their jobs.

Nevertheless, workers do rebel, and do so in many different ways—by strike action, by bans on overtime, go-slows, industrial sabotage, working to rule, sit-ins, occupations, the sequestration of managers, and whatever else may be thought to serve the purposes of struggle. In so far as some of these actions are illegal, they are inevitably opposed and repudiated by the unions. But even where action is legal and 'official', trade union leaders and officials are most likely, by the very nature of their role and location, to seek a restoration of business as usual. No doubt their eagerness to do so, and the price they are willing to pay by way of compromise and retreat, will vary according to ideological dispositions and circumstances. But the business of trade union leaders and officials is bargaining, compromise, conciliation: a strike and other manifestations of militancy are as much an interruption of normal business for trade union officials as it is for employers, and constitute a nuisance and a threat, to be averted if at all possible, or to be brought to an end at the earliest opportunity. Another factor which leads in the same direction is that strike action creates a more favourable climate for militants and critics of the union leadership. These are grounds enough for the ambiguity of the role of trade unions.

As for the leaders of social democratic parties, they have generally been quite firmly opposed to strikes and other forms of industrial militancy. In fact, they have been powerful advocates of conciliation and, quite often, particularly when in government, fierce and vociferous opponents of militancy in any shape or form. At best, they have sought to turn themselves into the architects of a 'political exchange' whereby industrial strife might be bought off or at least contained by means of various concessions and reforms.[12] The point is of wider application: the role which these leaders and their parties have traditionally performed in capitalist-democratic regimes has been that of advocates and agents of reform, which has also made it possible for them to be effective advocates and agents of social peace and stability.

Social democracy may well claim to have played a part in bringing about substantial improvements in the condition of the working class in the twentieth century, by virtue both of its activities when in opposition and of its policies and actions in government. Social democratic achievements have been particularly marked in Sweden, Norway, and Denmark, where social democratic parties have long established themselves as the 'normal' parties of government. But important advances have also been registered in other countries where social democracy was well established.

However, and without belittling what social democratic parties have been able to achieve in this realm, the point has to be made that a crucial factor in making these achievements possible was the strength, resilience, and pressure of organized labour and other social forces bent on reform. The correlation between pressure from below and reform is very strong: a greater percentage of GNP is likely to be spent on collective services and welfare programmes in countries where trade union organization is strong, or where other pressure from below is intense.[13]

The degree to which the key factor is the intensity of pressure from below is well illustrated by the experience of the sixties in the United States, where no social democratic party of any consequence exists, save in the very weak (and unacknowledged) version constituted by the Democratic Party. Frances Fox Piven and Richard Cloward note that in the sixties, the federal government responded because it was vulnerable. The Southern civil rights movement had already made it the object of black rage, and the Northern black movement soon followed suit. Moreover, Democratic administrations of the 1960s could not ignore intensifying conflict in the older cities that local governments were incapable of containing, for the New Deal realignment had made these cities the urban strongholds of the party . . . Over the next few years these new federal resources and the heightened awareness of federal responsibility they implied, combined with the smoldering anger of the ghetto, created enough political pressure to force a much enlarged flow of benefits from the social welfare program created in the 1930s, and to force the creation of new programs too . . . In brief, the framework of benefit programs created by the insurgent movements of the 1930s was elaborated and expanded by the insurgent movements of the 1960s.[14]

As T. B. Edsall also notes, 'the liberal-democratic agenda of the 1950s and 1960s—civil rights, housing, programs to alleviate hunger and malnutrition, federal aid to education, health coverage for the elderly and the poor, welfare assistance, job programs to counter recessions—was initiated by a wide range of forces'; but the one consistent element in all legislative battles was 'labor's active presence in each of the lobbying coalitions'.[15]

In other advanced capitalist countries, where social democratic parties do exist and occupy an important place in political life, they have traditionally given expression, shape, and coherence to demands for reform; and they have, in government, translated some at least of these demands into actual programmes. This is no small thing. But against this must be set the fact that social democratic governments have also tended to *limit* the scope of reform, and have given to the 'welfare state' a highly bureaucratic and often rebarbative character; and that, where economic circumstances have seemed to demand it, they have not hesitated to practise policies of retrenchment in collective and welfare services which have borne most heavily on those who could least afford it. Faced, as they saw it, with the need for 'austerity', they applied it in ways which made a bitter mockery of the 'equality of sacrifice' they also preached; and they thereby created a disaffection which brought conservative governments back to office, and helped these governments to go even further in the curtailment of services and benefits.

The point is not, of course, that social democracy has not made a socialist revolution anywhere: it is hardly reasonable to blame it for not doing something which it never had any intention of doing, if by revolution is meant a seizure of power outside the confines of the constitutional system. One country in the advanced capitalist world where a revolution might have succeeded was Germany in 1918, when the constitutional system of Wilhelmine Germany had broken down, and where the social democrats were in a commanding position to lay the basis for a new social order. Instead, they turned themselves into the bulwark of the existing social order, and thereby rendered a momentous and priceless service to the German dominant class.

There is hardly another case in the twentieth century—at least in the advanced capitalist world—where such an opportunity clearly beckoned. But the point in any case is not that social democracy failed to press ahead with revolution by way of a seizure of power, but that it has for the most part failed to press ahead with reforms capable of advancing the 'structural' transformation of the social order; and where it has seemed disposed to embark on such a transformation, as in Britain in 1945, or in France in 1981, it has very rapidly desisted and retreated. The question this raises is why it has been so.

IV

The answer to that question lies above all in ideological and political positions induced and reinforced by the political context provided by bourgeois democracy.

Particular emphasis must be given here to the fact that class struggle in most of the countries of advanced capitalism has been waged in the context of bourgeois democracy. Many of the countries in question—Britain, the United States, Canada, and Scandinavia, the Low Countries, Australia, and New Zealand—have been capitalist democracies throughout this century, and even longer (save for the wartime occupation of Holland and Belgium). France has also had a capitalist-democratic regime for well over a hundred years, with only the wartime interruption of Vichy between 1940 and 1944. Germany, Italy, and Japan have had such regimes since 1945, and both Italy and Germany had the experience of weak parliamentary regimes before the Fascists took over in Italy and the Nazis in Germany. In short, this is the form of regime which has provided the main context of class struggle in the countries of advanced capitalism.

This means, broadly speaking, that labour movements, as they assumed their 'modern' form in the last decades of the nineteenth century, entered into a political system of representation which had not been devised by them or for them—a system intended to bring together people possessed of property, privilege, position, and power, so that they might discuss affairs of state and other matters of interest in a context of agreement about the sanctity of private property and the right of those who owned or controlled property to exploit those who worked for them (though this, needless to say, was not how such things were discussed). However much disagreement there might be over a multitude of issues great and small, there was at least agreement on this fundamental point; and this naturally fostered compromise, conciliation, and collaboration. There were occasions when the system broke down because interests became irreconcilable, or were believed to be so: the Civil War in the United States provides the most notable example of such a breakdown in the nineteenth century. For the most part, however, the system engendered political stability, nowhere more so than in Britain, where it proved capable of assimilating a new bourgeoisie in the early part of the nineteenth century.

Labour movements, representing exploited and subordinate classes, were by the end of the century expected (and did themselves expect) to enter into the system and to make use of it, even though they were, or came to be, formally committed to the radical transformation of the social order, a purpose altogether different from, and indeed opposed to, the purposes which had always moved the traditional representatives of propertied and dominant classes.

It would be impossible to exaggerate the importance of the fact that representatives of the working class found ready-made, so to speak, an institutional system which seemed capable of serving whatever purposes labour movements might seek to realize, including the socialist transformation of the social order. Whether the system was, or could ever be, thus flexible is not here the issue; the fact is that the mass membership of labour movements, and not only their leaders, believed that here indeed was the system which best affirmed the promise of democracy. No doubt further measures of 'democratization' were required at different points of the system; but these too, it was believed, could be achieved within the system itself, and by mechanisms which it provided.

It is, in this perspective, highly significant that the altogether different system envisaged by Marx in *The Civil War in France* and by Lenin in *The State and Revolution* should have found so little resonance in the labour movements of Western Europe and North America: this vision of a system akin to semi-direct democracy, in which the representative element would be minimal, failed to awaken any substantial response in working-class movements steeped in the tradition of bourgeois representative regimes. Soviet experience, and later the experience of all other Communist regimes, could only serve to confirm the view that, whatever its limitations might be thought to be, the Western system of government was the most 'democratic' of all conceivable political systems.

A factor of great importance in the attunement of many activists to bourgeois democracy was that it made possible insertion into political life not only at the national level, but at local or regional or provincial level as well. National politics might be remote and uncertain; but there were things that could be done, with effect, at sub-national level. Members of the petty bourgeoisie in bourgeois parties had long found their way into local politics, and had found there a real field of operation and a compensation for their relatively subordinate position in society. This, from the last decades of the nineteenth century onwards, also became increasingly true for activists in the labour movement. 'Municipal' or 'gas and water socialism' was crucially important in engaging activists in the political life of bourgeois democracy and in persuading them of its democratic possibilities; and for some of them at least, politics at this level offered a chance to exercise responsibility and a degree of power, and constituted in fact one of the very few avenues of responsibility and power (and of achieving a certain status) open to working-class activists. At first, it was mainly social democratic activists, in growing numbers, who were to be found in local government in most advanced capitalist countries. They were later followed by Communists as well. After World War II, in countries such as France and Italy,

Communists were in control of many cities and towns—and in Italy, regions—and in control, therefore, within strict limits, of a small but by no means negligible part of state power.[16]

Bourgeois democracy was well suited to the voicing of specific grievances and demands, and to the remedying of what were taken to be specific problems. Social democratic leaders, for their part (or at least, many of them) often proclaimed that they wanted much more than specific remedies for specific problems: nothing less, in fact, than the creation of a new social order based on equality, justice, fairness, compassion, co-operation, and so forth. Such a vision, however, was perfectly compatible with the concentration on the piecemeal, gradual, 'incremental' reforms whose pursuit bourgeois democracy encouraged. Indeed, the vision was also compatible with a fierce opposition to all strategies, proposals, and struggles designed to advance the radical trans-formation of the social order and to bring nearer the realization of the vision, on the ground that the strategies were self-defeating, dangerous, and irresponsible, that the policies were unrealistic, inopportune, or misconceived, that they would not only fail to achieve their aims, but place in jeopardy much that had already been achieved. There has never been a dearth of such arguments, which helped to turn social democratic leaders and their supporters into the scourge of their radical critics, and which enabled them to do so with a very good conscience.

Bourgeois democracy greatly fosters 'moderation', both in trade union leaders and in parliamentarians of social democratic disposition. The system functions by means of a considerable measure of collaboration between opponents who are colleagues as well as adversaries. A process of 'natural' or 'functional' selection is here at work. To begin with, the system attracts people who are in any case of 'moderate' disposition; and for those who are not, there is an immensely powerful pull towards the development of such a disposition. For those who submit to it, there is advancement, praise, honour; for those who resist it, there is denunciation, often of great virulence, from a multitude of sources. For people who aspire to a role of leadership in the labour movement, the lure of 'moderation' is unquestionably very strong; it is often resisted, of course, but at considerable cost.

Selection is also made by social democratic leaders themselves. From the vantage point of their position in parties or trade unions, they naturally do what they can to recruit and promote those people who share their own views, and to prevent the rise of those—most often on their left—who do not. The attempt may not always be successful, and other pulls towards 'moderation' then come into play; but the attempt to keep 'unsound' people out, successful or not, has always been an important part of the internal life of working-class organizations.

In terms of the politics of class struggle, this means that social democratic leaderships have been among the most important forces of opposition against anyone to their Left. It is thus from *within* labour movements themselves that have come some of the most powerful—and effective—voices to denounce radicals, militants, Communists—anyone on the Left critical of social democratic strategy and policies. This has obviously been of immense advantage to the forces of conservatism in advanced capitalist societies.

It has often been argued that 'moderation' and the drastic dilution of socialist policies which it entails has been imposed upon leaders of working-class parties by the democratic process itself: 'the electorate', it has been said, simply would not vote for the kind of policies which left socialists, not to speak of 'ultra-left' ones, chose to advocate. There are many different versions of this theme; but the essence of it is that not enough voters are at all likely to find socialist policies sufficiently acceptable to give parties who advocate these policies the command of parliamentary assemblies.[17]

Much obviously depends on what is meant by socialist policies. I have already noted that parties committed to a revolutionary agenda, and to an ultimate seizure of power, have indeed found little support (in so far as they have sought it) at the polls. But I also noted that this has hardly ever been the issue. The real issue has mostly been the more humane management of capitalism on the one hand, or radical reform on the other. On *this* issue, it cannot be said that 'the electorate' has spoken with an unequivocal voice. In fact, a majority of voters has quite often, especially since World War II, given electoral support to parties committed precisely to programmes of radical reform.

The problem does not lie with the voters, but with leaders who do not themselves *believe* in the radical programmes they find themselves saddled with; and they are therefore all the less likely to defend them with the vigour and conviction which the advocacy of such programmes requires. The reasons why they do not believe in them has much to do with their 'moderate' ideological dispositions, which lead them to look with great suspicion upon all radical policies. In addition, they harbour the deep conviction that such policies would be exceedingly difficult to put into practice, that the attempt to do so would call forth fierce and effective opposition from very powerful interests, and that a government seeking to do so would very rapidly face extremely heavy odds. *This is perfectly true.* Radical reform in the power structure of advanced capitalism is a very arduous business indeed. Robert Keohane remarks that what he calls liberal capitalism 'generates a systematic bias against social-democratic solutions to economic problems in advanced industrial countries . . . a sort of Gresham's law may operate in which policies which reinforce the position of capital drive out policies that reduce its dominance and distribute wealth more equally';[18] faced with this 'bias', and with all the difficulties social democratic governments, however 'moderate', tend to confront, such governments can either decide to fight for the policies to which they are committed by their electoral programmes and pledges, or to retreat. Social democratic governments, given the nature of their leaderships, have always chosen the latter option.

A good deal more needs to be said about the social democratic record, both in opposition and in government. One item in this record is the response of social democratic leaderships to the threat from the Right. Social democratic leaders have of course been profound believers in parliamentary democracy, and resolute in their rhetoric against its enemies, not least against what they took to be its enemies on the Left. But the fact remains that when capitalist democracy has been threatened from the Right, their response has been hesitant and prevaricating.

The country where social democratic failure in this respect was most dramatic was Germany in the years preceding Hitler's assumption of power. Again and again, social democratic leaders showed themselves desperately weak in the face of an ever more direct and definite threat. In July 1932, for instance, the Chancellor, Franz von Papen, dissolved the Social Democratic Government of Prussia. This was a crucial moment in the developing crisis. It was in fact one of the last opportunities for an effective mobilization against the rising tide of reaction. Whether any action would have been successful is of course an unanswerable question. But the Social Democrats chose to do nothing. At the last conference of the Party, in June 1933, after Hitler had been in power for some months and just before the Social Democratic Party was dissolved, one of its leaders, Carl Severing, delivered the following verdict on the Party's inaction:

It is gruesome when I think of it today, what blood I thought had to be avoided in July 1932 . . . I could not justify what, in my opinion, would have been needlessly spent blood of our followers . . . Now I have to tell you, nothing was avoided thereby. Now it will be an ocean of blood and tears. From the enemy no mercy is to be expected.[19]

The case of Austria offers striking parallels. Austrian Social Democracy had emerged from World War I as the overwhelmingly dominant force in the labour movement, and proceeded at once to use its power to contain the workers' movement. One historian of Austrian Social Democracy has noted that in 1919, 'with the establishment of the Hungarian Soviet Republic on March 21 and the proclamation of the Bavarian Soviet Republic on April 5 . . . the Socialists saw their most important task to be the prevention of a dictatorship of workers' councils in Austria'.[20]

The task was duly accomplished. But having saved bourgeois democracy, the Social Democrats were in due course presented with a dire threat to it from the Right. In March 1933, Chancellor Dolfuss virtually abrogated parliamentary government in Austria: throughout the crisis which preceded his action, the Social Democratic Party prevaricated and failed to respond. Later, in exile, Otto Bauer, one of the most prestigious figures in Austrian—indeed in European—socialism, said the following about social democratic inaction in the face of the threat of dictatorship:

We could have responded on March 15 by calling a general strike. Never were the conditions for a successful strike so favourable as on that day. The counter-revolution which was then reaching its full development in Germany had aroused the Austrian masses. The masses of the workers were awaiting the signal for battle . . . The railwaymen were not yet so crushed as they were eleven months later. The government's military organization was far weaker than in February 1934. At that time we might have won. But we shrank back, dismayed, from the battle . . . We

postponed the fight because we wanted to spare the country the
of a bloody civil war.[21]

The wish to avoid civil war is entirely honourable; but what it
leaves out of account is that there are circumstances when the
best—even the only way—to avoid civil war is to mobilize all
available forces for the struggle, and thus compel the Right to
pause and possibly to retreat; and preparing for struggle is also
a condition for winning, if a confrontation becomes inevitable.
Recklessness in these matters is criminal and stupid; but pre-
varication and paralysis spell certain disaster.

Nor in any case is the fear of civil war a sufficient explanation
of the ways in which social democracy faces—or rather refuses to
face—a serious threat to parliamentary democracy from the Right.
What is involved here is a whole style and temper of politics.
David Beetham makes the point very well:

> . . . the fact that Social Democrats, whether of left, right or centre, all
> made the same choices when confronted with the slide to fascist
> dictatorship cannot be attributed just to the logic of events, but to some
> basic characteristic of Social Democracy itself. It was the conditioning
> effect of every day routines and practices in the parliamentary arena that
> led them to prefer the familiar processes of negotiation and compromise
> at the highest level, even with those who were undermining parliament,
> rather than rely on the less controllable extra-parliamentary mass
> struggle, even in defence of parliament.[22]

Beetham is referring to the inter-war years. But the point is
also relevant for later years, and applies not only to the threat of
fascism, which has been negligible in the post-war decades, but
also to all struggles from below. Social democratic leaders are
quite simply extremely uncomfortable with all extra-parliamentary
struggles, and seek by all possible means to contain and reduce
them.

It has also to be said that the social democratic recoil from
violence and bloodshed has been extremely selective. Social
democracy everywhere has not felt the same qualms when a
'national' struggle, as distinct from a class struggle, was at issue.
World War I set a precedent that has been faithfully followed
ever since. Not only did most social democratic leaders (and most
of their followers) whole-heartedly support 'their' governments
in 1914; even more remarkable is the fact that most social

democratic leaders found no difficulty whatever in continuing to support these governments, and indeed to take part in them, through four years of mass slaughter, in one of the most murderous and useless wars ever fought. Millions upon millions of young men died on the battlefields, with the full support of European Social Democracy. The danger of class politics leading to bloodshed evokes a—very reasonable—recoil from social democrats; but the reality of bloodshed, on a huge scale, in the course of 'national' politics and 'national' purposes has generally evoked strong support. Here is where 'integration' acquires its full meaning.

There is one area of 'national' politics which needs to be mentioned in this connection: the area of colonial and imperialist wars waged in the course of the twentieth century by France, Britain, Belgium, and Holland. In such cases, not only has social democratic support been generally forthcoming, but it is social democratic governments, or governments which included social democrats, which have often waged these wars.

The most notable social democratic involvement in colonial and imperialist ventures was that of the French Socialist Party, whose leaders played a major role in the years following World War II in the horrendously bloody struggles against the independence movements of Indo-China, North Africa, and Madagascar, with social democratic ministers having the ultimate political responsibility for military enterprises which included the usual catalogue of torture and massacre.

For its part, the Labour Government of 1945-51 in Britain avoided major colonial wars by accepting, initially with considerable reluctance, the inevitability of independence for India, Burma, and Ceylon. In Malaysia, on the other hand, the Labour Government waged a bitter 'counter-insurgency' struggle, accompanied by considerable repression, against a Communist-led independence guerrilla movement; and the Labour leaders gave staunch support, after leaving office, to the continuation of the war by the Conservative Government. So too did they support the military campaign against the 'Mau Mau' rebellion in Kenya between 1952 and 1955; and they barely raised any opposition to the suspension of the Constitution of British Guiana in 1953, after Dr Cheddi Jagan's People's Progressive Party had won an election there. Dr Jagan was viewed by the Government (and the

United States) as dangerously left-wing and pro-Communist; this was also the view of the Labour leaders.[23] Throughout, Labour's colonial policies were inspired by a mixture of imperial concerns, anti-communism, and a weak paternalist reformism.

Finally, there is the crucial role which social democracy has played in the Cold War since 1945. Ever since then, social democratic leaders, in trade unions and political parties, have been among the firmest and most ardent supporters of the United States in what was proclaimed to be a struggle against Soviet aggression and expansionism. I shall argue in Chapter 6 that the United States was in fact engaged in a global conservative crusade against revolution and radical reform; and social democratic support for this enterprise was extremely precious to the United States, for it greatly helped to obscure the real nature of the enterprise, and mobilized labour movements whose support would otherwise have been much more difficult or even impossible to obtain.

This social democratic support for the United States has also had a great impact on the politics of labour, and on class struggle in general; for it has for all practical purposes removed from serious debate between social democrats and their conservative opponents any fundamental question of foreign and defence policy, from the end of World War II until the eighties. It is only in the last few years that this basic consensus has begun— but only begun—to fray at the edges.

Moreover, the adoption by social democratic movements of the American perspectives on the nature of the Cold War greatly helped to cast deep suspicion, as 'Communist-inspired', on any demand or policy on home or foreign or defence or imperial issues which departed from the 'conventional wisdom' in any of these fields. The change which has occurred in this respect in recent years is very substantial: it is not now possible, as it was in the great days of the Cold War, to dispose of left arguments and proposals simply by declaring them to be 'Communist-inspired'; or at least, it is now much more difficult to do so.

It may well be said at this point that social democratic leaders were only able to pursue the 'moderate' policies they favoured because they enjoyed the support of a majority of their activists; and that their left critics were always an unrepresentative minority, even in their own parties. There is no question that this has often been the case in the ebb and flow of political life.

Nevertheless, this argument ignores the fact that, in the constant struggle between social democratic leaders located on the Right and Centre of their parties on the one hand, and their left critics on the other, the leaders have always enjoyed an enormous advantage, by reason of their command of the party apparatus. This makes possible the extensive and effective use of that apparatus in the struggle against opponents; and leaders are in any case very well placed to denounce their critics as divisive, disruptive, disloyal, and heedless of the 'unity' which, they proclaim, is an indispensable ingredient for electoral and political success. This is particularly effective when these leaders are also in government, and subject to attack from their conservative opponents. The appeal for loyalty is also supported by a rhetoric intended to suggest the leaders' own fervent adherence to the party's ideals, but an adherence combined with the sense of realism and practicality so woefully and evidently lacking in the critics.

Nor should it be forgotten that the struggle between Left and Right/Centre in social democratic parties is not confined to the protagonists in the parties themselves. It is also conducted in the bourgeois press. However much anti-socialist papers may dislike social democratic leaders, they dislike these leaders' left critics a lot more; and while they may not support with any enthusiasm social democratic leaders in struggle with left opponents, they can be relied on to attack left critics with great violence. A climate of opinion is thus fostered which is highly favourable to leaders, and this is likely to have an effect on large numbers of activists, whose main concern is with the winning of elections, at local as well as national level, and who come to resent the constant 'rocking of the boat' in which left activists seem to be engaged.

Given all this, it is only very inept leaders who would not be able to prevail in party struggles. The point is that party leaders do have considerable powers of manipulation and manœuvre. Social democratic leaders have always used these powers to contain and defeat opposition from the Left. In so doing, they have made a major contribution to the de-radicalization of political life in their countries.

V

The only other parties on the Left which have ever managed to carve a place for themselves in labour movements, and therefore to offer external opposition to social democratic leaderships, are Communist parties; and we must further consider the contribution of these parties to class struggle.

We left Communist parties, it will be recalled, at the point of their turn from the Third Period to Popular Fronts in 1934/5. The turn was taken for tactical reasons, in the face of the threat of Fascism, and Communist parties now not only sought alliances with the social democrats they had so recently denounced as 'social fascists', but also with anyone who was willing to co-operate with them in the struggle against Fascism. Where there had been harsh rejection, there was now warm embrace.

As was, however, noted earlier, the turn had much more than tactical significance. It also marked the installation of Communist parties in the framework of bourgeois democracy, and a new willingness to operate within its political system. What this meant, in effect, was the abandonment of the notion of revolution in its strong, insurrectionary meaning; and, concomitantly, the abandonment of the vision of an altogether different political system, as sketched out by Marx and Lenin. How much of a departure this was is well indicated in a letter embodying earlier perspectives, which the Central Committee of the French Communist Party sent in 1934 to the Permanent Administrative Commission of the Socialist Party during negotiations on the formation of the Popular Front. Notwithstanding the Communist party's wish for alliance, the letter insisted that, in the perspective of the Party,

in place of the present state and its organs will be substituted the organs of a true democracy of workers, peasants and soldiers, the *French soviets*. From bottom to top, from the local level and the factory to the department or the region, right up to workers' and peasants' government, *all power* will belong to councils elected by wage-earners, both legislative and executive power.[24]

George Lavau notes that from 1935 on, the PCF was 'never again to write anything like this statement'; 'no official PCF

document', he also writes, 'ever contains even the most sur-
reptitious allusion to the withering of the state under the socialism
to be engendered in France, nor to French "Soviets", nor to the
popular judiciary, nor to the transfer of power to elected councils,
even at the local level or in the factory.'[25] This is, broadly
speaking, accurate; and the same kind of evolution is also to be
found in other western Communist parties. By 1936, Togliatti,
who was then an important figure in the Comintern and who was
to play a crucial role in post-liberation Italy, was referring to the
Republic in Spain as no longer a 'bourgeois democratic Republic
of the common type', but as a 'new type of democracy'.[26]

Events in France in 1936 provided an early demonstration of
the dilemmas this new perspective was likely to create. The
Popular Front coalition of Socialists, Communists, and Radicals
won an absolute majority of seats in the second round of the
general election of that year. This second round was held on 3
May, but Léon Blum, the Socialist Prime Minister designate,
only took office a month later. The election itself was immediately
followed by a formidable wave of strikes all over France, with
the occupation by workers of many enterprises. At his later trial
under the Vichy regime, Blum spoke of the strike wave as 'the
social explosion which hit my government in the face'; and his
first concern on assuming office was to bring the strikes to an end
at all costs. This was achieved with the Matignon accords of
7/8 June, which conceded greater trade union recognition by
employers, some wage increases, and the famous *congés payés*, the
fortnight's holiday with pay which was one of the most visible
achievements of the Popular Front Government.

The Communist Party had refused to participate in the
Blum Government. But it played a profoundly moderating role
throughout the 'social explosion', and placed its whole weight on
the side of accommodation and settlement, an attitude epitomized
by the often-quoted remark of Maurice Thorez: 'Il faut savoir
terminer une grève dès que satisfaction a été obtenue' ('One must
know how to end a strike as soon as demands have been met').
A left-wing Socialist, Marceau Pivert, had coined the phrase at
the beginning of the strike wave, 'Tout est possible'. On the
contrary, said the leadership of the Communist Party, 'tout
n'est pas possible', and they denounced what they took to be
manifestations of Trotskyism and ultra-leftism.[27]

The acceptance by western Communist parties of the framework of bourgeois democracy was a matter of the greatest importance for the politics of class struggle from below. But its significance remained hidden by some of the characteristics of these parties. One such characteristic, already noted, was their unconditional support of Soviet policies. This not only distinguished them from all other parties and exposed them to the accusation of foreign allegiance; it also forced them into positions which could relegate them to the periphery of the political system, or even extrude them from it altogether. The most notable and dramatic example of this was the acceptance by western Communist parties of the Soviet view, following the Nazi–Soviet Pact of August 1939 (which Communist parties also supported), that the war which had begun in September 1939 between Britain and France against Germany was an imperialist war, which it was the duty of all Communists to oppose—a duty made all the more onerous because it required these parties to reverse their initial support of the war. Even before the switch, the French Government had dissolved the Communist Party, suspended 300 Communist-controlled municipal councils, removed 2,270 councillors from office, banned all Communist periodicals, and generally engaged in the fierce repression of Communists everywhere, including that of Communist parliamentarians.[28]

The German attack on the USSR in June 1941 rescued Communist parties from an intolerable situation, and made it possible for them to assume a leading position in resistance movements throughout occupied Europe. But it also enabled them, with the full encouragement of the Soviet leadership, to resume their earlier strategy. By the end of World War II, western Communist parties, and notably the Italian and French parties, greatly strengthened in membership, popular support, and prestige because of their heroic resistance record, had come to be part of governmental coalitions in which they only formed a subordinate element. This inevitably involved them in the assumption of responsibility without real power—and in the compromises which such involvement imperatively demanded.

In the crucial years immediately following liberation, Communist parties, guided by the 'spirit of Yalta', undoubtedly played an important stabilizing role, and greatly helped to contain the radicalism and the militancy engendered by the experience of war. That role, in the case of France, was readily acknowledged by General de Gaulle, who had, precisely with this purpose in mind, eased the return of Maurice Thorez to France from the Soviet Union, where he had taken refuge after fleeing from certain arrest while in the army at the beginning of the war. As de Gaulle said in his Memoirs to explain the Communists' inclusion in his government, 'at least for a certain time, their participation under my leadership would help to assure social peace, of which the country had such great need.'[29]

In effect, this Communist participation in coalitions in which they occupied subordinate positions involved what may rightly be called class collaboration and vigorous opposition to class struggle, all for the sake of hypothetical influence in a 're-construction' that was, in practice, strictly capitalist reconstruction. In the French case, it also meant the acceptance of French foreign and colonial policies which included the violent repression of colonial liberation movements, notably in Indo-China; and ministerial responsibility reinforced a 'national vocation' among the leaders of the PCF which ran sharply counter to the 'proletarian internationalism' and the resolute anti-imperialism which was supposed to move Communist parties.[30]

It has always been argued that the French, Italian, and other western Communist parties took the path of class collaboration because the road to revolution was insuperably blocked by the presence of allied armies in their countries; and because the attempt to seize power or to seek revolutionary change would have been crushed in blood. However, the assumption that this was the determining factor in the strategy of the Communist parties in Italy, France, and other western countries needs to be questioned. Of course, it is impossible to say conclusively what Communist parties would have done had allied armies not been present in their countries. But the evidence very strongly suggests that their leaders at least had no thought of seizing power, and that they were fully committed to advance by electoral and parliamentary means. This was also the strategy favoured by Stalin. But there was no need whatever for Soviet pressure: western Communist leaderships were themselves convinced that this was the only course open to them.

It is extremely unlikely that a revolutionary conquest of power by Communist parties was possible in the circumstances of liberation. But this can hardly be taken to mean that the kind of whole-hearted class collaboration which Communist leaders pursued was the only other alternative open to them. At a time when traditional elites were deeply discredited and the bourgeois state unusually weakened, and with strong popular support for great changes in economic and social life, major advances seemed possible, even if revolution was not. Communist parties, it seems reasonable to argue, could have achieved a great deal more than they did, had they held out for far-reaching reforms; and success could have opened the way for further advances. Instead, they— or rather their leaders—chose the illusory power of (non-strategic) ministerial positions in governments whose main concern was, in essence, the restoration of a damaged bourgeois social order. As a result of their choice, Communist parties made a valuable contribution to the realization of that restoration. In the Italian case in particular, but also in the French one, that contribution could be said to have been absolutely crucial.

By 1947, the bourgeois social order had been restored, and with the aggravation of the Cold War, Communist ministers in Italy, France, and elsewhere in western Europe were unceremoniously expelled from the government, and their parties duly resumed an oppositional role. But notwithstanding the insistence of their enemies, particularly in France, that they were bent on violent revolution, as witnessed by the strikes and demonstrations which they organized, no such design formed any part of their purpose.

Nor has it at any time since then formed part of their purpose. Time and again, and most notably in periods of great crisis, as in France in May 1968, they have demonstrated quite clearly how real was their abhorrence of extra-parliamentary actions which were not under their control, and which they therefore took, almost by definition, to be ill-conceived or 'adventurist'.[31]

Both the French and the Italian Communist leaderships have also remained very keen to become members of coalition governments, even as junior partners. The PCF was glad to accept four rather peripheral ministries in the government that came into being when François Mitterand won the presidency in May 1981; and both ministers and Party were therefore implicated in the retreats which marked the Mitterand presidency after its initial period of reform. As for the PCI, its overtures to the Christian Democrats, notably in 1976, were always spurned, not least because of American hostility to any inclusion of Communists in an Italian government;[32] but the Communists always offered a co-operative kind of opposition.[33]

Professor Blackmer speaks in this connection of 'the classical dilemma faced by the Communist and Socialist parties in Europe':

> Can they somehow remain 'revolutionary', in at least the minimal sense of working effectively for the economic, social and political transformation of these societies, or are they fated to become (if this has not happened already) largely or totally integrated into those societies, adapting to existing institutions and values rather than seriously challenging them?[34]

But a distinction surely needs to be made here between two forms of 'integration'. On the one hand, there is the assumption of responsibility without real power in coalition governments, which certainly entails a drastic erosion of purpose. On the other, there is involvement and struggle in various parts of the political system as well as outside it, which is a rather different matter. Thus it has been noted in relation to the PCI that

> in July 1976, the Chamber of Deputies elected a Communist President, and the PCI obtained the chairmanship of six parliamentary committees. In the following months it secured its share of governmental patronage in appointing its nominees to the Constitutional Court and the Supreme Judicial Council, the national radio-TV organisation, and the boards of many corporations.[35]

In addition, the PCI then also held power in six of Italy's twenty regions, and in most large cities.[36]

Insertion of *this* kind, in a capitalist-democratic regime, is unavoidable for a mass working-class party. The dangers this presents, of adaptation to 'existing institutions and values', and of oligarchy, nepotism, and corruption, are obvious, and require effective check and control by the exercise of democratic, grassroots accountability. But insertion at the local, regional, or even parliamentary level need not ineluctably entail the erosion of purpose which minority participation in government does produce. A great deal here depends on the general perspectives of the party, and on its ideological and political firmness. The loss of purpose and even of identity which is implicit in Professor Blackmer's question is the result not of insertion into the system, but of *previous* ideological and political choices. These choices may be confirmed and enhanced by insertion; but they are not produced by it. In other words, the capture of cities and regions, and of parliamentary positions, by a party possessed of a strong transformative vocation, and held to that vocation by an effective democratic life, can be used for the purpose of significant reform, challenge, and further advance.

VI

There is one further aspect of the role which working-class parties perform, or are supposed to perform, which requires consideration: namely, their educational role. The working class is permanently subjected to a thousand different influences which are intended to bring about its acceptance and endorsement of the social order, and its rejection not only of revolutionary upheaval, which is not very difficult to obtain, but also of radical reform and socialist purposes, which is a different matter. This will be considered further in Chapter 5, as part of the discussion of the politics of class struggle from above. But what, it may be asked at this point, do parties purporting to advance the interests of the working class do to counter these influences, and to offer radically different alternatives to bourgeois ideology?

In seeking to answer this question, it may be useful to recall first Lenin's famous remark in *What is to be Done?* (1902) that 'the history of all countries shows that the working class, exclusively by its own effort, is able to develop only trade union consciousness', a 'consciousness' which he counterposed to socialist or revolutionary consciousness.[37] In saying this, Lenin had followed what he called the 'profoundly true and important words' of Karl Kautsky in *Neue Zeit*, which he quoted at length and which categorically denied that 'socialist consciousness' was a 'necessary and direct result of the proletarian class struggle':

'Of course, Socialism, as a doctrine, has its roots in modern economic relationships just as the class struggle of the proletariat has, and like the latter emerges from the struggle against the capitalist-created poverty and misery of the masses. But Socialism and the class struggle arise side by side and not one out of the other; each arises out of different conditions.'[38]

Both Kautsky and Lenin deduced from their separation of socialism from the class struggle that 'socialist consciousness' had to be brought into the labour movement 'from outside'. 'Socialist consciousness', Kautsky had said, 'is something introduced into the proletarian class struggle from without and not something that arose within it spontaneously.'[39]

The distinction between 'trade union consciousness' and 'socialist' or 'revolutionary' consciousness lies in the sharp differentiation between aims which are intended to improve the condition of the working class within the framework of capitalism; and aims which are intended to transcend that framework. 'Trade union consciousness' has often stood in strong opposition to 'socialist consciousness'. The labour movement in the United States provides an obvious example of such opposition; but it has also been common, to one degree or another, in the labour movements of other advanced capitalist countries. As noted earlier, however, the aims which inform 'trade union consciousness' are by no-means incompatible with those which inspire 'socialist consciousness'. The crucial distinction here lies between the view that a wholesale transformation of the social order can occur relatively smoothly, as a result of a series of gradual advances and reforms, so that these become the royal road to the achievement of a socialist society; as against the view that even though reforms are valuable, both in themselves and as part of the struggle, they cannot obviate the need for a much more radical break with the existing social order than is usually envisaged in the 'gradualist' perspective.

The opposition of 'trade union consciousness' to 'socialist consciousness' runs the risk of underestimating the importance which even limited 'economic' struggles may have, and the political consequences which they may produce. However, it is nevertheless true that these struggles are for the most part very limited in scope, intent, and consequences, however important the demands expressed may be for the people who make them. Nor, more generally, can the failings of capitalism be relied on to produce a 'socialist consciousness' on a large scale. These failings do provide the essential *basis* on which such a consciousness may come to be generated; but all experience clearly shows that even though a minority of activists may deduce from the wrongs of capitalism the need to transcend it, these wrongs, however deep and grievous they may be, cannot by themselves create a vast *socialist* movement, whose members and supporters have really 'interiorized' a 'socialist consciousness'.

In order for this to come about, specific agencies are required. Frank Parkin has suggested that it is 'the mass political party based on the working class' which must be the source of a radical value system capable of providing 'a moral framework which promotes an *oppositional* interpretation of class inequalities'.[40] This is right, even though other agencies and movements can obviously contribute to the process.

In this respect, however, the working class has been very poorly served by the main parties of the Left. In fact, social democratic parties, far from being agencies of dissemination of 'radical value systems', have (at least since World War I, and in some cases, for instance, Britain, even earlier) turned themselves into fierce opponents of any such system. For radical value systems, and the programmes and policies which they produce, unfortunately *challenge* the 'moderate' positions which social democratic leaderships have favoured, and have therefore regularly been denounced by these leaderships as irresponsible, nonsensical, utopian, fellow travelling, Trotskyist, and so forth. Social democratic parties have generally been unable to produce a plausible alternative to the doctrines and policies they have opposed, and they have as a result played an important role in weaning organized labour and the working class in general *away* from anything that could even minimally be called 'socialist consciousness'.

For their part, Communist parties have been very concerned to foster and disseminate a 'socialist consciousness' in the working class, and beyond, particularly among activists; and they did, particularly in their early days, seek to turn themselves into 'schools of socialism' as well as agencies of class struggle, by way of party schools and other educational activities.[41] However, these endeavours did no more escape the blight of Stalinism than did other areas of party activity. Party members were therefore taught a peculiarly rigid and mechanical version of Marxism, inspired by Stalin's own pronouncements on the subject; and they were also imbued with a discipline which required them to accept, as part of their political education, whatever lies and calumnies originated in Moscow. Nevertheless, Communist Parties and their youth organizations, in the inter-war years, were the main source of dissemination of ideas which, for all the distortions and limitations which they suffered, did constitute an alternative 'world view', and which provided a source of inspiration and confidence to vast numbers of activists in labour movements everywhere.

Communist parties have long been released from the grip of Stalinist constraints. But the uncertainties and crises which have attended their life since the late fifties have also been reflected in their educational activity, and have made this a much more problematic enterprise. Work in the realm of socialist education nowadays, if taken seriously, inevitably involves controversy and dissent; and this too is likely to reduce its attractions to party leaderships concerned with the affirmation of the Party's positions. The old certainties produced a fierce insistence on rigorous orthodoxy and an unquestioning acceptance of 'the line' Later uncertainties appear to have made for a relative neglect of political education.[42]

As for the parties, groups, and sects to the left of Communist parties, they have generally been too small to be able to play a substantial educational role in labour movements, whatever they might do for their own members; and most of them have in any case suffered from a sectarian narrowness and rigidity which encouraged sloganeering rather than fruitful education in socialist ideas.

There was a time, not so long ago, when the 'march of labour' was conceived in exceedingly 'triumphalist' terms. This was an obligatory theme of Stalinism; but it also pervaded labour movements at large. In this perspective, the Left might experience occasional setbacks, defeats, even disasters. But the future nevertheless belonged to it: its triumph was inevitable, inscribed in the logic of history itself.

In recent years, this belief in the inevitable triumph of the forces of light over the forces of darkness has been replaced in many parts of the Left by a profound disbelief in the capacity of labour to act as a prime agency of radical change. One by-product of this scepticism has been a displacement of attention towards other agencies of pressure and change, notably new social movements. Their role is considered in the next chapter.

4

New Social Movements and Class Struggle

I

My purpose in this chapter is to discuss the claim noted in Chapter 1, according to which the struggles in which new social movements are engaged must be taken to have at least as much significance for the shape and future of the social order as the struggles of labour movements and parties of the Left—or even greater significance.

New social movements encompass a great diversity of causes and concerns. The most notable are feminism, anti-racism, ecology, peace and disarmament, student movements, and sexual liberation. To these may be added liberation theology and the movements and currents of thought and action associated with it.[1] Of course, the cause and concerns associated with one new social movement are not exclusive to it: there is a great deal of ideological sharing between them.

A preliminary point needs to be made regarding any comparison between new social movements and labour movements. This is that the notion of the 'primacy' of the latter as agencies of radical change does not, in itself, at all require a devaluation of the importance of new social movements. It is unfortunately true that Marxists and others on the 'traditional' Left have often given the impression that they viewed the strivings and struggles of these movements as of no great consequence, or as an unwelcome 'diversion', at best, from the 'real' struggle. Sometimes the grievances and demands expressed by new social movements have been dismissed as mere bourgeois and petty-bourgeois preoccupations, of no great relevance to the concerns of labour movements; and people wedded to the notion of the primacy of the struggles in which labour engages with capital and the state have been inclined to suggest that demands from new social movements, in so far as they were relevant to labour movements, could easily be accommodated in the latter's programmes, or were already included in these programmes (or implied by them), and that the insistence of new social movements on autonomy and independence was therefore divisive and debilitating.

Such views are now rather less common than they used to be, not least because new social movements have endured and have carved a notable place for themselves on the political scene. But it is in any case perfectly possible to believe that if advanced capitalist societies are to be fundamentally transformed (a notion which will be further discussed presently), then labour movements and their agencies remain by far the most important factor in any such transformation; *and* to believe also that new social movements are themselves of great importance, and can make a real contribution to the achievement of fundamental change. This is what will be argued here.

New social movements are important because of the issues which they raise; because they mobilize masses of people around these issues; and because they can make—and indeed have already made—a notable impact on their societies. Most of them are bourgeois or petty-bourgeois in their leadership (but so for that matter are the main agencies of labour movements); and their constituencies are not mainly working class. Their appeal cuts across class; and one of the main points of contention which some new social movements have with Marxism is precisely on the question of the divisions in advanced capitalist societies. Marxists insist that the fundamental division in these societies remains that between dominant classes, at whose core is the class which owns and controls the main means of domination, and a subordinate class, at whose core are wage-earners who do not own or control such means. In the perspective of the new social movements, however, the notion of *one* fundamental division in society obscures what are taken to be other divisions just as 'fundamental', based on gender, or race, or other factors of division; and there are feminists and members of black movements who would go further, and argue that while there is indeed *a* fundamental division in society, it is not one based on class, but on gender or race.

Notwithstanding their diversity, new social movements have in common the crucial fact that they come up against prevailing structures of power, state-determined policies, and conventional modes of thought. Theirs is what might be called a dissenting vocation. It is in this sense that their activities constitute pressure from below, because they speak for sections of the population which are subject to exploitation and discrimination, or on behalf of minority causes.

There are many aspects of this pressure from below which are closely related to class struggle, and which are indeed part of class struggle—for instance, the struggle of black workers (men and women) and of white women workers against super-exploitation, or against state policies and actions. Class struggle and pressure from below exercised by members of new social movements intersect at many points. It may be best, nevertheless, to treat them as distinct forms of pressure and struggle, and to limit the meaning of class struggle to the encounter between labour on the one hand, and capital and the state on the other. But the distinction is in many ways somewhat artificial.[2]

Most new social movements are not of course new. At one time or another, there have throughout the history of capitalism (and earlier) been movements of protest and reform concerned with some at least of the issues which have been taken up by new social movements: the women's movement (or movements) has a long history; and so too have anti-racist, peace, and student movements. On the other hand, it is clear that the new social movements of recent decades have been immeasurably larger, stronger, more vigorous and ambitious, and also more effective, than any of their predecessors. In this sense, they are 'new', and represent a remarkable phenomenon, with a deep reach into the moral and political culture of contemporary societies.

Why this phenomenon should have occurred in the latter part of the twentieth century requires an answer which comprises many different factors: the immense shake-up represented by World War II; changes in the social structure and the labour process; the erosion of deference and the growth of expectations; the recoil from bureaucratic organization and faceless hierarchies; the threat posed to human survival by environmental vandalism and the arms race; the new technologies of birth control; the search for open, democratic, grassroots forms of organization and existence, and the general affirmation of individual uniqueness against depersonalized bigness. New social movements emphasize different themes, and some of these themes are in conflict with others. But all of them embody a protest against one aspect or other of the status quo.

In this catalogue of factors, there is, however, one factor missing: this is the rejection by all new social movements of the view that *labour* movements could be the appropriate instrument for the advancement of their own aims. In a sense, the emergence of new social movements is a dramatic vote of no confidence in the ability of labour movements and socialist parties to represent adequately, or at all, the grievances, interests, and demands of new social movements, and of the constituencies which they have mobilized. To put it somewhat differently, their emergence is an implicit (and often an explicit) rejection of the claim that the working class is a 'universal' class, and that labour movements claiming to represent it are themselves possessed of a universal vocation and role, capable of encompassing all demands directed at human emancipation. What the new social movements said, or implied by their very existence, was that this claim was unacceptable, and that even though trade unions and parties of the Left might be willing to endorse the concerns of new social movements, experience had shown that they could not be relied on to champion them effectively. The critique often went further, and entailed a virulent rejection of the idea that labour movements dominated by white men steeped in 'traditional' modes of thought could conceivably understand, let alone support, the demands made by new social movements. The claim to 'universalism' was, in this vein, dismissed as an arrogant and absurd presumption, in any case belied by the record of discrimination and exclusion and neglect on the part of labour movements.

The validity of this indictment will be discussed presently. For the moment, I turn to the strengths and limitations of new social movements themselves.

II

New social movements, I have already suggested, affect their societies in various ways, and may legitimately claim some responsibility, at least, for advances and reforms achieved in the areas of life and policy which concern them. The improvements which have occurred, for instance, in the ways in which white society relates to black people in the United States must, to a decisive degree, be attributed to the struggles in which black movements have been engaged since the fifties. Without the freedom marches, the demonstrations, rallies, and other activities of black activists, and on frequent occasions their defiance of the law, with all the sacrifices which their activism entailed, it is safe to say that the black condition in the United States would be far worse than it actually is. This is not to say that the black condition is now good. The advances which have been achieved have been exceedingly limited; and the vast majority of black men and women continue to experience discrimination and super-exploitation, with a degree of unemployment and poverty far higher than is found in the white population. Also, racism—not only against black people, but against all ethnic minorities—continues to suffuse American life. Nevertheless, there has been progress; and the basis has been laid for more.

Much the same may be said, even more definitely, about the advances which have been registered by feminists in the countries where they have been most active. Feminists, in evaluating what has happened to women in recent decades, rightly point to an enduring and pervasive sexism, to the bitter opposition which the assertion of women's rights (notably the right to abortion) encounters, and to the quite overt super-exploitation and discrimination to which they continue to be subjected. Yet what was no more than a distant and blurred memory of suffragette struggles when Simone de Beauvoir first published *The Second Sex* in 1949 (first English translation in 1953) has turned into a real presence on the moral, political, and cultural scene; and feminists may well claim to have been responsible for a cultural revolution of major proportions. It is a cultural revolution which still has a very long way to go; and like all revolutions, it is subject to setbacks and retreats. Nor has it borne sufficient fruit, at work or beyond it. All the same, there is progress here too, and promise of further and more substantial advances.

So too may movements for sexual liberation, for ecological redemption, and for disarmament point to advances, and simultaneously bemoan the fact that they have not accomplished more, and that progress in their chosen fields is so slow and beset by so many obstacles of every kind. In the same context, reference also must be made to the impact which student movements in the sixties were able to exercise in a number of countries, notably in the United States and France. The New Left in the United States began as a student movement, and was a major element in the movement against the war in Vietnam; and the 'May events' in France in 1968 began purely as a Parisian student movement, which then turned into a vast youth rebellion, which was eventually taken up by trade unions and parties of the Left, with a general strike that for a time paralysed France and seemed to threaten the regime itself.[3]

The question, then, is not whether new social movements can achieve certain changes in their societies: this may by now be taken for granted. The question is rather what the changes they seek, *even if they could be fully realized*, would mean in terms of the *distribution of power, property, privilege, and position* in their societies—in other words, in the structure of domination and exploitation.

In one sense, new social movements are well entitled to claim that they are pursuing 'revolutionary' aims, and that the achievement of these aims would have a 'revolutionary' effect on their societies. For it is certainly true, for instance, that to bring about the end of women's oppression, or even to reduce it drastically, would represent an immense, unprecedented change in the nature and texture of individual and social life. Similarly, the end of discrimination and super-exploitation of black people and other minorities, and the general elimination or drastic reduction of racism would be an immense transformation. Again, it would be no exaggeration to describe the elimination or radical curtailment of environmental perils or the dangers of nuclear annihilation as a revolutionary change in the prospects of the human race.

We may leave aside for the moment the question of how such aims are to be realized, and focus rather on the question asked earlier: namely, what bearing their achievement would have on the general structure of domination and exploitation in capitalist societies.

In seeking to answer that question, it is necessary to take account of the different currents of thought which are to be found in new social movements. The feminist movement, for instance, has often been seen as divided between radical, socialist, and liberal currents; and even though the separation between them is often blurred, the positions which the labels portray are nevertheless distinct.[4] Much the same kind of division is to be found in other social movements.

Liberal feminism has constituted the largest element in the women's movement. Its basic aim has been to achieve equality with men in every field, at work, in the home, and before the law; and also to achieve certain reforms of central concern to women, for instance, the right of women to control their reproductive lives, maternity leave, child care centres, equal job-training opportunities, and so on.

The importance of all such demands (for men as well as women) is not in question. But it is a matter of considerable importance in the present context that liberal feminism conceives the achievement of these aims as occurring within the framework of capitalism, without any thought of radical transformation in other respects. Liberal feminists are, quite rightly, sharply critical of a social and political system which allows the oppression, exclusion, and discrimination from which women suffer, but their critique does not extend to the system as a whole, and to the dynamic which fosters the evils which liberal feminism opposes.

If liberal feminists could succeed in the achievement of all their aims, or even in the achievement of a substantial part of their aims, there would undoubtedly occur important changes in the composition of the power elite of advanced capitalist societies, and in the distribution of power as between men and women in general, with the accession of many more women to command posts in economic and political life; and there would also occur a considerable improvement in the general condition of women in relation to men. But it is in no way to belittle the importance of such advances to note that capitalism itself, as a system of domination and exploitation, would remain in being. As workers, women wage-earners would have achieved equality of exploitation, and even this should not be belittled. But most women would remain subordinate and exploited.

Moreover, it needs to be said that many women who are part of liberal feminism are by no means to be taken as 'liberal' on issues other than the condition of women. Women who feel passionately about their own grievances may also support quite reactionary policies on other issues of home and foreign policy. Liberal feminism is not in the least incompatible with highly

conservative views in other areas and may even be quite indifferent
to (or may even support) the discrimination, oppression, and
injustices suffered by other sections of society, for instance, black
people.

Liberal feminism is distinguished from radical or socialist feminism by its belief that what stands in the way of women's
emancipation is ancient tradition, deep-rooted prejudice, and
political resistance. All this, in the liberal feminist perspective,
can be changed by pressure, propaganda, persuasion, organization,
and energetic lobbying. The notion of structural constraints and
of a dynamic which drives *capitalism* as a system towards the
continued oppression of women is alien to this mode of thought.

Radical feminism, for its part, attributes crucial importance to
what might be called structural factors, but finds them embedded
in structures which are not simply those of capitalism. Capitalism
may reinforce these other structures, but is not responsible for
them. The crucial factor is gender division, and the oppression
which men visit upon women in economic, social, political, and
sexual terms. Here, for radical feminism, is the fundamental line
of cleavage in society: the original class division, according to this
view, was between the sexes, and the motive force of history has
always been and remains the striving of men for domination over
women. For some radical feminists, it is male nature itself which
is taken to be aggressive, violent, alienated, and directed against
women. For others, it is an ancient and deep-rooted patriarchal
tradition and culture which has nurtured men into being the
oppressors of women, with very scant hope that most men could
be so 'de-nurtured' as to cease being compulsive sexists. As a
result, the transformation which socialists seek in the economic,
social, and political realms, whatever value it may otherwise have,
is fundamentally flawed because it fails to address the main,
supreme issue: namely, men's oppression of women. Socialism,
viewed thus, is merely a different name for yet another system of
patriarchy, for yet another mode of exploitation of women, for
yet another legitimation of permanent violence against them.

What resolution there could ever be to this gender-determined
version of the war of all (men) against all (women) is not clear.
What alleviation of women's oppression may be possible in a
system in which patriarchy rules is by definition negligible, and

is in any case always vulnerable to annulment; and the logical alternative must therefore be the creation of a space in which women so inclined might live and function autonomously from men, in alternative communities and networks free from the evils that form part of male-dominated societies.

Not all radical feminists take such a negative view of the relations between men and women; and the distance which separates many radical feminists from socialist feminists is in fact short. Socialist feminists are more likely to locate the roots of women's oppression in economic, social, and political structures than in the alleged psychology of men; and they are likely to be more optimistic about the possibilities of alleviating and eventually doing away with the oppression of women in a socialist society. Also, socialist feminists are much more inclined to believe that work in or with the labour movement is both possible and necessary, without loss of autonomy and distinctiveness. Radical feminists, on the other hand, are hostile to what they view as organizations which, for all their declarations of belief in gender equality, are pervaded by sexism and are solidly male-dominated. These differences between the socialist and radical currents in feminism are not negligible. But neither, for the most part, do they create altogether separate universes of thought and practice, between which dialogue, not to speak of co-operation, is impossible.

One of the great strengths of socialist feminism, as compared with other feminist currents, is its emphasis on class as well as gender. For class impinges on all questions relating to gender (and to race) in absolutely critical ways.

It should be obvious that gender cannot be abstracted from class. It is true that most women, as a gender, are subject to various forms of oppression and discrimination. But they experience this very unequally, in different ways, with very different degrees of intensity, *depending on their class location.* The notion of 'women', as such, tends to obscure vast class differences, which create very different contexts for bourgeois women as compared with working-class women. Bourgeois women do suffer various forms of oppression; but the differences between their experience of it and that of working-class women is very great indeed. For bourgeois women, whether by virtue of their own achievements, or through marriage, are part of the dominant class, and share in the advantages which accrue to membership of that class. They may well do so less fully than men in comparable positions on the social scale; and they may be subject to forms of oppression or discrimination which make them subordinate members of the dominant class. But this does not place them on the same level as working-class women or, for that matter, working-class men.[5] Frank Parkin notes that 'if the wives and daughters unskilled labourers have some things in common with the wives and daughters of wealthy landowners, there can be no doubt that the *differences* in their overall situation are far more striking and significant.' 'Only if the disabilities attaching to female status', he adds, 'were felt to be so great as to override differences of a class kind would it be realistic to regard sex as an important dimension of stratification.'[6] Sex *is* an important dimension of stratification; but it cannot, all the same, be separated from class location.

In fact, the point needs to be made somewhat more strongly. As two Marxist feminists put it, 'though women are placed simultaneously in two separate but linked structures, those of class and patriarchy, *it is their class position which limits the conditions of the forms of patriarchy they will be objectively subjected to.*'[7] In this perspective, the notion of women as a 'sexual class' is a misconception. 'What better proof can there be that women are a sexual class', Zillah Eisenstein asks, 'than women organizing across political orientations to build a unified feminist movement?'; and this, she adds, 'is the real proof of feminism that no marxist will be able to explain away'.[8] But nowhere has it in fact been possible to build a 'unified feminist movement'. Nor is there any reason to believe that such a movement can be built, given the deep class and other divisions which stand in its way. The notion of sexual class seeks to obliterate these divisions; but it comes up against their harsh reality.

Two other feminist writers have noted that 'women of color realize that they are never oppressed simply as women but always as women who are not white. Consequently, they regard racism as an enemy that is at least as powerful as male dominance and ultimately inseparable from it.'[9] But class enters here too: for black working-class women are far more disadvantaged than bourgeois black women, not to speak of bourgeois white women.

This is not to deny that women do have certain common

interests—for instance, the right to reproductive choice, or the struggle against male violence. But class, in relation to women, is nevertheless a major dividing factor, whereas wage-earners, men and women, do constitute one class, however divided by gender, race, ethnicity, religion, that class may be. As a class, wage-earners have the *potential* for a degree of unity, at least, which women, as such, cannot hope to achieve.

There is another sense in which class enters (or should enter) into the discussion of gender oppression. This is that the notion of 'men' as the oppressors of women also suffers from a damaging abstractionism. It is quite true that both bourgeois and working-class men oppress women; but it is also the case that they do so *unequally*, because of *their* class location. This is not, of course, because working-class men are 'nicer' or 'kinder' to women than their bourgeois counterparts. It is rather that some men, by virtue of their position and power in the process of production and in society at large, are much more directly and effectively implicated in the oppression and exploitation of women than are other men who do not have this position and power. In this sense, patriarchy, understood as the domination of women by men, is not at all classless. For its exercise is in many very important ways determined by the *area of power* which men command; and power is very unequally distributed among men. Working-class men may oppress and exploit their wives and daughters, and wield some limited power over women at work, or engage in sexual harassment; and nothing of this is negligible. But the power thus exercised, however arbitrary and objectionable, is much more circumscribed than the power which bourgeois men, as employers, have over women. After all, it is not 'men' in the abstract whose location in the upper reaches of the process of production drives them to the super-exploitation of women workers: it is men *as employers* (and also, it may be added, the small minority of women who are also employers). Nor is it 'men' in the abstract who exercise supervisory functions over women (and men) in factories or offices, but *some* men, entrusted with these functions from above, and expected and required to carry them out.

Similarly, it is not simply 'men' who are in charge of the state apparatus and who make policy in ways which all feminists rightly denounce as deeply detrimental to women: it is particular men who are for the most part located in the upper and uppermost reaches of the state; and so too it is some men (and some women) who staff the regulatory agencies of the state at lower levels. The state plays a major role in the regulation of welfare, property, marriage, the custody of children, abortion, rape, and pornography. On all such issues, the state acts in ways which are often contradictory. As Varda Burstyn notes, 'one part of the state may attempt on a local level to set up child care facilities, rape crisis centres, community enterprises and local decision-making bodies . . . while another level of the state, inevitably a "higher", more centralized level, will cut off the funds for these projects, or declare them illegal, or otherwise swamp, contain or dismantle them.'[10] But neither at the higher nor at the lower levels of the state is it working-class men who make and carry out policy. They may support the government which makes policy; but then so do many women as well.

The point may be extended to sexual exploitation. Men of all classes have always engaged in it; but the area of power which some men have and which most men do not have is here, too, crucially relevant. Gerda Lerner makes the point that 'from the earliest period of class development to the present, sexual dominance of higher class males over lower class women has been the very mark of women's class oppression. Clearly, class oppression cannot ever be considered the same condition for men and women.'[11]

But class oppression here means oppression by 'higher class males', and cannot be taken to encompass all men. This does not in any way mean that working-class men do not oppress and exploit women, or that they are not complicit in the oppression and exploitation of women exercised by men 'higher up'. What it means is simply that the power to oppress and exploit wielded by working-class men is much smaller than that of bourgeois (and petty-bourgeois) men. This is no consolation or comfort to a wife battered by her working-class husband, or to a daughter sexually abused by her working-class father, or to a woman worker sexually harassed or bullied by her working-class male 'fellow' worker. Nevertheless, a great inequality of power, in this as in all other realms, is a dimension which the notion of 'patriarchy' and the oppression of women by 'men' altogether ignores.

Many of the considerations relating to feminism are also directly relevant to another main source of oppression: namely, race. In this instance, too, class is a matter of paramount importance. All black people are exposed to discrimination and various forms of oppression.[12] But black working-class men and women (particularly women) are subject to far greater exploitation and oppression than petty-bourgeois and bourgeois black people. In advanced capitalist societies, such people have been able to gain at least some degree of protection from the disadvantages and sufferings which white societies visit upon black people, and to enjoy some of the benefits, comforts, and privileges associated with their class position in the social structure. The people who constitute the black bourgeoisie and petty bourgeoisie may be capitalists, usually on a medium or small scale; or they may be professional or sub-professional men and women, often within the 'black community', sometimes outside it. They may in fact be part of the cultural universe of that community, and be acutely aware, from personal experience and observation, of the racism which suffuses their society. But the fact nevertheless remains that, because of their own class position, they experience racism very differently from working-class blacks. Indeed, a great many black men and women act, professionally, as intermediaries between the power structure and black people, and are inevitably drawn into the system—and may even acquire a vested interest in it.

As in the case of the feminist movement, it is possible to discern three broad currents in the black movement. The first—by far the most important—is concerned to advance the economic, civic, and political rights of black people within the existing social order, without much or any thought regarding its radical transformation in other respects. In other words, this 'liberal' black current seeks for black people the same treatment which capitalist society accords to whites.

A second current of thought, marginal but nevertheless persistent and vocal, has always been that of black people who believe that black emancipation is impossible in a white-dominated society in which racism is so deep as to be virtually ineradicable. Like that of radical feminism, this position does not offer any very obvious answer to the question of what then is to be done. In the United States, it has occasionally led to the advocacy of a black nation in the southern states of the country, or of a return to

Africa. Both such notions clearly belong to the realm of fantasy rather than serious politics. A less extreme alternative is the strengthening of the black community, economically, politically, and culturally, so that it might constitute a more solid, less vulnerable enclave in white society, with its own identity, means of defence, and influence in the political life of society.

The third position, akin to socialist feminism, insists on the crucial importance which needs to be attributed to the struggle against racism; but it also sees the labour movement, for all the latter's own racism, as the major (though not the only) vehicle of that struggle; and it further believes that only a socialist transformation can bring about the rooting-out of the basic sources of racism.

Divisions in black movements based on class or ideology or other differences are profound; and even conditions of extreme oppression, as in South Africa, can only partially subdue them. Black movements have nevertheless demonstrated that they can be effective pressure groups and can bring about improvements in the condition of those for whom they speak. In the exceptional conditions of South Africa, where the regime has itself officially turned colour into a stigma, 'blackness' has also served as a rallying-point for a movement which, on its record in recent years, will in due course topple the apartheid regime. In other countries, on the other hand—notably in advanced capitalist countries with capitalist-democratic regimes—black movements cannot, by themselves, hope to achieve more than limited advances. These advances are valuable; but they do not amount to a decisive breach in the structures of racial oppression and exploitation.

It is not very difficult to find ideological and political differences in ecological and peace movements, or in sexual liberation movements, which are broadly similar to those which exist in feminist and black movements. In their case, too, there are those people whose concerns do not extend to the nature of the social order itself, and who seek reform in the particular fields which are of interest to them. Secondly, there are those—notably in the ecological movement—who are moved by the search for entirely new ways of life, for a fundamentally new relationship to nature, for face-to-face communities in which the multiple alienations of contemporary life will have been conquered. But for all their transformative aspirations—or, as many would see it, *because* of their transformative aspirations—the people thus inspired reject the socialism on offer as quite incapable of bringing about the kind of society they want, and see it indeed as replicating rather than curing the evils they oppose. Thirdly, there are the people in the 'green' movements who situate their ecological concerns within a socialist framework and see the struggle for ecological salvation and other emancipatory concerns as part and parcel of the struggle for a socialist society, but who believe that labour movements have been and are inadequately alert to the issues that concern the 'green' movement, and who therefore feel that they must retain their autonomy.

Even so, there are strong grounds for saying that if they are to achieve their aims, the 'greens' and all other new social movements are absolutely and inescapably dependent on the potential strength of labour movements and their political agencies.

III

I have already noted that new social movements have made significant advances in recent decades; and they may reasonably hope to make more in the years to come. But what they cannot reasonably expect is that societies whose main dynamic is the pursuit of private profit and whose whole mode of being is suffused by deep inequalities of every kind can be made to do away with exploitation, discrimination, violence against vulnerable sections of the population, ecological vandalism, international strife, and all the other evils which have brought new social movements into being.

This is not to suggest that 'socialism' is a magic formula and a cure-all for everything that is wrong in the world. It is to say, rather, that actually existing capitalist societies are incapable of curing the evils which concern new social movements; and that the necessary—but not sufficient—condition for the cure or drastic alleviation of these evils is the creation of societies very different in their social structure, dynamic, organization, and ethos.

But if such a radical transformation is required, then it is quite certain that labour movements are indispensable for the purpose. Here again, the argument is not that labour movements in

advanced capitalist countries *will* necessarily play this transformative role. Nor is it to accord some kind of arbitrarily
'privileged' place to labour movements, out of metaphysical belief
in the 'mission' of the working class. The argument is that without
labour movements organized as political forces, no fundamental
challenge to the existing social order can ever be mounted. For
organized labour does have a greater potential strength, cohesion,
and capacity to act as a transformative force than any other force
in society. Whether it is ever likely to realize its potential, and
what that realization would mean, will be discussed in the last
chapter. But it does at least seem reasonable to argue that so long
as organized labour and its political agencies refuse to fulfil their
transformative potential, so long will the existing social order
remain safe from revolutionary challenge, whatever feminists, or
black people, or gays and lesbians, or environmentalists, or peace
activists, or any other group may choose to do, and even though
their actions may well produce advances and reforms. It is in this
sense that it is necessary to speak of the 'primacy' of labour
movements in regard to social change.

'Primacy' does not mean domination or absorption. Nor certainly does it devalue the work of new social movements, whose
support labour movements would undoubtedly require in the
advancement of their transformative endeavours. This support is
not only a matter of additional numbers—even though new social
movements can activate constituencies which labour movements
are unable to reach. It is also a matter of the contribution which
new social movements can make—and have in fact already made—
to the enrichment of the theory and practices of labour movements.
For there can surely be no question that new social movements
are the bearers of many ideas and practices which must form part
of any emancipatory project worthy of the name, but which labour
movements have traditionally tended to neglect or which, in some
countries, they have opposed.

To speak thus, however, is to assume certain affinities and
possibilities of co-operation and alliance between labour movements on the one hand and new social movements on the other.
It is an assumption which many people in new social movements
have questioned, not least because labour movements themselves
have exhibited many of the deformations and vices against which
feminists, black people, and others are struggling. But much here

depends on what are thought to be the reasons for these deformations and vices.

Among these reasons, a central place needs to be accorded to the context in which deformations and vices occur. That context exercises a very strong pull in the direction of sectionalism, fragmentation, competition, and struggle among workers themselves, and also in the direction of discrimination and closure exercised against vulnerable minorities. Throughout the history of capitalism, workers have sought to improve their bargaining position *vis-à-vis* employers by preventing the access of women, black people, Catholics, Irishmen, or whoever, to their occupations. The roots of such discrimination lie in the attempt to protect jobs and conditions; and the divisions and fragmentations and hostilities this causes are frequently encouraged or even fostered by employers. Discrimination is then rationalized by ideological constructs and racist or sexist stereotypes according to which women are unsuited to particular forms of work, black people are stupid, Irishmen are shiftless, and so on; and these constructs acquire a life of their own and become an autonomous part of the culture. To ignore this economic dimension in the history of racist or sexist discrimination is to leave a crucial facet of reality out of account.[13]

It is nevertheless true that a great deal of oppression, discrimination, aggression, and violence exercised by white men, whether workers or bourgeois, against women, black people, ethnic minorities, gays and lesbians, cannot be traced back in any plausible way to direct or even indirect economic pressures. A different explanation is required, and must be sought, I would argue, in traditional ideological prejudices and positions, nurtured over many generations, and reinforced by the multiple alienations, frustrations, and anxieties generated by societies whose dynamic is ruthless competition and frantic acquisition, and whose ethos constitutes a permanent denial, in practice, of co-operation, fellowship, and solidarity. Such societies provide a fertile ground for the festering of the 'injuries of class' and for the development of pathological deformations: mechanisms of legitimation for these deformations readily come into play and designate victims as themselves responsible for the sufferings inflicted upon them, and for diverse social ills.

Feminists and others rightly point out that pre-capitalist

societies were similarly deformed, and that Communist societies are also afflicted by racism and sexism. From this, it is but a small step to the claim that such phenomena are trans-historical, and rooted in human nature, or in male nature, rather than in social processes susceptible to drastic attenuation and to eventual extirpation. But this ignores the fact that pre-capitalist societies were also class societies marked by domination and exploitation, with their own 'injuries of class'. As for Communist societies, the circumstances in which they came into being, their economic, social, and political conditions, and the circumstances in which they have developed as Communist regimes have made them exceedingly prone to the perpetuation of deformations which they have inherited and are formally pledged to eliminate, and which are deeply rooted in their tradition and culture.

In short, explanations for enduring evils such as sexism and racism must be sought in the social context in which they occur. To seek them outside that context, and to invoke for their explanation trans-historical and supposedly immutable traits of human nature or male nature is to retreat from rational analysis.

The case against 'generic' explanations (or rather pseudo-explanations) for such phenomena as racism and sexism is reinforced by much historical experience. The point bears repeating: there have been innumerable instances everywhere of workers, male and female, white and black, Catholic and Protestant, Muslim and Jewish, acting together in struggle and achieving a high, if temporary, level of solidarity.

The pulls against the maintenance of solidarity are very strong, but they have been proved again and again not to be insuperable. Workers divided by gender, race, ethnicity, and religion *have* come together in trade unions and parties and other organizations of labour movements, and have found common ground and solidarity in common struggles against employers and the state.

A crucial responsibility in this area, too, falls upon trade unions and political parties of the Left; and the record on this score is not quite as bleak as is often suggested. It is true that the history of trade unionism is spattered with instances of prejudice and discrimination, much more virulent in some countries (for instance, the United States, not to speak of South Africa) than in others, but nowhere negligible. But given the economic context in which trade unions operate, and the sexism and racism which pervade the culture of all societies, the remarkable thing is not that trade unionists should have been affected by these prejudices, but that the organizations of which they are members should, in country after country, have been in the forefront of the opposition to racial and gender discrimination. Nor are the labour movements worst affected by such evils frozen in immutable positions: it is enough for instance to compare the level of racism prevalent in American trade unions before World War II with its level in more recent times to see that however slow and limited progress may be, it does occur.

As for labour and socialist parties, they have, from their very beginnings, been among the most consistent forces opposing the prejudices prevalent in their societies. It was the leader of the German Social Democratic Party, August Bebel, who published in 1878 one of the major feminist texts of the nineteenth century, *Women and Socialism*, which became the essential statement on the subject for party members and others; and Angela Weir and Elizabeth Wilson note that 'the German SPD had a women's movement with 175,000 members in 1914 and had introduced the first motion calling for the enfranchisement of women in the Reichstag in 1895. The SPD was formally committed to creches for working mothers, equal pay for equal work, the education of women, relaxation of the abortion laws and availability of contraceptives.'[14]

At different levels of commitment, the same story can be repeated for all parties of the Left everywhere. In terms of formal commitment at least, and often in practice as well, parties of the Left have proved to be the staunch supporters of many of the causes and concerns which move the new social movements; and it is worth adding that Communist parties in particular, for all their great shortcomings and failings, have been in the vanguard of the struggle against oppression and discrimination in their societies, often in exceptionally harsh and dangerous conditions— for instance, in the southern states of the United States (or in the North for that matter) and in South Africa. The policies and strategies of Communist parties might often be mistaken; but this does not diminish the reality of the commitment of their members to a vision of human emancipation which knows no boundaries of gender or race. Much the same vision has inspired socialists everywhere.

Against this, feminists and members of racial or ethnic minorities are well entitled to point to lapses, in practice, from formal party commitments, or to practices which belie the commitments; and members of new social movements in general may well argue that the issues which concern them are not granted an adequate place in the range of concerns of the parties of the Left. But however justified these grievances may be, the failings to which they point are clearly not irremediable; and they do not preclude, given some flexibility, the waging of common struggles over mutually agreed policies and aims. Suspicions, disagreements, and rivalries will endure; but they need not be crippling.

It must, however, be said that labour movements will remain at the core of the struggle for radical reform and revolutionary change in advanced capitalist societies. New social movements may doubt this, or deny it. But all conservative forces in these societies do not doubt it. For them, the main antagonist, as always, remains organized labour and the socialist Left: it is they who must above all be contained, repelled, and, if need be, crushed. It is to these ends that class struggle from above is mainly directed; and it is to the ways in which this struggle is conducted that I now turn.

5

The Politics of Class Struggle, II

What I have called class struggle from above is in fact waged by many different protagonists—by employers, power-holders in the state, political agencies such as parties, lobbies, newspapers, and journals, and by many other agencies which may declare themselves to be 'non-political' (and which may truly believe that they are), but which do nevertheless contribute to the struggle. There are innumerable ways in which individuals and groups may do so; and many of those involved in the struggle are not members of the dominant class or power elite at all, but of the petty bourgeoisie, and include a host of journalists, 'commentators', and others in semi-professional occupations, who may be among the most vocal and most ardent combatants in the struggle. So, too, many of its foot soldiers are drawn from the working class. However, the reason for speaking of 'class struggle from above' is that the crucial protagonists are usually those who own or control the main means of domination in capitalist society— employers on the one hand and the state on the other, with the hands usually clasped in a firm grip. Even in those cases where the main impulse seems to be provided from elsewhere than 'above', as, for instance, in the fascist movements in the inter-war years, the acquiescence, support, or complicity of traditional elites has always been critical for the success of these movements.[1]

There are of course great differences among the people engaged in this struggle, but they can all nevertheless be encompassed under the label 'conservative'. For most of them are consciously and explicitly intent on the maintenance, defence, and re-inforcement of the existing social order against challenge from the Left. The rhetoric of some of the people concerned may be 'radical' or 'revolutionary', the extreme case being that of the Fascists in Italy and the Nazis in Germany. But their 'radicalism' is allied to the bitterest enmity against labour movements, left parties, and all other forces of radical change in their society; and even more important, the result of authoritarian and fascist rule, notwithstanding the rhetoric, is always the consolidation of the capitalist social order. The same applies to 'radical' conservatism of the Thatcher variety.

The problem which capitalist democracy poses to conservative forces is how to defend great concentrations of power and privilege against pressure from below for radical reform or revolutionary change, in regimes which offer such pressure many opportunities to manifest itself and to develop. How, to put the same point somewhat differently, is a relatively small minority of people, enjoying a vastly disproportionate amount of power and privilege, to continue enjoying this in circumstances which make pressure and challenge from below a legitimate enterprise, rendered all the more legitimate by a democratic rhetoric which it is very difficult— in fact, virtually impossible—to reject.

It is a problem which greatly exercised conservative politicians and others in the last decades of the nineteenth century, the years which saw the rise of the contemporary labour movement, the extension of the suffrage, and the arrival of organized labour on the political and parliamentary scene; and it is a problem which has ever since preoccupied power-holders everywhere.

Capitalist democracy not only makes pressure from below possible: it also imposes certain constraints upon the ways in which that pressure is met and countered; and much conservative effort therefore goes into the endeavour to circumvent, overcome, manipulate, or erode these constraints, and to do this within the framework of democratic forms.

Of course, this is not how those who speak for conservatism have for the most part perceived, let alone articulated, the problem: they have seen it instead as a struggle in defence of freedom, justice, the national interest, democracy, reason, the rule of law, decency, and so forth. This has provided conservative forces with the crucial element of self-legitimation which dominant classes and their allies in other classes need; and this element of self-legitimation has been powerfully reinforced by the conviction that behind their internal opponents and enemies there lurked the threat of 'communism' and Soviet aggression.

At one level, the democratic forms of capitalist democracy are a nuisance to dominant classes. At another level, these forms are highly 'functional'; for they help to 'routinize' conflict and to 'integrate' challenge in the ways discussed earlier. This being the case, the constraints imposed upon conservative forces by democratic forms are a relatively small price to pay for the advantages which this type of political system affords to dominant classes. All the more is this so in that the system is flexible enough to allow the bending and circumventing of these forms when required. There is always the danger that pressure from below and class struggle might become so intense as to render democratic forms exceedingly 'dysfunctional': but only crises of great magnitude producing massive shifts of opinion are likely to bring this about. Leaving this aside for the moment, we may turn to the ways in which containment is assured, and class struggle from above waged, in 'normal' times.

II

We begin with what was described in an earlier chapter as the 'primary cell' of class struggle: namely, conflict at the point of production, but this time in the perspective of class struggle from above.

I noted in Chapter 1 that employers are inevitably, 'structurally', engaged in struggle with their workers, because of the fundamentally contradictory aims of each side. But it must also be said that employers are engaged in forms of pressure, in relation to their workers, whether the workers themselves are engaged in struggle or not. The reason for this one-sidedness is that employers are ineluctably driven, by virtue of their position in the productive process and the inner dynamic of that process, to seek better returns from their workers for the wages they pay them. Employers seek, and must seek, ways of keeping down wage costs, of improving productivity, of reducing overhead costs, and of affirming the managerial prerogatives and the supervisory control upon which the fulfilment of these and similar aims depends. In other words, pressure is built into the employers' role, just as resistance is built into that of their workers.

In seeking to further their aims, employers enjoy a great number of advantages. One of these, of primary importance, is the advantage of being able to take initiatives, to make decisions, to manifest their will and demands to their workers. Employers act, workers react; and employers act in the knowledge that they are in charge, in command.

On the other hand, this employers' advantage has to be constantly defended, sustained, assured, enforced: formal command has to be translated into effective control, and this, given the nature of labour as a 'peculiar commodity', raises problems. To resolve the problem, many different devices need to be employed, involving a mixture of detailed supervision and control, coercion and intimidation, cajoling and enticement. At one end of the spectrum, there is what has, in the American case, been called 'the daily terrorism exercised by foremen and company security departments (or even internal vigilante organisations, as at Goodyear)'.[2] This 'daily terrorism' is found in even more pronounced form in Japanese 'industrial relations', which have had so many admirers in the West in recent years:

Japanese factories have an extremely high number of supervisory staff. Repression inside the plant is sustained through constant espionage on militant workers and the sabotage of contesting workers' organisations— such as splitting a combative union or forming a subsidized 'second' union to bribe or terrorize away wavering workers from the militant line—and also through the constant 'family-like' interference in workers' everyday lives. In many cases companies hire gangsters and goon squads, which operate off the shop floor as well as on it. Terror in and around the plant by private companies is complemented by massive police repression against militants in society in general.[3]

At the other end of the spectrum, there are bonus and welfare schemes, sports and entertainment facilities, and anything else that may induce in workers, or at least among sections of workers, a sense of gratitude and 'loyalty'.[4]

The power bestowed by the right to take policy decisions has, in recent decades, also been manifested in the threat that a firm faced with recalcitrant and over-demanding workers would move elsewhere. Thus Michael Burawoy speaks of 'the new despotism' constituted by 'the "rational" tyranny of capital over the *collective* worker . . . the fear of being fired is replaced by the fear of capital flight, plant closure, transfer of operations, and plant disinvestment.'[5]

The main obstacle to the power which employers seek to wield over their workers is the spontaneous and many-faceted resistance of the workers themselves. But their resistance needs to be given shape and coherence, and this is done, well or badly, by trade unions. This is why the attitude of employers to trade unions ranges from reluctant and qualified acceptance to bitter hostility and rejection. In some countries, notably Sweden, trade unions have become an uncontroversial part of the industrial landscape, even if employers remain vigilantly concerned that trade unions should not impinge too greatly upon what employers take to be their own prerogatives. In other countries, notably the United States, employers fight a bitter and tireless battle to prevent unionization at all, or seek to get rid of trade unions in their firms if there is any possibility of doing so. It is only in some parts of the economy that trade unionism has achieved acceptance by employers, and within strictly limited terms: the overwhelming majority of American workers (some 85 per cent) are non-unionized and very poorly placed to resist their employers' pressure.

Even where unionism cannot be prevented among manual workers, it may be possible to prevent it among other employees. Thus Richard Hyman writes, in relation to Britain:

Private employers have often fiercely resisted staff unionisation, even where unions exist among the manual labour force. Staff are then inhibited from taking up union membership; either through identification with the employer's viewpoint; or from fear of dismissal, damage to personal prospects of promotion, or other forms of victimisation; or simply because a weak and unrecognized union can win no improvements in conditions from the employer and therefore has no concrete inducements to offer the potential member.[6]

He also notes the contrast between the public sector in Britain, with a high degree of unionization of white-collar workers, and the private sector, where for much of the post-war period the proportion was only 12 per cent. Privatization, in this respect, offers, among other advantages to employers, the hope that the rate of union membership might, in due course, be drastically reduced.

However, trade unions, as was noted in Chapter 3, can be a help rather than a hindrance to employers; for they are agencies of conciliation and containment as well as agencies of pressure and conflict. Even shop stewards, often viewed as incurable 'trouble-makers', have in fact proved to be of great help in smoothing out the innumerable micro-problems which arise at the point of production.[7] The real problem, from the point of view of employers, is not activists as such, but activists who, though possibly playing a part in resolving problems on the shop floor, are moved by strong left-wing convictions, belong to left-wing organizations, are disposed to question and challenge managerial prerogatives, and are potential leaders in conflict situations. From the earliest days of capitalism, employers have been at war with such people, and have done everything they could to eliminate them from their enterprises, or at least to marginalize them, to isolate them, and to exile them as far as possible to departments of the enterprise where they would be least likely to poison the minds of their fellow workers. Again, how this is done, with what degree of determination, brutality, and success, varies from country to country; but known (or suspected) left activists, whether in capitalist enterprises or state ones, have always known blacklisting, persecution, harassment, often physical violence—occasionally in some countries, for instance the United States, murder at the hands of goons and security men. There is nothing very remarkable about much of this: it must be taken to form a 'natural' part of class struggle from above in the capitalist system.

So too must efforts of employers to find all possible means of dividing workers from each other by differential treatment and concessions, by preventing the creation of stable relationships at the workplace, by multi-tier wage levels, and by any other means likely to reduce the solidarity of workers with each other. This too must be taken to be a 'natural' part of industrial relations under capitalism.

Yet, despite all endeavours by employers, conflict does flare up and strikes do occur. When they do, and particularly when they are on a substantial scale, class struggle from above assumes more intense forms, with the deployment of many different weapons in the employers' arsenal. This too varies from country to country, from industry to industry, and is also subject to prevailing economic and other circumstances. But the arsenal includes such weapons as lay-offs, the dismissal of strikers or the threat of dismissal, the threat of plant closures or their actual closure, the employment wherever possible of strike-breakers and so on.

All this, however, leaves out of the reckoning what is the most important aspect of any major strike: the fact that *employers do not have to fight it alone.* For with them in the struggle are to be found other and formidable forces—in society on the one hand, and in the state on the other.

In society, employers can rely on whatever help, direct or indirect, employers' associations may be able to extend to them. So too can they count on the endeavours of lobbies, 'freedom associations', and other such organizations whose main purpose is precisely to counter trade unionism, to help defeat strikes, and to influence public opinion against both trade unions and strikes. In the event of a major industrial conflagration, notably in a general strike, a host of organizations moved by the same purposes may be expected to come into being for the maintenance of essential services, the support of strike-breakers, and whatever else may contribute to the defeat of the strike. In the same vein, the overwhelming majority of the press can be counted on to add its weight to the creation of a climate hostile to strikers, activists, trade union leaders, and anybody else supporting the action.

All such endeavours are proclaimed to be undertaken out of concern for 'the community', 'the public', and so forth, whose welfare and convenience suffer as a result of the strike. But the fact remains that it is workers in struggle with their employers, using the only effective weapon they have, who are the target of denunciation and abuse, and whose defeat is being sought.

In any major dispute, there are also voices raised—for instance, that of churchmen—whose plea is for conciliation, compromise, settlement. Such pleas may well be made by people who are not unsympathetic to the strikers; but however well-meaning they may be, their efforts tend nevertheless to have an adverse effect on the workers' side, in so far as a refusal on the part of the strikers to retreat (and this is what is commonly involved) strengthens the image of strikers as obdurate and indifferent to the inconvenience they are causing.

In combination, all such efforts can constitute a formidable mobilization of forces on the employers' side. But the most decisive help to employers, whether in the private sector or in state enterprise, is that provided by the state. Its own intervention is defended in the same terms as are used by the press and others against trade unions and strikes—the defence of 'law and order', the maintenance of essential services, the inconvenience of 'the public', and the protection of 'the right to work' (of strike-breakers).

This is not necessarily mere rhetoric. Essential services may well be jeopardized by a major strike, and the 'public' may indeed be greatly inconvenienced by it. 'Law and order' may be greatly disturbed in conditions of conflict, though its disturbance is very often the result of police behaviour and actions rather than the responsibility of strikers. Again, it is true that the right to work of strike-breakers may well be placed at risk as a result of mass picketing designed to prevent the weakening or defeat of the strike. Right is here pitted against right, with each side defending what are in effect contradictory interests.

This is something which is consistently overlooked in industrial disputes. The state's intervention occurs in a particular social context—a context of class domination, exploitation, and great inequality which inevitably turns such notions as 'the public', 'the community', 'the national interest', into obfuscating abstractions. What is being protected is not a 'community'—a term laden with strong intimations of fellowship—but a particular social order, marked by deep class divisions, vast inequalities of every kind, and contradictory class interests. Strikes, in such a context, are a 'natural' part of industrial relations; and any substantial strike is indeed likely to visit inconvenience on 'the public': but the fault for this lies in a system which breeds conflict and which empties the notion of community of its meaning.

State intervention in industrial relations is not of course confined to industrial disputes. It pervades every aspect of these relations at all times, by way of the legislative and regulatory provisions which the state lays down and enforces. Whether an industrial dispute occurs or not, there is a legal framework which governs the 'relations of production'; and that framework is pre-eminently concerned with the protection of employers' rights and pre-rogatives. By comparison, the rights of wage-earners and the prerogatives of trade unions are infinitely more modest and precarious. There is a real sense in which unions are intruders— and are treated as intruders—in a relationship between employer and worker sanctified by the notion of 'freedom of contract'; and unions are in any case enmeshed in a thick web of contractual and legally enforceable rules and obligations, nowhere more so than in the United States, where, as Davis observes, the contract between the union and the employer 'usually contains no-strike provisions, is non-extensive, and above all, is extremely detailed in its specifications; fixing the actual, not merely the minimal, conditions'.[8]

Such contracts require the unions to employ large staffs of legal experts and officials;[9] and employers, whose own legal resources may be expected to match or exceed those of unions, can normally anticipate a sympathetic hearing from arbitration boards and the courts. The Reagan years have in fact seen a very marked tilting of the balance in favour of management by the conscious and deliberate appointment of people favourable to business to such bodies as the National Labor Relations Board. In any case, as Davis also notes,

the Justice Department has moved aggressively to reverse labor reforms by administrative fiat: exempting certain categories of federal contractors from minimum wage provisions; weakening affirmative action requirements; cutting Occupational Safety and Health Administration standards; removing seventy-year old restrictions on child labor and home work; replacing CETA with a low-cost job training bill.[10]

These attacks, it should be recalled, occur in the context of a legislative framework, notably the Taft-Hartley Act of 1947, which drastically constrains union power.[11]

Ever since it came to office in 1979, the Thatcher Government has been just as determined and consistent in its attack on trade unions, industrial activism, and gains previously made in the field of industrial relations. Thus in relation to employment protection, the period of continuous employment required before workers could complain to a tribunal against unfair dismissal was repeatedly extended, so that 'these gradually increasing qualifying periods excluded millions of workers from the protection not to be unfairly dismissed.'[12] In relation to minimum wages, measures were taken which 'amounted to a major withdrawal of legal support from collective bargaining by removing a minimum floor in favour of the pursuit of market forces'.[13] Picketing was drastically restricted and sympathy action altogether banned. The power of employers to dismiss strikers was considerably extended.

Strike action has been made contingent on strict ballot provisions; and the closed shop has been eliminated.

The state has on occasion played an important role in overcoming the opposition of employers to trade unions and in limiting the prerogatives of employers. Given sufficient pressure from below, and in circumstances favourable to labour, there are, as noted earlier, concessions to be had, in this field as in others; and limited though these concessions may be, they are none the less valuable in so far as they help redress somewhat the balance of power between employers and workers. But what the state gives, the state can also, in different circumstances, take away; and so it does. The right to strike exists everywhere in capitalist-democratic regimes; but it is everywhere greatly limited by a series of prohibitions and constraints which greatly weaken its meaning and practice, and which expose unions and strikers deemed to have infringed these prohibitions and constraints to severe penalties. Complex legal provisions do everywhere regulate when and how and by whom a strike may be called, according to what procedures and against what employer, with what requirements of notification, cooling-off periods, arbitration and conciliation procedures, ballots of workers, codes of conduct in regard to picketing, and much else which is intended to affect the capacity of workers to take action against their employers, however justified their grievances and demands may be; and there are also many countries in which large categories of workers, namely public and state employees, are denied the right to strike at all.

'The state' here means the different branches of the state system—the government, high-level civil servants, police and military chiefs, the judiciary, the legislative branch, local and regional government; and it is very notable that in no sphere of policy do these different branches of the state system work in greater harmony than in the defeat of a major strike. The separation of powers, in some capitalist-democratic regimes at least—for instance, the American—does produce genuine conflicts between different branches over specific issues of policy and action. In regard to industrial disputes, however, there is near-perfect co-operation. Governments intent on breaking strikes may rest assured that they will receive the fullest co-operation from police and, where required, military chiefs; that legislative bodies will give them the powers they may need; that the judiciary at all levels may be counted on to uphold 'law and order', and to do all it can to help the government's purposes. Local and regional authorities under left-wing control may not co-operate; but their recalcitrance can be circumvented or overcome by governments armed with the formidable power conferred upon them by emergency legislation.

All governments, whether conservative or social democratic, react with great hostility to major industrial disputes. The difference between them lies in the manner of their response to such episodes. A Labour Government faced with a strike like the miners' strike in 1984/5 could not have reacted to it with the ferocity and callousness displayed by the Thatcher Government.[14] All the same, Labour Governments have frequently invoked the power at their command to break strikes, and have never hesitated to denounce strikers in vehement terms.[15]

There is an aspect of the state's response to strikes which needs particular attention. This is the fact that 'upholding the law', whether by the police, the military, or the judiciary, is a formulation which conceals more than it reveals of what is involved. For not only is the law itself in this regard the product of powerful ideological and political motivations: more important in this context is that it inevitably requires interpretation. This means that those people in the state who are responsible for the application and the enforcement of the law have a considerable amount of *discretion* in the interpretation of its meaning. This has always been recognized in the case of the judiciary; but it is also of great relevance in regard to the police, whose direct encounter with strikers and pickets in a dispute gives crucial importance to the point. The manner in which police and judicial discretion are used differs according to circumstance, place, and the temper of the government of the day, which is likely to influence the ways in which the police (and the military) act. But the discretion which agents of the state have in the application of the law may confidently be expected to be used in ways which are detrimental to the strikers, however much within the law they seek to confine themselves. For what is, and what is not, within the law is precisely the subject of a great deal of discretion, so that what is legal is very often what the police or magistrates or judges choose to consider legal. These choices are not random or solely based on an 'objective' view of the evidence and the issues, however much the people concerned may believe that their decisions are thus based: these decisions are inevitably laden with powerful ideological assumptions and prejudices, held with an intensity commensurate with the sharpness of the conflict.

These considerations are not only relevant to situations of crisis and conflict: they also apply to the exercise of what I have called 'activist rights'[16] in general. The issue will be pursued further in Section v. ii of this chapter. For the moment, the point I wish to note is how vast are the resources which private and public employers enjoy in the crucial aspect of class struggle encompassed by the relations between employers and wage-earners. Here as everywhere else, there is an enormous disparity in the position of the contending parties. But equally remarkable is the fact that this disparity has often been surmounted by the collective determination of workers, and by their willingness to endure the sacrifices and sufferings which struggle entails.

There are occasions when employers and governments welcome or at least accept confrontation with workers and their unions over wages and other issues, in the belief that their success in such a confrontation would weaken the unions and activists, affirm managerial authority, and advance the policies on which employers and governments are bent. This is undoubtedly how the Thatcher Government envisaged the confrontation with the National Union of Mineworkers in the period before the miners' strike occurred.

On the other hand, confrontation is a costly and messy business; and governments and most employers would rather achieve their aims and ensure industrial peace by other means, particularly when the economic and political climate is not unambiguously favourable to them. In the three decades following World War II, governments in advanced capitalist countries accepted confrontation when it appeared unavoidable, and did their best to defeat industrial militancy; but they also sought to enmesh trade unions into networks of agreements, 'social contracts', 'incomes policies', and other such devices, whose basic purpose was to reduce pressure from below, particularly in relation to wage demands, and to turn trade unions into more or less official agencies for the maintenance of industrial peace and economic stability.[17]

For their part, trade union leaders were themselves very willing to enter into formal agreements with employers and the state, and saw such agreements as a means of strengthening their own position, of giving them a voice in the making of policy, and of achieving concessions for those on whose behalf they spoke.

The label under which these endeavours were subsumed was 'corporatism'.[18] It was in some ways a confusing label, in so far as corporatism and the 'corporate state' had been how Italian Fascism had described its own endeavours to bring about industrial peace and class collaboration. The main feature of Fascist corporatism had been its enforced, compulsory character, not to speak of the fact that labour organizations brought into being by Fascism were altogether subordinate to the Fascist regime. Compulsion has also been the main feature of the attempts of other right-wing authoritarian regimes—for instance, Salazar's Portugal—to introduce corporatism, under one label or another, into their country. Capitalist-democratic regimes, for their part, have sought to achieve a voluntary kind of corporatism, with trade unions having one foot in the state, the other outside it. However, the agreements reached under corporatist arrangements have often been given a legally sanctioned and compulsory character, with the imposition of 'norms' and 'ceilings' for wage increases over given periods, or the restriction of strike action under given agreements. This corporatism formally integrates trade unions into a tripartite system, in which capital and the state are the other partners: in effect, the unions in this system are for all practical purposes the junior allies of capital and the state, and the would-be guarantors of a precarious industrial peace, in return for concessions which are always highly problematic. One of the main theorists of corporatism has suggested that 'societal corporatism can be traced primarily to the imperative necessity for a stable bourgeois-democratic regime . . . to associate or incorporate subordinate classes and status groups more closely within the political process.'[19] It is refreshing to find that, in this formulation, there is no question of 'subordinate classes' ceasing to be subordinate by way of corporatism. But a good deal more than 'association' and 'incorporation' is involved in the process. As David Cameron has noted, 'corporatism can be seen as a system of institutionalised wage restraint in which labour, acting "responsibly", voluntarily participates in and legitimizes the transfer of income from labour to capital.'[20]

This negative view of corporatism needs some slight qualification. There are some cases, notably that of Sweden, where labour movements are exceptionally well entrenched and where social democratic government is the rule rather than the exception. In such cases, corporatism may turn out to have advantages over any other political strategy. An article in the *Economist* in 1987 entitled 'The Non-conformist State' ran as follows:

Sweden is an economic paradox. It has the biggest public sector of any industrial economy, the highest taxes, the most generous welfare state, the narrowest wage differentials, and powerful trade unions. According to prevailing economic wisdom, it ought to be suffering from an acute bout of 'eurosclerosis', with rigid labour markets and arthritic industry. Instead, Sweden has many large and vigorous companies, and one of the lowest unemployment rates in Europe.[21]

This does not amount to the end of exploitation or of subordination. But it clearly represents a set of real gains of great value to the working class; and it is reasonable to suppose that this owes a good deal to the corporatist policies pursued by the Swedish labour movement.

In other countries of advanced capitalism, on the other hand— for instance, Britain—corporatist policies have meant above all else wage restraint and other sacrifices for the working class. One crucial assumption on which corporatist policies have been defended is that all classes share a common interest which will presumably be impartially served by these policies. Thus a major study of the European experience of incomes policies, such policies being the cornerstone of corporatism, opens with the statement: 'This book is about trade-union power and efforts to restrain its use *in the general economic interest.*'[22] But as Leo Panitch observes, 'it is assumed, rather than demonstrated . . . that there is in fact an underlying social harmony in modern capitalist societies and that in the circumstances the concept of national or public interest is an unproblematic one.'[23]

It is in fact an exceedingly problematic assumption. For in societies which are class-divided and class-competitive, and in which labour movements are not nearly so well entrenched as in Sweden, the restraint of trade union power is much more likely to serve the interests of employers and of the dominant class in general than 'the general economic interest'.

An alternative defence of corporatist policies acknowledges the reality of conflict between major interests in capitalist society, but claims that corporatism provides a framework within which conflict may be negotiated and resolved—a framework, moreover, which could be advantageous to labour. Thus John Goldthorpe writes:

What corporatist institutions can be said to provide is a distinctive context within which the class conflicts of a capitalist society may be carried on. The eventual outcome of such conflicts will depend on the relative success of contending organizational leaderships in mobilizing and sustaining support within their constituencies; but under corporatism as here understood, labour attains a position in which it can at least make the attempt to convert its market strength into political measures designed to advanced working class interests in a wider-ranging and more permanent manner than could be achieved through action in the industrial sphere alone.[24]

The real question, however, is not whether labour should act in the industrial sphere alone; but whether the trade unions which represent its interests, or which purport to do so, are better able to advance these interests within a corporatist framework than outside it. The history of corporatist experience since World War II would seem to suggest that it is only in 'Swedish' circumstances, which are not reproduced in most advanced capitalist countries, that the corporatist framework could be turned into something more than a device to curb labour demands and gains; and even this would not produce the emancipation of labour from class domination and exploitation.

There is one exceptional circumstance in which policies of restraint could be demanded from labour—namely, where a government of the Left was seriously and very visibly engaged in the radical transformation of the social order in directions unambiguously advantageous to the vast majority of the population. Such a government, which would itself be the product of vast popular support, would be entitled to ask for restraint in the making of demands, and would undoubtedly be heeded.

It is significant that corporatism and incomes policies should have had the greatest vogue at a time when organized labour was in a relatively strong bargaining position, in the post-war decades of economic growth and a strong demand for labour. By the early seventies, the economic climate was worsening, the demand for

labour was beginning to slacken, and corporatism began to lose
its appeal. The appeal had in any case been reduced by the
resistances it had encountered within the ranks of labour itself,
and by the failures of policy which these resistances provoked.
Thus,

by the end of the 1960s, most of the first-generation experiments in the
United States and most European countries had been abandoned or
greatly de-emphasized. Although there were some instances of short-term
restraint of increases in money wages, these periods of apparent effectiveness were often terminated by waves of wildcat strikes, wage explo-
sions, and severe disruptions in national systems of industrial relations.[25]

Full (or near full) employment produces conditions favourable
to the advancement of labour demands. Mass unemployment, on
the other hand, may be expected to place severe constraints on
the militancy of labour. However wasteful it may be, and however
malignant its effect on the unemployed, mass unemployment thus
produces a climate of industrial relations which employers and
the state do not find at all unattractive, notwithstanding the
constant expressions of regret which they may proffer. As Michał
Kalecki observed of 'business leaders' in 1943, at a time when
full employment was being promised as a peacetime reward for
the sacrifices of war, 'their class instinct tells them that lasting
full employment is unsound from their point of view and that
unemployment is an integral part of the normal capitalist system.'[26]
It was not until the 1970s, however, that unemployment on a
really huge scale became again part of the 'normal capitalist
system' in advanced capitalist countries, and thus condemned
millions upon millions of people to enforced and debilitating
idleness, with horrendous rates of unemployment among young
people, notably young people in black and other minorities. What
has perhaps been most notable about this in the years since mass
unemployment descended upon these countries is the lack of
urgency and vigour with which governments have tackled the
blight. It might have been otherwise if *employers* had been
adversely affected by mass unemployment; or if the unemployed—
or organized labour—had been able or willing to pose a major
threat to social and political stability by the vigour of their
opposition to it. But they were not; and employers were thus able

to reap the benefits to be had from the weakening of labour to which mass unemployment undoubtedly contributed.

Mass unemployment is not only an 'economic' phenomenon, but a political one as well. Its level is greatly influenced by political circumstances and by the policies which the prevailing balance of forces dictates. 'Macro-economic outcomes', it has been said, 'are not altogether endogenous to the economy, but obviously are influenced to a significant extent by long- and short-term political choices.'[27] These political choices are crucially affected by the balance of class forces, and the weight which organized labour and parties of the Left are able or willing to bring to bear on the policy decisions of the state. This is one of the many areas in which supposedly insurmountable economic imperatives, declared to be beyond the reach of governments, suddenly become susceptible to drastic modification, provided that sufficient pressure from below and the threat of great trouble is directed at policy-makers.[28]

III

Social policy constitutes a crucial terrain of class struggle from above; and it is certainly seen to be such by power elites and dominant classes, even if the terms of the struggle are defined in rather different language. 'Social policy' encompasses a wide range of social and collective services and benefits for which the state has assumed responsibility in the twentieth century, and which has given rise to the emollient and apologetic label 'the welfare state';[29] and social policy may also be taken to encompass the vital area of the state's taxation policies.

State action in this realm assumes two distinct forms. The first involves the conscious pursuit by the state of policies designed to attenuate and defuse popular grievances and demands, and thereby to contain pressure from below. It is from this point of view no accident that the contemporary 'welfare state' should have begun to be built in the last decades of the nineteenth century, at a time when the modern labour movement itself was being constituted. The hope of governments then and ever since has been that moderate doses of social reform would still the demand for more radical policies, and that the working class would thus be persuaded to shun parties which advocated such policies.

The second form which state action assumes is precisely the *limitation* of the scope and substance of social policies and benefits. Having assumed a benevolent and 'caring' stance, the state also and simultaneously seeks to ensure that the bounties which it confers should not inhibit the operation of capitalist rationality and the predominance of the market.

The state in this realm is subject to a permanent tension between contradictory pressures. On the one hand, it is strongly pressed by capital and other conservative forces to reduce its expenditure on social, collective, and other such services; and pressures in the same direction are generated within the state itself. Some governments are less parsimonious than others; but it is only in very unusual circumstances that parsimoniousness is not the rule. On the other hand, there is constant pressure from below, which power-holders cannot afford to ignore and which, in many cases, they have no wish to ignore, both in their own interest, and also because expectations must not be altogether disappointed if the state is to fulfil its essential stabilizing function. It is this tension which finds expression in the character of the state's measures in relation to welfare, benefits, and services: provision has to be made, and it is made; but it is made grudgingly.

It may be noted that the working class itself mostly pays in direct and indirect taxes for the services and benefits which accrue to it. What occurs is very largely a redistribution of income within the working class itself. This does not make social and collective services any less valuable: but it does put in a different perspective the impression conveyed by constant conservative laments that the 'welfare state' is one vast gift which the 'middle class' makes to the working class. Such gift as occurs is for the most part made by some sections of the working class to other, more deprived sections of it.

Also, benefits and services are of advantage to the bourgeoisie and the petty bourgeoisie as well as to the working class. So too are the social services and benefits which the state provides in the field of health, education, transport, housing, the environment, and so on of advantage not only to the immediate beneficiaries, but also to corporate power and business in general. For these benefits and services clearly play a major role in enabling workers to take their place in the process of production and to perform efficiently the tasks allotted to them. The state here plays an indispensable role and supplements the work which is done by women in the home.

Yet conservative forces have always displayed a powerful, visceral dislike of public expenditure *for welfare purposes*. The qualification is essential because dislike in this instance of public expenditure, and concern for the 'taxpayer's money', is replaced by strong support when it comes to expenditure on defence, military operations, subsidies to private enterprise, and the strengthening of the police, surveillance, and intelligence agencies.

However, the conservative dislike of public expenditure on welfare services and benefits is quite understandable. For such services and benefits raise expectations; they enhance the notion of state responsibility and social rights against the notion of individual competition and striving; they render their beneficiaries in the working class less vulnerable to the rigours of the market, and to the dictates of employers; and they could even involve greater tax burdens on the well-to-do.

Had matters been left to the capitalist class itself, the chances are that its opposition to social reform and its resistance to the extension of social and collective services would have produced much greater strife and turmoil than has in fact occurred in advanced capitalist countries. But it is the state which has, in this field as in others, acted as the 'conscience of the rich', and taken upon itself the responsibility of protecting the dominant class from its own short-sightedness. This is yet another instance of the need which the state has, notwithstanding its partnership with capital, to act independently of it.

As was noted earlier, however, the state acts in these matters with deep concern for the public purse, and is guided by 'what the nation can afford'. 'What the nation can afford' is an interesting notion. For, far from being an objectively determined quantity, it is something which is very largely determined by highly subjective and deeply class-bound considerations, however much these considerations may be believed to be rigorously objective. The most obvious instance of this is that what 'the nation' cannot afford in relation to social services and benefits, it can well afford in relation to expenditure on arms. Astronomical sums, almost beyond belief, have been spent by such countries as the United

States, Britain, France, and other advanced capitalist countries since World War II, with very little if any thought of what the nation could afford, on the manufacture or purchase from abroad of weapons of war. Enormous sums of money have not only been spent, but totally wasted on defence projects which have eventually been abandoned. So too, in the United States, money has been no object in the financing of military interventionism, covert operations, and support for reactionary groups and 'freedom fighters' in 'third world' countries.[30] As noted, such expenditure has in the past raised little opposition from most journalists and politicians, let alone businessmen who have found the defence industries a uniquely plentiful trough at which to feed, with the fodder provided by the state.

The basis of this remarkable discrepancy is what I have called class-bound thinking. Such thinking finds it easy to rationalize and legitimate the denunciation of expenditure on the 'welfare state' as profligate, wasteful, ruinous, and so forth because it runs counter to the rule of the market and 'decommodifies' important areas of life; whereas expenditure on defence is justified (in so far as it is thought to require justification at all) by such trigger words as 'national security', 'the Soviet threat', and similar narcotic formulations.

Even in the decades following World War II—the golden age of advanced capitalism—there had been a great deal of conservative resistance to public expenditure on welfare, though that resistance could then only limit the expansion of state interventionism in this area. With the end of the era of economic expansion, the opportunity came to launch a much more sustained and successful attack on welfare and collective services, and on the assumptions which lay behind them.

One of the most notable features of that attack is that it was often initiated by social democratic governments—for instance, by the governments of Harold Wilson and James Callaghan in Britain between 1974 and 1979, or by the Mitterand regime in France after the first year of reforming endeavours following the Socialist Party's sweeping electoral victory in 1981. Faced with serious economic difficulties, such governments always find it easiest to practise 'retrenchment' in terms which are injurious to the working class and offensive to their own party activists, but which have the approval and support of conservative opinion at home and abroad. However, it was the conservative governments elected in the late seventies and early eighties which really bent their energies, in the name of freedom, free enterprise, efficiency, and individual initiative, to undo some at least of the gains which had been made in the previous decades in citizenship rights, collective services, state regulation of capitalist enterprise, and welfare advances.

The most emphatic of such endeavours were those of the Thatcher Government in Britain from the time of its first election in 1979, and of the Reagan Presidency from 1981 onwards.[31] As early as 1982, Frances Fox Piven and Richard Cloward remarked that, in the United States, 'the budgets and powers of agencies responsible for controlling the polluting effects of industry, enforcing health and safety standards in the workplace, overseeing guidelines for the hiring of women and minorities, prosecuting anti-trust suits, and limiting the exploitation of mineral resources on federal lands . . . were all reduced or abolished.'[32] The following years saw an intensification of these policies, and an ever more determined effort to achieve the 're-commodification' and the privatization of welfare and collective services, the erosion of citizenship rights, and an ever more sustained attack on the poor, the sick, the disabled, the young, the unemployed, the weak. An important part of this attack was the loosening and abdication of the state's powers of regulation and control of capitalist enterprise, the deliberate weakening of the already weak regulatory agencies, and the further reduction of the constraints—in any case, not at all onerous—which business had had to endure in such areas as health and safety at work, or in reducing the pollution for which it was responsible.[33]

Much the same story may be told about Britain in the Thatcher years. There too, a Conservative Government, faced with continuous and accelerated economic decline and social malaise, sought remedy in the weakening of trade unions and the reassertion of managerial authority, and in the waging of a relentless war of attrition against the public sector, both in the economic and social spheres. As D. Hall succinctly puts it, 'the whole structure of policy was designed to give maximum freedom to profitable activity while curbing public services.'[34] The privatization which was at the centre of these policies was of great value to corporate finance and greatly strengthened the capitalist sector. A conspicuous feature of this 'sale of the family silver', as Harold Macmillan, a Conservative of an earlier vintage, put it, was the bargain price at which public assets were sold off.

The experience of the eighties in the area of social policy clearly demonstrates how substantial the variations in the state's performance can be. Whether they are conservative, or 'liberal', or social democratic, all governments in advanced capitalist countries with capitalist-democratic regimes *must* intervene in economic life, administer welfare and collective services, perform regulatory functions in relation to capital. But they can do so within a fairly broad spectrum of possible policies, at one end of which there is the social democratic brand of interventionism, and at the other end of which there is the conservative stance of minimal interventionism, at least in regard to policies which do not favour capital and which do not accord with conservative wishes and inclinations. What the state does or does not do may be determined by many different factors: but the crucial factor is the strength, resilience, determination, and pressure from below, notably from organized labour. Where this is lacking or weak, the state is able to reduce the scope and substance of its social and economic interventionism. Correspondingly, it then increases what might be called coercive interventionism, police powers and repression. Its own policies produce a marked brutalization of society and the proliferation of criminal activity, which in turn produces frantic calls for more and harsher repression. Less welfare equals more crime equals more police: the relationship is inescapable—and none of the real problems are touched.

There is one item of social and economic policy which has through the ages been exceptionally important as an issue of class struggle from above: namely, taxation. Dominant classes everywhere have naturally always sought to reduce to the greatest possible extent the amount of money they have to pay in taxes. They seek this for themselves; and, in a capitalist context, those who are in charge of capitalist enterprise seek it for their firms. One of the most truly remarkable aspects of the history of capitalist democracies in the twentieth century is how successful dominant classes have been in these strivings, notwithstanding the constant complaints and wailings of business and the rich about the tax burdens they have to bear; or perhaps it is not so remarkable, given the consideration, generosity, and partiality with which the state in these societies has always treated both business and the rich.

The state, to paraphrase Max Weber, has a monopoly of legitimate appropriation by way of taxation. What it has to decide is how much is to be 'pumped out' in taxation from different classes and 'income groups'. Governments differ, because of their political complexion, in the policies they pursue in this respect. Some are particularly well disposed towards corporations and high 'income groups'; others less so. But the spectrum of choices has in this realm always been very narrow; or, more accurately, it has always been accepted by governments—including social democratic ones—as being very narrow. As a result, the burdens which corporations and the rich have had to bear have never been particularly onerous. Social democratic governments have always displayed weak redistributive propensities, whereas conservative governments have often displayed considerable vigour in tilting the balance even further in favour of the higher income groups.

Taxation is an area where governments are peculiarly subject to intense pressure from capital and its lobbies; and the commitment which governments have to capitalist enterprise in any case dictates a respectful hearing for the warnings by business and its allies that harshness in respect of the tax burdens imposed upon it is bound to 'kill the goose that lays the golden eggs'. The question which never seems to arise is for whom the golden eggs are being laid: the assumption is unquestioned that everybody is included in the feast. Governments themselves are well aware that a resolute attack on the privileges, allowances, and exemptions of business will mean a loss of 'business confidence', with all the dangers this entails of non-co-operation, and even of departure for more friendly climes.

Personal taxation must of course be taken to mean a lot more than direct taxation of income. It includes everywhere what in Britain goes under the label of national insurance contributions, Value Added Tax, custom and excise duties, local government rates, all of which are regressive taxes; the so-called community charge (i.e. the poll tax) will greatly increase this regressive feature of taxation. Whatever element of redistribution is entailed in income taxation is thus countered or neutralized by indirect taxation.

In the same vein, Westergaard and Resler noted in 1975 that

dependent allowance apart, the arrangements for which tax concessions are available are ones used mainly, and most effectively, by people on comfortable to high incomes. Ordinary wage-earners and the poor do not set expenses against income from fees. They are either not enrolled in private insurance schemes set up by their employers, or they are enrolled on comparatively unfavourable terms. They are not usually in a position to take advantage of covenants with tax reliefs attached. They either cannot afford to buy homes at all, or have only relatively small mortgages for house purchases. They do not on the whole finance expenditure beyond their immediately disposable incomes from bank loans and overdrafts, but have to rely on hire purchase and savings clubs at high rates of interest and without tax concessions. Working-class credit, in short, is very expensive, both because high rates of interest have to be paid, and because tax concessions are not generally available to reduce the effective cost. Upper- and middle-class credit is much cheaper on both scores.[35]

Not much in all this, save in relation to house purchase, has changed since this was written. The years of the Thatcher Governments and of the Reagan Administration have also been marked by a particularly strong redistributive bias in favour of the higher and highest income groups. In the case of the United States, Joshua Cohen and Joel Rogers note on the basis of official statistics that 'by 1985, the top 20 per cent of American families were receiving 43.5 per cent of total income—the highest level on records that go back to 1947—while the bottom 60 per cent were receiving only 32.4 per cent, the lowest share on record';[36] similarly, 'across income groups, the results [of taxation policy] were consistently regressive. Including inflation effects and Social Security taxes, the tax burden for those making under $10,000 a year increased 22 per cent; for those making $200,000 a year it decreased 15 per cent.'[37] Precisely the same regressive bias has been reflected in the taxation policies of the Thatcher Governments: as John Rentoul puts it, 'every single new tax relief, tax perk or tax subsidy introduced in Britain since 1979 has benefited the rich rather than the poor.'[38]

The point made in Chapter 2 concerning tax avoidance may also be recalled. Both business taxation and the taxation of the rich are greatly reduced by virtue of the many loopholes which armies of lawyers and accountants are able to discover or invent in the tax system, or by the interpretation they are able to place on tax legislation. Corporate enterprise has been remarkably successful in reducing its tax burdens, and in many cases has managed, quite legally, to shed the burden altogether.

In any case, taxation figures inevitably leave out of account the enormous amount of income which is not declared. Thus Lester Thurow noted in 1985 that 'for every dollar of tax not paid on illegal income the Internal Revenue Service estimates that nine dollars of taxes are not paid on legal income. Unreported legal income reached $250 billion in 1981; by now it is considerably higher.'[39]

Taxation is an intrinsic part of class struggle. But it is a struggle which is mainly waged by the bourgeoisie and parts of the petty bourgeoisie, and from which the working class is largely precluded. Moreover, business—particularly big business—and the rich in general are infinitely better able to defend themselves against the demands of the tax authorities than are workers and the poor; and they can also count on much more guarded and deferential treatment—not for them the dawn raids on the homes of Supplementary Benefits claimants to discover whether their circumstances *really* warrant the pittance they claim.[40]

IV

In any class society, those who control the main means of domination and exploitation naturally seek to reduce as much as possible the manifestations of struggle and pressure emanating from below. It may be possible to achieve this by relying almost exclusively on rule by force: but such rule is bound to be very difficult, uncertain, and liable to sudden termination.

Capitalist-democratic regimes, for their part, are very dependent on a high level of social pacification, on the routinization of conflict within 'safe' channels, and on the acceptance by the subordinate population of the legitimacy of the social order. Rule by force in these regimes, though a perfectly 'normal' part of the process of government, is, as already noted, subject to various constraints, and is in any case liable to produce more conflict and confrontation. Far better, clearly, to 'win the hearts and minds' of as many people in the subordinate population as possible.

Winning hearts and minds is the ideal, in so far as it betokens a positive, even an enthusiastic, endorsement of the social order. But this, though welcome, is not actually essential, or even necessary. Mere acceptance, with a resigned sense that not much is possible by way of pressure and challenge, allied to a sense that, however unsatisfactory things may be, any alternative would be at least as bad and probably a great deal worse, will do almost as well. For such sentiments, preferably deeply interiorized, make for passivity rather than activism, submission rather than rebellion, a disbelief that radical alternatives are possible.

It is in this light that the notion of 'hegemony' is nowadays best understood. Gramsci used the term in a much stronger sense to denote the capacity of dominant classes to disseminate their values and ideas throughout society, and thus to persuade the subordinate class to conceive the world in their own, bourgeois, terms. No doubt, hegemony did in the early decades of the twentieth century have something of that nature; and in some measure it still has. But it seems more realistic to see it today as the capacity of dominant classes to persuade subordinate ones not that the existing social order is splendid, but rather that whatever may be wrong with it is remediable without any need for any major structural change, and that any radical alternative that may be proposed—meaning in effect a socialist alternative—is in any case bound to be worse, indeed catastrophically worse. Hegemony does not need much more than this to be a reality.

The supreme example of this kind of hegemony in the capitalist world is the United States. No doubt, the United States is also a country where hegemony in its strong sense is widespread throughout the population. But hegemony in its second, weaker, sense is common as well. For there are vast layers of the population who do not join in what C. Wright Mills once called the great American celebration, and who are very critical of many aspects of the 'American way of life', but who are also bereft of any sense that there is much they can do to change things, and who therefore do not vote, and retreat into political passivity and indifference. The best proof of the fact is that the United States, alone of all advanced capitalist countries with capitalist-democratic regimes, does not have a labour and socialist movement with a marked political presence; or, to put the matter in its proper perspective, it is the only country in the advanced capitalist world whose dominant class has managed to avert the implantation in political life of a party of the Left capable of mounting a serious challenge to the predominance of the bourgeois parties. This is not at all synonymous with the absence of opposition, pressure, and struggle from many sources, including the labour movement. But it does mean that most such opposition occurs within a framework of thought from which all sense of radical alternatives has been effectively banished. That is hegemony. A very large question, which will be discussed in the concluding chapter, is whether other capitalist countries are destined to follow the American path and undergo a process of 'Americanization' in this respect; or whether, on the contrary, it is the United States which will 'catch up' with other advanced capitalist countries and develop (or rather re-develop) a substantial labour and socialist movement, with a real political weight and substance.

In seeking to achieve hegemony, dominant classes enjoy some formidable initial advantages. A social order which has endured for a considerable length of time tends to be seen by the largest part of the subordinate population—as well, of course, as by the dominant class—as 'natural'. 'Habit', William James noted long ago, 'is the enormous flywheel of society, its most precious conservative agent.'[41] It takes a major convulsion—economic crisis and collapse, the experience of war, massive and disruptive technological change—to bring about a radical questioning of the social framework in which life is lived.

Also, members of subordinate classes, for all the grievances and demands they may have, are, not surprisingly, highly suspicious and fearful of vast changes which hold the certainty of dislocations whose advantageous effects are inevitably problematic. Bertolt Brecht wrote as follows about this in 1943:

History shows that peoples do not lightly undertake radical changes in the economic system. The people are not gamblers. They do not speculate. They hate and fear the disorder which accompanies social change. Only when the order under which they have lived turns to an indubitable and intolerable disorder do the people dare, and even then nervously, uncertainly, again and again shrinking back in turn, to change the situation.[42]

To speak of this as 'popular conservatism' is somewhat misleading. The effect may be conservative; yet the impulse is
produced not by a worked-out conservative ideology or by support
for conservatism, but by fear of the unknown. Moreover, the
distinction noted earlier again needs to be made between popular
resistance to revolutionary change, in the strong, insurrectionary,
or let's-start-all-over-again sense, and popular attitudes to far-
reaching reforms which do not appear to mean convulsion and
possible chaos. This is why conservative ideologists and politicians
always seek to portray even moderate proposals for reform as
'extreme' as well as foolish, or as steps on the road to upheaval
and ruin. It is precisely because popular fear of revolutionary
change does not necessarily betoken a rejection of proposals. for
radical reform that hegemony can never be taken for granted; and
conservative forces do not indeed take it for granted. They know
full well that it is something that has permanently to be fought
for, in what amounts to an unrelenting *ideological class struggle
from above.*

In that struggle, conservative forces are also greatly helped by
a factor akin to habit: namely, tradition. But tradition does not
simply happen: in *The Invention of Tradition*, Hobsbawm and
Ranger have very usefully provided a reminder that tradition is
something that is indeed 'invented', used, manipulated, and that
it serves ideological and political purposes; and that where it does
not exist, it is contrived and affirmed by ceremonies, rituals, codes
of behaviour, costumes, language, all of which are intended in
one way or another to encourage the worship of what Aneurin
Bevan once called 'the most conservative of all religions—ancestor
worship'.[43]

The 'invention' of tradition must, in the present context, be
linked to the need felt by dominant classes to use it as one more
response to the rise of labour movements in the second half of
the nineteenth century, and to the dangers that were thought to
arise from the extension of the suffrage to the working class. Thus
Hobsbawm notes that 'the widespread progress of electoral
democracy and the consequent emergence of mass politics . . .
dominated the invention of official traditions in the period 1870-
1914';[44] and he also notes that 'after the 1870s . . . and almost
certainly in connection with the emergence of mass politics,
rulers and middle class observers rediscovered the importance of

"irrational" elements in the maintenance of the social fabric and the social order.'[45] Among the most important of these elements is a nationalism which is barely distinguishable from chauvinism, and which is fostered by the state and by a host of organizations in society. One expression of the cult of nationalism is the commemoration of the men who fell in the wars which have punctuated the history of all the countries of advanced capitalism. It is typical of the ceremonies associated with these wars that the question is never raised of the morality of the enterprises which doomed those being commemorated.

Ideological class struggle from above is not conducted from a single source. Nor does it present a single, 'monolithic' message. On the contrary, it is conducted by a multitude of very diverse agencies; and these agencies speak with many, often discordant, voices. Yet neither the diversity of voices, nor that of the messages which they seek to convey, should be allowed to obscure the fact that they do nevertheless share a set of underlying beliefs; and the fact also that there is at work here a very powerful endeavour to persuade the subordinate population to endorse these underlying beliefs, or at least to reject contrary (and by definition subversive) ones.

I suggested in an earlier chapter what these core beliefs were: the virtues of 'free enterprise' and its associated qualities—competition, individualism, freedom, efficiency; the evils of socialism and its associated vices—statism stagnation, incompetence, oppression; the horrors of communism and the threat of Soviet aggression and domination.

The beliefs in question are held in stronger or weaker versions, depending on the brand of conservatism being advanced. One such brand, for instance, which enjoyed considerable currency in the post-war decades, readily incorporated the notion that state intervention in economic and social life was imperatively needed. Its Keynesianism was the point of junction with social democratic interventionism. Similarly, there were substantial differences in the ways in which diverse currents of conservatism approached the question of the 'Soviet threat'. But all such differences, whether over home or foreign policy, occurred within a broadly agreed conservative 'world view'. It is this 'world view', in its different versions, which ideological class struggle from above is intended to disseminate; and this struggle has always been conducted with a determination and coherence which the Left has never been able to match. This is not simply a matter of resources, important though that is; it is also related to the fact that the divisions which have existed on the Left, and the ambiguity of purpose which has marked its largest formations, have inevitably produced an uncertain sound.

There is one item in this conservative ideological struggle which may be singled out, since it has had such a tremendous (and effective) place in the arsenal of conservatism in the twentieth century: anti-communism.[46]

Already in 1848 Marx and Engels had proclaimed in the *Communist Manifesto* that the 'spectre' of communism was haunting Europe. But this was then no more than hyperbole: it was not until 1917 and the Bolshevik Revolution that the spectre assumed real, substantive, corporeal existence in the shape of the Soviet Union, as the centre of what was then proclaimed by the Bolsheviks to be a world movement dedicated to the overthrow of capitalism everywhere.

From then onwards, conservative forces in the advanced capitalist world (and everywhere else in the capitalist world as well) have made anti-communism the centrepiece of their ideological struggles, and denounced 'communism' as an urgent threat to freedom, democracy, religion, prosperity, and all that was decent and good in these societies. From 1945 onwards, 'communism' was linked to the threat of Soviet subversion, aggression, and expansionism, and could also be denounced as akin to, or as synonymous with, treasonable intent. More will be said about this in the next chapter.

The value of this propaganda, from a conservative point of view, has been enormous. For one thing, it created a bogey of huge proportions. For another, it could be used to attack not only Communists, but the whole Left, including social democracy, however much social democrats might themselves proclaim and demonstrate their own anti-communist credentials. Anti-communism was an ideal weapon with which to disorient and divide the Left, and liberals as well, and place them on the defensive; and it had the additional advantage of nurturing the claim that the Right alone was the true defender of freedom and democracy against their enemies, at home and abroad.

The struggle would have been more arduous had 'communism'

in the Soviet Union and, later, elsewhere, offered a more attractive picture to the working class of advanced capitalist countries. But it did not; and Soviet policies and actions after 1945 gave to the notion of a Soviet threat a sufficient degree of plausibility to turn it into a major weapon in the conservative repertoire.

Ideological class struggle from above constitutes a gigantic enterprise in political socialization and indoctrination, and amounts in effect to a daily, massive assault on popular consciousness. Among all the many different forces which are involved in this enterprise, two require particular attention in the present context, since they are the ones most directly engaged in the struggle: one of them is the communications industry under private ownership and control; the other is the state.

The resources of the people who command the many diverse parts of the communications industry are truly immense. Some of the people in question are more concerned with politics than others; but none of them, it is safe to say, are indifferent to politics, and to what, by way of politics, is written or transmitted or performed in the media they control. The concern may well be perfunctory, in so far as owners and controllers may confidently rely on editors, journalists, producers, and others who work for them to remain within a well-understood ideological spectrum of thought, which stretches from mild social democracy at one end to far right conservatism at the other. Such a framework allows for diversity and 'pluralism', and may even be allowed to include the expression of strongly dissident and critical thought. Moreover, the media under capitalist control, though most emphatic and virulent about the derelictions and sins of the Left, particularly when a left government is in office, quite commonly attack bourgeois governments as well for their own sins of commission and omission, and assert thereby their own independence and professionalism.

There is, of course, considerable value in having a press, radio, television, and other parts of the communications industry which are not totally subservient to the wishes or dictates of capitalist owners and controllers or the state; and any exercise of an independent and critical spirit in any part of the industry is therefore to be welcomed. But it is precisely because there is not nearly enough independence from capitalist control or the state

that notions of openness and pluralism in relation to the communications industry must be taken, at best, to be dubious, and
for the most part, to be plainly false.

The point is of particular application to newspapers. In the
case of the United States, for instance, it is a remarkable
illustration of the meaning of hegemony that, with some minor
exceptions, the fifteen hundred-odd newspapers which appear
every morning from one end of the country to the other span a
quite narrow spectrum of political discourse. The narrowness
of the spectrum is concealed by innumerable differences of
presentation, emphasis, policy, allegiance, substance—some newspapers are more 'liberal', others more conservative. But this does
not prevent the existence of a consensus on all really fundamental
issues: anything resembling a radically alternative viewpoint from
the Left is only allowed fleeting appearances in some 'quality'
newspapers, and is totally excluded from most others. Much the
same is true of radio and television; or for that matter of political
debate in general in the United States. Here too, there is strong,
often passionate and bitter disagreement between people who
differ on a multitude of questions, and who are in fierce
competition, in the case of politicians, for election and office. But
the differences between them have been firmly located inside a
broad consensus on the virtues of 'free enterprise', the evils of
socialism, not to speak of 'communism', the reality of the Soviet
threat, the need for the strongest possible defence, the basic thrust
of American foreign policy, and other such crucial issues.

Newspapers in Britain do not have a much broader span; and
the notion of a daily assault on the consciousness of the working
class is particularly apposite in the case of most British tabloids,
whose virulence, mendacity, and partisanship on behalf of conservatism, and whose viciousness in the denigration of any other
political position, leave most 'popular' newspapers in the rest of
the advanced capitalist world far behind in this particular form
of yellow journalism.

Capitalist ownership and control of a large part of the media
is a crucial weapon in the waging of ideological class struggle.
But corporate power, outside the media, also affords to those who
wield it various other ways of waging that struggle. There is, for
instance, the power which business has of withholding advertising
revenue from media which have incurred its displeasure, and the

acute awareness of media which depend on this revenue that anything which appears to be 'anti-business', or which for some other reason greatly displeases important advertisers, is likely to have disagreeable consequences.

In any case, newspapers whose readership is made up of people with low purchasing power—in other words, the working class— must, if they are to attract advertisers from the world of business (and this is a *sine qua non* of survival), achieve a mass circulation. Their recipe for the purpose is gossip, scandal, and sport, all of it heavily seasoned with sex. These tabloids can only be called newspapers in a loose sense. The version of Gresham's Law which operates here is closely related to the requirements of 'free enterprise'.

Corporate power is also increasingly given to advertising not only its products, but also its philosophy and views. 'Corporations', Piven and Cloward have noted for the United States, 'now spend approximately one-third of their tax-deductible advertising dollars to influence people as "citizens" rather than just as consumers';[47] and this 'advocacy advertising' obviously carries a heavy conservative, pro-business message.[48]

Again, major corporations are able to mobilize vast armies of people for the purpose of influencing legislators, newspapers, and 'public opinion' at large. Thus T. B. Edsall notes that major companies in the United States 'each have networks of plants, suppliers, retailer outfits, sub-contractors, salesmen, and distributors in every congressional district in the nation, as well as thousands of dispersed shareholders'.[49] So too can corporate power arrange for such things as 'the organized creation of seemingly spontaneous outporings of public opinion for or against specific legislative proposals, voiced through coordinated letter writing, telegrams, and telephone campaigns—all deluging members of Congress'.[50]

In addition to these endeavours by individual firms, some 150,000 professional lobbyists for corporate and trade associations were at work in the United States in the early eighties.[51] Their main concern was no doubt for their particular employers; but this was perfectly compatible with the celebration of capitalist enterprise in general, and the denigration of all attempts to tax, regulate, or otherwise constrain business.

The President and Chief Executive of Chase Manhattan Bank

stated very plainly what was required of business: 'We must take
our message directly into American homes, to the people, to the
ultimate deciders of our society's fate. We need nothing less than
a major and sustained effort in the market place of ideas.'[52] It is
this concern which impels corporate power to be the major
contributor to a host of research institutes, foundations, councils,
associations, and other such bodies, which seek to influence
government or society at large, or both. In their case, too, the
ideological spectrum that is being spanned is very narrow, ranging
as it does from the mildest sort of 'liberalism' to extreme
conservatism; and it is the conservative institutions, such as the
notorious Heritage Foundation, which have fared best in the
Reagan years.

The reach of corporate power extends to all areas of intellectual
activity, however remote such activity might be from the specific
concerns of business. Michael Useem notes this involvement in
the following terms:

The involvement of corporate leadership in the affairs of nonprofit
organizations constitutes a seldom acknowledged but highly important
part of business's political outreach. The programs of universities, arts
organizations, medical centers, and civic institutions can have a critical
bearing on the business climate.[53]

He also notes, in this context, that in 1968, a survey conducted
of more than 5,000 trustees of a cross-section of American colleges
and universities found that 1,307 were executives or directors of
large corporations.[54]

The influence thus wielded by business need not be heavy-
handed: all that is usually required is for the institutions concerned
to exercise a degree of self-censorship so as not to offend the
sponsors on whose benefactions they depend. That is normally
enough. If more is needed, that too will be forthcoming.

American business has been more deeply and more pervasively
engaged in ideological class struggle from above than business in
other advanced capitalist countries. This, however, is simply a
matter of degree: at one level or another, business in all these
countries wages the same kind of ideological class struggle as
its American counterparts. Obviously, the 'Americanization' of
politics, were it to occur, would have as one of its features the

further extension of the ideological reach of corporate power in all areas of intellectual and artistic activity.

The essentially conservative message which business seeks to foster requires the collaboration of journalists, commentators, academics, intellectuals, and artists, whose task it is to articulate it: the striving for hegemony in any sense would be impossible without their collaboration. In *The German Ideology* (1846), Marx and Engels noted that a dominant class must seek 'to present its interest as the common interest of all the members of society . . . it has to give its ideas the form of universality, and present them as the only rational, universally valid ones';[55] and they also spoke of the division of labour which 'manifests itself also in the ruling class as the division of mental and material labour, so that inside this class one part appears as the thinkers of the class (its active, conceptive ideologists, who make the formation of the illusions of the class about itself their chief source of livelihood), while the others' attitude to these ideas and illusions is more passive and receptive, because they are in reality the active members of this class and have less time to make up illusions and ideas about themselves'.[56]

Those to whom Marx and Engels refer are not necessarily members of the ruling or dominant class: they may be members of the bourgeoisie or of the petty bourgeoisie. But their task is indeed the one stated; and that task is not less well performed because many—perhaps most—of the people concerned *share* the illusion that the defence, strengthening, and celebration of the existing social order, and the denunciation of its socialist alternative, which also means the strengthening of the position of the dominant class, *is* in the general interest, and *does* represent 'the only rational, universally valid' ideas about the proper organization of society. In *Capital*, Marx had some bitter things to say about bourgeois economists after 1830 in France and England, when 'the class struggle took on more and more explicit and threatening forms, both in practice and in theory'. This, he wrote,

sounded the knell of scientific bourgeois economics. It was thenceforth no longer a question whether this or that theorem was true, but whether it was useful to capital or harmful, expedient or inexpedient, in accordance with police regulations or contrary to them. In place of disinterested inquirers there stepped hired prize-fighters; in place of genuine scientific research, the bad conscience and evil intent of apologetics.[57]

The point Marx was making remained valid ever after, and hardly applied to economists alone, or to France and England only.[58] But the characterization is nevertheless over-simple and does not take into account the complexity of the thought-processes involved. No doubt, there are ideological 'hired prize-fighters' who write what is wanted of them without belief in what they are writing. Such people develop a profound cynicism about their craft, and about the world around them, a stance which they need if they are to live with themselves. For the most part, however, it is more likely that the processes of thought are more complex, and that ideologists do believe what they are saying, or believe enough of it to render it legitimate in their own eyes. Moreover, and of great importance, what matters is not only what is being said, but what is *not* being said: apologetics may be couched in positive terms; but there is also considerable value in the suppression of inconvenient facts, or in the manipulation, adapt- ation, moulding, and bending of facts or ideas in such a way as to reduce or annul the 'unhelpful' effects which facts or ideas might have. There are endless ways in which apologetics can be advanced with an excellent conscience.

This also makes it possible for the people concerned to believe that the rewards for their work are entirely merited. For the point has to be made that there are considerable rewards to be had for remaining within the framework of acceptable opinion— acceptable, that is, first of all to the powers that be. Within that framework, there are jobs, grants, promotion, travel, prestige, even fame. Outside it, there is likely to be trouble, discrimination, harassment, even persecution. This is not necessarily the only inducement towards ideological conformity; but it would be naïve to ignore its weight—and conformity is all the more attractive because there is no requirement that it be rigid and undeviating, and it is in fact quite compatible with the expression of critical views on this or that aspect of the social order and the policies of governments. That too provides the ingredient of self-legitimation which ideologists, like most other people, do require.

In addition to the struggle waged in the ideological realm by corporate power and other agencies in society, there is also the formidable power of the state. For in this realm as in all others, there has occurred a steady process of 'statization', meaning that official agencies have assumed ever greater responsibilities in the business of persuasion, indoctrination, and the striving for hegemony.

Here too, the forms which this process assumes are extremely varied. Thus presidents, prime ministers, and their ministerial colleagues make the fullest use of radio and television for the propagation of ideas and policy proposals, and for the defence of their government's policies and actions. In so far as the governments in question are mostly conservative, what they have to say is naturally couched in conservative terms; and what they have to say amounts to a torrent of conservative propaganda. Nor can the contribution of social democratic leaders in office (or in opposition) be said to counterbalance this conservative bias with their own socialist pronouncements, since their pronouncements very seldom bear any such mark, and are very often much more congruent with prevailing orthodoxies than with any kind of socialist non-conformity.

Also, ministerial departments in all advanced capitalist countries have developed their own propaganda facilities, on a huge and ever-growing scale, so much so that the Department of Defence in the United States can be described as the 'largest advertising agency in the world'.[59] Furthermore, these departments, and the offices of presidents, prime ministers, and other ministers are also powerful agencies of pressure on the media—newspapers, radio, television—and seek to influence them in the desired directions by a mixture of blandishments and threats. Governments themselves manipulate the news; and they also seek to manipulate journalists and commentators.[60] They do not always succeed, but occasional failure should not disguise the degree of co-operation they are able to obtain, and indeed how much such co-operation is willingly, even enthusiastically, given, by men and women who believe that they are serving a good cause, and who are at the same time doing themselves some good—a very agreeable combination.

Taken together, the endeavours of corporate power in the realm of communications, of other agencies in society, and of the state amount to what has earlier been referred to as a gigantic enterprise in indoctrination. But this is not to say that the enterprise has actually achieved the desired effect. It is true that the system as a whole is not at present seriously questioned by the majority of people in advanced capitalist countries, though the level of legitimation varies from country to country. But even where the level is high, there constantly occurs strong resistance from below to particular policies and actions, which sometimes leads to questioning of the social order itself, but often does not. This is what has often happened in the United States, and elsewhere as well.

In other words, social pacification and the conquest of the hearts and minds of the subordinate populations of advanced capitalist countries, *even in conditions of hegemony*, remains something of a permanently elusive goal. Protest, challenge, and dissent endure, and need to be contained and subdued. This is why repression and the threat of repression remain an essential element of class struggle from above, and indeed occupy a growing place in the political life of these countries.

V.i

Political repression forms a large and indispensable part of class struggle from above; and I am concerned here with the forms which it has assumed in the regimes of advanced capitalism since World War II. But something needs to be said first about the authoritarian forms which capitalist regimes assumed in Europe in the inter-ways years.

The very first thing that needs to be noted is how *prevalent* authoritarian regimes of the Right were in Europe after 1918. In country after country, weak, unstable bourgeois-democratic regimes were replaced by authoritarian or fascist ones.[61] By 1939, the majority of European countries were ruled by such regimes. Only the Scandinavian countries, the Low Countries, Switzerland, Britain, and France remained bourgeois democracies; and by 1940, the Low Countries, and Norway and Denmark had been occupied by Germany, and France had acquired its own authoritarian regime.

A common feature of these authoritarian regimes of the Right— indeed, their common distinguishing characteristic—was their violent repression of the Left, and particularly of Communists, with the widespread use of imprisonment, torture, and summary execution. Others suffered as well; but it was above all the Left, and notably the 'extreme' Left, which was the main target of state repression. Relatedly, all such regimes had in common the abrogation of civic and political rights, the dissolution of trade unions and parties, the banning of strikes, and other such measures designed to paralyse and crush opposition and challenge to capitalist and state power.

Another common—and crucial—feature of these authoritarian regimes was the support which their rulers received from traditional bourgeois elites—economic, administrative, professional, and cultural. This raises the question of what might be called the *propensity to authoritarianism* of traditional elites in bourgeois-democratic regimes.

These traditional elites tend to be suspicious of democratic forms, and seek to place effective constraints upon them; but it is clearly not the case that dominant classes in these regimes wish, in normal circumstances, to see these democratic forms altogether abrogated. Particularly is this so in long-established capitalist-democratic regimes. On the contrary, dominant classes in such regimes are content to dwell within these political structures, but always on one major condition: that these structures should be able to guarantee the stability of the social order, that they should prevent any serious encroachment on existing arrangements regarding power, property, and privilege, and that the government should pursue 'reasonable' policies at home and abroad. Where these conditions are no longer met, and where the likelihood of restoring them within the existing political system seems dim, dominant classes naturally become very worried, and the notion of a 'strong' regime, able to put an end to crisis and instability and to reaffirm their predominance (which is taken to be synonymous with the national interest, law and order, and the proper scheme of things) acquires considerable attraction. This is particularly true where bourgeois democracy is in any case weak, unstable, and visibly unable to control events.

A great deal has been made in recent years of the fact that capitalist support for the Nazis was not nearly as straightforward as has often been suggested in Marxist writings on the subject: indeed, it has been very strongly argued that capitalists did not really help the Nazis in any very significant way at all. One of the main proponents of this thesis, Professor H. A. Turner, has provided a very detailed account of the attitude of German big business to the Nazis before their assumption of power.[62] But far from sustaining the thesis, his account shows well how strong was the propensity of German big business (and not so big business as well) towards *some* form of authoritarianism, and how real in fact was the contribution which German business did make to the Nazis' assumption of power. The same is true of other sectors of Germany's traditional elites: there were plenty of aristocrats and professional members of the bourgeoisie who also supported the Nazis on their way to power.[63]

In support of his thesis, Professor Turner adduces much evidence to show that, on the whole, German big business was rather uneasy about the Nazis in the years preceding their conquest of power. It is well worth noting, however, what big business was uneasy about: *not* about the anti-parliamentary, anti-liberal, authoritarian, racist, and expansionist purposes of the Nazis, but about their demagogic denunciations of big business and their threats (usually accompanied by private assurances that the threats need not be taken seriously) of intervention, control, and appropriation. It was the 'socialism' in National Socialism that worried them: for the rest, all that the Nazis proclaimed and denounced disturbed them very little.[64]

Moreover, Professor Turner clearly shows that the Nazis did receive money from big business: 'during the spring and early summer of 1932,' he writes, 'more money than ever before flowed from the business community to various Nazis.'[65] Further financial support was forthcoming once Hitler had become Chancellor on 30 January 1933. Elections were to be held on March 5. During the election campaign, which left no doubt at all about the Nazis' methods and ends, a meeting was held between Hitler, Goering, and other top Nazis, and several dozen prominent industrialists headed by Krupp von Bohlen. The industrialists were treated to a one-and-a-half-hour harangue from Hitler about the incompatibility of free enterprise and political democracy; the necessity to 'extirpate Marxism'; the need to have a 'martially prepared nation'; and about Hitler's intention not to surrender power even if the forthcoming election failed to provide a majority for his Cabinet. In reply, Krupp merely 'stated that a detailed discussion did not seem desirable and improvised polite words of thanks and some innocuous generalizations about the need for a strong and independent state that could clarify the domestic political situation and impartially serve the general welfare'. Hitler then left, and Goering told the industrialists that they had an obligation to make some financial sacrifices to help the Nazi election campaign. 'Such sacrifices could be borne more easily,' he also said, 'if one kept in mind that the balloting of March 5 would be "the last for the next five years, even probably for the next hundred years".' The sum stipulated was 3 million marks; and this was duly delivered.[66] This, Professor Turner notes, was 'the first significant material contribution by organized big business interests to the Nazi cause. That contribution unquestionably helped the Nazis tighten their grip on power.'[67]

Even so, it is no doubt true that financial help was not decisive in the Nazis' advance to power, for they had themselves developed a remarkable set of mechanisms for raising money—collections at meetings, dues and donations from members, the sale of 'officially certified paraphernalia', such as 'brown shirts, caps, swastika armbands, and other accoutrements indispensable to the well-equipped storm trooper, such as brass knuckles, daggers and first aid kits', the endorsement of a razor blades, margarine, and cigarettes, and the sale of pamphlets and leaflets.[68]

But there were *other ways* than financial help whereby German capitalists helped the Nazis. One of them was simply by failing to use their vast resources *to oppose* them, and by giving Hitler and other leading Nazis a respectful hearing (as well as *some* financial support). Of great importance too was the support which big business gave to *other* right-wing parties, such as the Deutschnazionale Volkspartei (DNVP) and the Deutsche Volkspartei (DVP): for these parties regarded the Nazis not at all as their implacable opponents, but on the contrary as potential allies.[69] Indeed, there were examples of such partnership before 1933, as in Thuringia, where a prominent Nazi became Minister of the Interior and Education in a coalition government installed with the votes of four bourgeois parties and the Nazis.[70] Big business hoped to 'tame' the Nazis, notably in relation to the latter's 'socialistic' policies: in the process, they gave the Nazis valuable legitimacy and eased their way into the political system and the apparatus of power. That was a tremendous service. In fact, the government which Hitler formed when he became Chancellor was itself a coalition of bourgeois parties with the Nazis, in which the Nazis only held three seats, including Hitler's own. In this context, the notion put forward by Professor Hamilton, that 'most of the political money of big business went, throughout the last years of the republic, to the conservative opponents of the Nazis',[71] is formally correct but rather misleading: for these 'opponents' included many people whom the Nazis could quite confidently expect to become allies and partners, as indeed happened. Professor Hamilton also refers to an article by Professor Turner, written a good many years before the publication of the latter's book, in which he argued that 'on balance, big business money went overwhelmingly against the Nazis'.[72] This formulation too suggests a degree of opposition to the Nazis on the part of business which is belied by the evidence later provided by Professor Turner himself. The more accurate judgement is that the 'business community' *strengthened political forces that would eventually play key roles in installing Hitler in power.*'[73] Nor should it be forgotten that once he was in power, Hitler could count on the full co-operation of the 'business community'. As Professor Turner also writes, without a hint of irony, 'the improvement in economic conditions brought with it the profits that ultimately serve as the measure of success or failure in the business world.'[74]

The enthusiasm with which the traditional elites in France supported the authoritarian option represented by Marshal Pétain in 1940 has been explained (or rather explained away) by the circumstances of a sudden and catastrophic defeat in war. But as Professor Paxton has rightly noted, the Vichy regime should rather be seen 'as another act in the long French drama of internal conflict opened in 1789 and still raging with the Popular Front Election of 1936'.[75] After 1936 and the fright it gave the bourgeoisie, there were many people on the Right who mouthed the slogan 'Rather Hitler than the Popular Front',[76] or 'Rather Hitler than Stalin.' In actual fact, it was not Hitler that the Right wanted, but its own *French* authoritarian regime; and defeat not only made this possible, but also produced support for it on the part of the overwhelming majority of the dominant class, including those people who had not hitherto been attracted to any such regime.[77] But as de Gaulle showed as early as 18 June 1940, there was nothing inevitable about this authoritarian option. Nor was it Hitler who imposed such a regime upon France. It was the

French Right which deliberately chose that option, because of its determination to exploit defeat as a means of ridding the country at long last of Communists, socialists, trade unions, strikes, inconvenient civic freedoms, and all other democratic features of bourgeois democracy.[78] Nor, it should be stressed, was this simply the option chosen by the pro-fascist Right. Most of the French Establishment was pro-Vichy, often ardently so. Debate has gone on in France over the question of collaboration with the Germans during the war. But at least as significant was the collaboration and support that was accorded to Pétain and the 'National Revolution' by the bulk of the French business and professional bourgeoisie.[79]

Another and more recent instance of the propensity to authoritarianism which dominant classes display in appropriate circumstances is provided by Chile in the last stages of the Allende regime. I will have occasion to refer in the next chapter to the involvement of the United States in the overthrow of the Allende Government in September 1973. But it may be noted here that American intervention only *supplemented* what Chilean conservative forces were themselves seeking to achieve. However decisive American support and encouragement for the *coup* may have been, its perpetration wholly depended on its Chilean instigators. Also, the *coup* was not simply a matter of military men acting unconstitutionally; the military were supported and encouraged by civilian politicians, who had hitherto operated within the constitutional framework, but who were now willing to step outside it. In so doing, they were undoubtedly representing faithfully the sentiments of the bulk of the Chilean bourgeoisie; and once the *coup* had succeeded, the new regime could rely, at the very least, on the acquiescence of that same bourgeoisie.

V.ii

Nowhere in the advanced capitalist world has there been any real threat since World War II of an authoritarian bid for power on the pattern of Chile (or Greece in 1967). The only such attempt, by French generals in Algeria in 1958 against the Fourth Republic, resulted in the renewed assumption of power by de Gaulle, who created a regime that was by no means the proto-fascist regime that had been widely feared. Another rebellion by French generals in Algeria, in 1961, was put down without any difficulty.

This absence of an authoritarian threat to bourgeois democracy cannot unfortunately be taken to mean that the propensity to authoritarianism of traditional elites has been finally subdued. It means rather that there has been no need for them to give serious thought to an authoritarian alternative to bourgeois democracy. This is why the neo-fascist groupings and sects which are at large have not obtained the kind of support from business and other conservative sources which they badly need if they are to achieve real success. But it is significant that the Gaullist leader, Jacques Chirac, and other Gaullist notables, should have shown an 'understanding' attitude towards the neo-fascist Jean-Marie Le Pen and his National Front in the period of the presidential and legislative elections in France in May/June 1988; and that some of these Gaullist notables should have entered into electoral alliances with candidates of the National Front. As in Germany in the years preceding Hitler's access to power, most members of traditional elites in bourgeois democracies are likely to find the language and the demands of racist and authoritarian neo-fascist demagogues much too crude, vulgar, unpleasant, and extreme for their taste. But such squeamishness tends to get eroded in situations of acute crisis; and it tends to get eroded not least because substantial numbers of people in the bourgeoisie have a lurking sympathy for some of the main themes which form part of neo-fascist rhetoric—the attacks on the Left, the denunciation of weak and vacillating politicians and the system which they run, the nationalist exaltation, the insistence on the need to transcend class divisions for the sake of a national rebirth ever more greatly imperilled by subversive and alien forces, and so on. Such themes strike a chord, notably among military, police, and surveillance agencies within the state, whose members are particularly—one might say professionally—prone to share such notions; and the same themes also strike a chord among traditional elites, and create, in the right circumstances, the possibility of understandings and alliances.

Even in quite 'normal' circumstances, capitalist-democratic regimes do use a great deal of political repression, and use it mainly against left activists and revolutionaries. It is in this sense that repression should be seen as a an important weapon in class struggle from above.

It was noted earlier that a large array of forces in society as well as the state are mobilized when a major strike occurs. The same point applies to the containment and repression of the radical and revolutionary Left. This takes many different forms, depending on the country and particular circumstances; but the extent and virulence of political repression is, generally speaking, inversely related to the depth of implantation, strength, and resilience of labour and left movements in the political life and political culture of given countries. It is where these movements have achieved real strength and a substantial measure of popular support that political repression, either by the state or by different forces in society, has been least pronounced and effective, at least within the framework of capitalist democracy. Thus anti-Communist witch-hunting has been much less pronounced since World War II in France and Italy, where Communist parties and the Left in general had acquired a mass basis and an important place in political life, than in the United States, where the labour movement was relatively weak, and where Communists outside a few major cities were very thin on the ground, or non-existent. It is in the United States, where Communists, members of other 'far left' groups, trade union activists, and other activists, did not have a deep implantation or a substantial measure of popular support, that political repression against them, by way of social and political exclusion, discrimination, harassment, and persecution, has been most vigorous.[80]

It may be said that it is not only the Left which is subject to political repression, and that the far Right is also affected by it. But while it is true that fascist-type organizations and activists of the far Right may attract the occasional attention of agencies of the state, and be subjected to repression because of some of their activities, there is in this realm a dramatic asymmetry of treatment of Right and Left. Nor is this very surprising: the views of the far Right, unless so extreme as to be right out of the political spectrum altogether, do not automatically brand those who hold them as wholly beyond acceptable discourse. To hold ultra-conservative and reactionary views is not generally liable to discrimination anywhere in the capitalist world. Nor even does membership of organizations of the far Right, provided they are legal, necessarily create problems for their members. By contrast, to hold and express strong left-wing views, and to belong to 'extreme' (or even not so 'extreme') left organizations, and to engage in activism on behalf of these views or organizations is very likely to entail a distinct element of risk, in terms of employment, career prospects, and encounter with the coercive agencies of the state.

Quite naturally, dominant classes everywhere have always sought to repress those whom they perceived (rightly or wrongly) as a threat to the existing social order: repressive action against trouble-makers, dissenters, revolutionaries, is as old as class society itself. So too has it been throughout the history of capitalism.[81] However, repression of radicals and revolutionaries in capitalist democratic regimes has assumed much more extensive, organized, and systematic forms since the Bolshevik Revolution, and particularly since World War II. What was still a relatively modest enterprise until then (almost a cottage industry) has turned into a massive one, which engages a huge personnel and vast resources, nowhere more so than in the United States.

In the containment, surveillance, and repression of the Left, capitalist democracies are still a fairly long way from being police states; but they are certainly very highly policed states, in which phone-tapping, mail-opening, surveillance, and internal spying, as well as direct and physical repression by state agencies, have become a familiar, habitual, and increasingly accepted part of the political scene and culture.

In the climate engendered by the Cold War after 1945, Communists provided a convenient target for a repressive enterprise that was intended to reach far beyond them. That enterprise assumed immeasurably larger dimensions in the United States than anywhere else in the advanced capitalist world, and left no sphere of American life untouched. Well before Senator McCarthy got going in 1949, the ground had been thoroughly prepared for him by the Truman Administration, notably with the promulgation in 1947 of the loyalty-security programme: 'No other event, no political trial or congressional hearing,' Professor Ellen Schrecker notes, 'was to shape the internal Cold War as decisively as the Truman Administration's loyalty-security program.'[82] Another notable milestone in the pre-McCarthy campaign was the prosecution of Communist leaders in 1948 under the Smith Act of 1940. The Act had made it a crime to teach and advocate the overthrow of the government by force, or to belong to a group advocating such overthrow. The Act had been invoked twice before 1948, once against some Trotskyists in 1941, and another time against some alleged Fascist sympathizers. The Trotskyists were convicted (their conviction being supported by the Communist Party), and the action against the Fascists ended in a mistrial. The trial against the Communist leaders, who denied that they advocated the overthrow of the government, also ended in their conviction and imprisonment. Following it,

the Justice Department resorted to an extensive use of the Smith Act and secured 126 indictments against other Party officials in the next few years. In a series of trials spread throughout the country, juries acquitted only ten of those charged. The convictions were devastating for the Communist Party, and they certainly are crucial to any explanation for the party's virtual demise in the 1950s.[83]

However, the struggle of the American state against 'communism' and 'Communists' (terms of great flexibility) did more than ensure the 'virtual demise' of the Communist Party. It also frightened, divided, and demoralized socialists, liberals, and New Deal progressives, and it decisively weakened the whole part of the political spectrum occupied by such people. Indeed, many of them, notably those whom C. Wright Mills aptly called 'Cold War liberals', themselves took part in the anti-Communist witchhunt, in the hope that this might put beyond question their own credentials as 'loyal' Americans. From the early days of the Cold War, the crucial fact was thus established that political non-conformity of a kind that could be construed as indicating a left-wing bias (or too pronounced a 'liberal' bias) could well be a barrier to government employment, or even to employment in many areas of non-government service as well; and that it might well bring trouble to those people who displayed such a bias.

It was not until the late fifties that this miasma began to lift, and that protest and agitation, on a growing scale, again became part of political life, over such issues as the virtual *apartheid* prevailing in the American South, and later over the American involvement in Vietnam. But it was a *new* Left that was summoned into existence by these and other issues. The old Left had been effectively subdued.

The excesses of McCarthyism are now part of history, and often deplored by some of the very people who then acquiesced, to say the least, in them. But the struggle against the Left has gone on, in more routinized, systematized, computerized forms, less crudely than in the days of McCarthy and J. Edgar Hoover, but no less persistently.[84]

The struggle against 'communism' assumed less intense, fevered, and hysterical forms in other advanced capitalist countries; but it was—particularly at the height of the Cold War— conducted with great energy and determination; and it has become an intrinsic part of what the state does and is expected to do.[85] In Britain, the process began under the Attlee Labour Government soon after World War II, and involved the 'purging' of civil servants in 'sensitive' posts for suspected 'communist' affiliations, connections, and inclinations.

It is no doubt true that all states inevitably seek to protect themselves against 'security risks', and are bound to do so. But the real issue has always been a very different one: namely, the struggle of the state against left-wing dissent and activism. At the end of January 1985, the then Home Secretary, Leon Brittan, thus told the Home Affairs Committee of the House of Commons, which was inquiring into the Special Branch, that political activists and other campaigners who were concerned that they were the object of security surveillance should ask themselves two questions:

Did they intend to harm the safety or well-being of the state? and did they intend to undermine or overthrow parliamentary democracy? If the answer was yes, they must expect to become legitimate targets of Special Branch attention.[86]

These criteria could obviously be made to include practically any left-wing activity which officers of the Special Branch deemed deserving of their attention; and the Home Secretary was careful to note that the criteria had first been drawn up by a Labour Government in 1975, and that he was 'broadly happy' with them, as well he might be.[87]

It was also a Social Democratic-Liberal coalition (in which the Social Democrats were the senior partners) which introduced a

major piece of repressive legislation in the German Federal
Republic in 1972, the *Berufsverbot* legislation. Long before then—
in fact, almost as soon as the state had been created in 1949—
Communists and 'fellow-travellers' had been excluded from the
civil service; and the Communist Party itself had been declared
to be 'hostile to the Constitution' by a Constitutional Court ruling
in 1956, and therefore illegal. The Party was reconstituted in
1968. Four years later, however, the *Berufsverbot* legislation
banned from public service at federal, provincial, and local level
all persons defined as 'extremists', 'radicals', and 'anti-democrats',
whether of the Right or of the Left. William Graf has noted that
one-tenth of the labour force in the Federal Republic is made up
of public servants, from railway workers to university teachers.
He also notes the 'consistent use of the *Berufsverbot* against the
Left in stark contrast to the law's favourable treatment of
neo-fascist organisations'; and also that ' "hostility to the constitution" has been steadily extended to include not only communists (a legal party since 1968) and their sympathisers, but
also pacifists, Greens, practitioners of alternative life-styles,
members of GDR-oriented groups, militant trade unionists,
radical journalists, critical teachers, and so on.'[88]

Political repression by the state would be much more difficult
to implement, or it would at least be much less effective, if it did
not engage the willing support and co-operation of people in
positions of power in society—in regional and local government,
in business, in the universities and schools, in the newspaper
world, in radio, television, the cinema, the theatre, and also in
trade unions and social democratic parties. In the United States,
the support which the state received from such sources for the
witch-hunt, and their co-operation in it, was one of the most
notable features of that episode.[89] In Britain, some trade unions
under strong right-wing leadership—for instance, the giant transport and General Workers Union—took it upon themselves
formally to exclude Communists from holding official union
positions. The Labour Party had ever since the twenties had a
list of 'proscribed' organizations, membership of which was
incompatible with membership of the Labour Party. The list was
greatly extended as the Cold War got under way; and the
prohibition proved to be a very effective way of isolating
Communist-led or Communist-influenced organizations, many of

them engaged in anti-colonial and anti-imperialist agitation, from the bulk of the labour movement.[90]

The political repression in which the state engages has nothing to do with security, defence, spying, and so on. Its purpose is to wage war against 'subversion', another highly elastic term which can be made to cover activities, associations, and pronouncements which are perfectly legal, but of which the agents of the state, and notably the agencies of internal espionage, disapprove. The net is wide enough to catch anyone and anything to the left of the most innocuous forms of social democracy.[91] It is this which makes the struggle against 'subversion' part of the class struggle in which conservative forces are engaged, of course in the name of 'national security', 'law and order', and the 'national interest'.

The phenomenon of terrorism has greatly helped the state to extend the ambit of its repressive functions; and it has also helped anyone so minded to suggest or imply affinities between terrorism and such activities as mass picketing, demonstrations, marches, and other political activities which are readily assimilated to subversion. As Mrs Thatcher put it in November 1984, at the time of the miners' strike: 'We are drawing to the end of a year in which our people have seen violence and intimidation in our midst; the cruelty of the terrorists; the violence of the picket-line; the deliberate flouting of the law of the land.'[92]

It is unlikely that the sandwiching of picketing between the cruelty of the terrorists and the deliberate flouting of the law of the land was purely accidental.

The state in capitalist democracies has always had formidable reserve powers to deal with such challenges as major industrial strikes, large-scale civil strife, and, of course, conditions of war. In any such circumstances, these regimes have easily turned themselves into what Clinton Rossiter aptly called 'constitutional dictatorships', with the appropriation by the state of sweeping emergency powers and the drastic curtailment or abrogation of civil and political freedoms.[93] But some at least of the powers which were granted to the state in 'exceptional' circumstances have come to be granted to the surveillance, police, para-military, and other repressive agencies as part of the state's habitual, 'normal' functioning.

Even so, state repression in capitalist-democratic regimes has been nowhere near as massive and murderous as the kind of repression which is familiar in authoritarian regimes of the Right, and which has also so deeply disfigured Communist regimes. The constraints and limits which democratic forms and struggles have placed upon repression by the state or conservative forces in society need to be fully acknowledged and valued. But there is a great danger that in saying this, much may be obscured in a fog of complacency and self-congratulation. A student of Italian terrorism makes an important point in this connection: 'It is one of the paradoxes of the Italian political system', he writes, 'that the formal guarantees of a liberal democracy and a relatively open political culture should co-exist with a state executive that can be arbitrary, partial and violent in its authoritarianism.'[94] The point is highly relevant to all capitalist-democratic regimes. For notwithstanding their democratic forms, political repression in these regimes is often arbitrary, brutal, and vindictive. Left activists do get arrested, beaten up, and killed by police and military or para-military forces in demonstrations, on picket-lines, in police stations or barracks; and repressive action is almost always 'covered' by ministers: it is only in rare circumstances involving the grossest abuses that policemen and other members of the state's coercive agencies need to worry about being called to account for their deeds. When they are, they usually find themselves treated by the courts with a degree of sympathy and understanding which contrast very sharply with the treatment accorded to left activists.

Nor does the point apply to political activists only: it is also valid for black people and other minorities whose own non-conformity is likely to incur the suspicion and hostility of conservative police and other state agencies. Capitalist democracy is an arena in which a permanent struggle is waged, from below on the one hand, for the defence, the strengthening, and the extension of civic and political rights, and from above on the other hand, for the limitation, erosion, and even, where deemed necessary, the abrogation of such rights.

The record of the Thatcher Government since 1979 shows well how far class struggle from above can be carried in 'normal' times, when opposition is divided, uncertain, and weak. Reference was made earlier to the erosion of trade union freedoms, the curbing of activist rights, regressive taxation policies, and the wholesale privatization of public industries and services. To this must be added the vast inflation of police powers and the militarization of the police; the systematic covering up of police and military abuses; the extension of the field of activity of security and surveillance agencies; the attempt by way of injunction and other means to prevent the publication by newspapers, magazines, and in book form, of certain material, on the ground of 'national security'; and, in the same vein, the intense pressure by ministers on such institutions as the BBC and the Independent Broadcasting Authority to curb the presentation of certain material, on the same ground.

These years have also witnessed the drastic curbing of the powers of local government and the abolition of major local authorities, notably the Greater London Council; the centralization of education at primary, secondary, and tertiary level, with a major attack on the independence of institutions of higher education; the habitual manipulation of news by ministers and their officials; the systematic exclusion from official and quasi-official bodies of people whose ideological pliability might be doubtful; and the fostering of a political climate, much encouraged by a press overwhelmingly attuned to government purposes, in which dissent from official policy is treated as eccentric, perverse, or subversive.

All this occurs in the name of freedom and democracy, and under traditional constitutional arrangements and trappings. It amounts neither to fascism nor to a police state. But it points in the direction of a regime in which democratic forms have ceased to provide effective constraints upon state power.

6

The International Dimension of Class Struggle

I

A realistic account of class struggle in the twentieth century must accord a central place to its international aspects. This is so because power elites of advanced capitalist countries have been deeply involved in class struggles beyond their own frontiers. In the post-World War II era in particular, there has been no country in the world, large or small, important or insignificant, which has not felt the impact of that involvement on its own internal struggles. Conversely, international relations have themselves been decisively affected by the class struggles which have occurred throughout the world since the end of World War II, and notably in the 'third world'. It is in fact impossible to understand the nature of international relations in the twentieth century aside from the dynamic imparted to them by class struggle.

The international dimension of class struggle is of course not new. The war which began in 1792 between revolutionary France and the old regimes in Europe (to go back no further) was to a very large extent directly related to the class struggles then occurring in France; and the war in turn had a decisive impact on the further development of the Revolution itself. Similarly, the fate of the 1848 revolutions in Germany, Austria, Hungary, and Italy was sealed by military intervention; and it was also repeated American interventions which often determined the outcomes of class struggles in Latin and Central America.

It is, however, in the twentieth century that the international dimension of class struggle has assumed extraordinary, unprecedented importance. What has above all been responsible for this is the fear of radical change and revolution which has haunted power elites in advanced capitalist countries since the Bolshevik Revolution: after 1917, the felt need to contain the spread of 'communism' became a major factor in international relations. The post-war settlement set the pattern: as Arno Mayer has noted, 'the Paris Peace Conference made a host of decisions, all of which in varying degrees were designed to check Bolshevism.'[1]

Conflict between states in the nineteenth century had mainly been inter-state rather than inter-class in character: in other words, international conflicts between states, for all their intensity, did not call into question the nature of the *social order* in each camp. The rivalries between capitalist states endured in the twentieth century, and proved ultimately too great to prevent two world wars. With 1917 and beyond, however, a different form of international conflict assumed ever-greater importance, based, on the capitalist side, on the notion that the capitalist world faced a massive, unprecedented challenge from revolutionary forces directed by the Soviet Union.

The first attempt to check Bolshevism involved the sending of British, French, American, and Japanese troops, together with troops from a dozen other countries, to help bring down the new regime. This intervention, together with the blockade imposed upon Bolshevik Russia, exacerbated the civil war that followed the Bolshevik seizure of power, aggravated the dislocations of every kind that confronted the regime, and greatly sharpened the repressive tendencies of Bolshevism. Here was the first instance after 1917 of the impact of external intervention upon an internal class struggle. There were others in the aftermath of war, one of the most notable being the contribution which external intervention made to the overthrow of the Communist regime in Hungary in 1919.[2]

Once the turmoil of the immediate post-war years had subsided, the leading powers had no urgent threat of revolution to confront and repel until well into World War II. The only crisis that might conceivably have threatened revolutionary upheaval was in Spain, in the Civil War; and even this was a fairly remote possibility. Nevertheless, it helped to persuade the Conservative Government in Britain, with the acquiescence of the Popular Front Government of Léon Blum in France, to adopt the policy of 'non-intervention' which, in the face of German and Italian intervention, doomed the Republic to defeat. One of the notable aspects of that lamentable story is the extreme caution displayed by the Soviet Union in the help which it extended to the Republic; another is the fierce opposition of Stalin (and of the Spanish Communist Party) to the 'radicalization' of the struggle.

Even though the threat of revolution was in effect non-existent in the inter-war years, fear of the extension of Communist influence and subversion did exercise the minds of bourgeois (and social-democratic) governments throughout those years. They feared it in their own countries; and also in colonial territories.[3] Communist parties, it will be recalled, had come into being after World War I everywhere in what had not yet come to be called the 'third world', and their activities were naturally a matter of deep concern to all colonial powers. Communist parties in all colonial territories were banned; and all activities of the Left were severely constrained and repressed. Repression of the Left might be inhibited at home; but it could be much more freely exercised in subject territories.

The same fear must also be held to have been a factor of crucial importance in determining the attitude of capitalist-democratic governments to Fascist and Nazi aggression and expansionism in the late thirties. Whatever might be said against the Fascists in Italy and the Nazis in Germany (and not much was in any case said against them by conservatives),[4] they were at least fiercely anti-communist, anti-Left and anti-Soviet; and there was also the possibility, indeed the hope, that Hitler would turn eastwards and manifest his declared expansionist ambitions in that direction, without greatly affecting the interests of the Western powers. There were many different concerns that went into the making of the policy of 'appeasement' which the British and French Governments (with the support of the United States) made the essence of their foreign diplomacy in the late thirties, in the face of repeated German and Italian aggression; but anti-communism was undoubtedly one such factor, of very great importance. The culmination of that policy was the Munich Agreement of September 1938 between Hitler, Mussolini, Chamberlain, and Daladier, which delivered Czechoslovakia into the hands of Hitler, and which testified to the determination of Britain and France to continue the 'appeasement' of the Nazi and Fascist dictators, and to exclude the Soviet Union from any arrangement they might make.[5]

It is also relevant to note here the striking contrast between the attitude of Western governments towards Fascist and Nazi aggression, right up to 1939, and the bellicose fury they displayed when Russia went to war with Finland at the end of November 1939, over the latter's refusal to grant Russia some strategic bases the Russians wanted for the defence of Leningrad. Whereas the League of Nations, under British and French leadership, had failed to react to fascist aggression, it promptly found the will to expel the Soviet Union; and both the French and British governments, though formally at war with Germany (this was the period of the 'phoney war'), did not fail to promise military help to Finland.[6] The war in Finland came to an end in March 1940. Had it gone on much longer, Britain and France might well have been embroiled in conflict with the USSR. It requires no great depth of thought to see how much ideological dispositions had to do with indulgence and acquiescence on the one side, and indignation and belligerency on the other.

In the end, Britain and France were forced into war by the inability of their governments to pursue 'appeasement' in the face of continued German aggression. What made it impossible was popular revulsion, particularly in Britain, against a policy that had been shown, with the German invasion of Czechoslovakia in March 1939, to have been totally bankrupt; and this was combined with a growing awareness among many Conservatives, for whom Churchill was the main spokesman, that Hitler threatened British national interests.

The war, as many people feared, was bound to produce an upsurge of radicalism. This was further reinforced by the German attack on Russia in June 1941; or rather, it was greatly reinforced by the epic struggle put up by Soviet armies against the German onslaught, and by Soviet military successes. From the time of the Soviet victory at Stalingrad in 1943, the question of the post-war settlement in Europe, and everywhere else for that matter, which had preoccupied the Western allies from the end of 1941 onwards, when the United States came into the war, became a central issue, indeed *the* central issue of the war. Victory over Germany, however long it took to achieve, was now certain: but what was to follow?

On this most vital question, there were bound to be great differences between the leading Western powers. One of the paramount concerns of the British and French governments, for instance, was to retain, or, in a number of cases, to repossess their colonial territories. For its part, the United States, clearly destined to be the leading capitalist power in the post-war world, had no reason to favour these colonial purposes, all the more so since it could and did confidently expect, in terms of economic and political influence, to supplant Britain, France, and other colonial powers in the territories freed from the latter's rule. Notwithstanding these and other divergencies, however, there was at least one supreme matter upon which the Western powers were in complete agreement: namely, the need to ensure by all possible means that the radicalism produced or enhanced by the war should be strictly contained, and prevented from bringing about revolutionary change anywhere in the world. Shorn of all inflated rhetoric, the ultimate purpose of Western governments was essentially the maintenance of the old order: such reforms as they were willing to countenance were not intended to transform the old order, but on the contrary, to ensure its survival. Nor, as has already been argued in Chapter 3, does the point have to be greatly modified in the case of social democratic governments: their desire for reform, and their implementation of reforming measures, never threatened the existing structure of power and property. In international terms, the preservation of the old order required the acceptance of American leadership by power elites everywhere. For the United States, given its immense strength at the end of the war, provided a much-needed guarantee of support to conservative forces, particularly in countries dislocated by the war, and in those where traditional elites had come to be deeply discredited by their collaboration with the Nazi occupiers. Acceptance of American leadership, meaning in effect American hegemony, had in this perspective a crucial class basis: in conditions where the status quo might be seriously threatened, the United States provided conservative forces with a measure of strength which they would otherwise have lacked.

It is this class dimension that helps to explain why power elites, who found much that was deeply unwelcome in America's economic and financial policies at the end of World War II, nevertheless readily accepted its leadership. Nowhere was this more evident than in Britain, whose traditional elites, under the inspiration of Winston Churchill, groped their way during the war to the acceptance of American predominance. The essentially junior position which this entailed for Britain was obscured, not least for the actors themselves, at least on the British side, by a grandiloquent rhetoric about a 'special relationship', 'the unity of Anglo-Saxon peoples', and other such sedative formulations.

Nor is it at all remarkable that social democratic leaders everywhere readily accepted American leadership. Quite apart from their ancient detestation of 'communism', there was also the fact that rejection of that leadership, and the attempt to carve out a 'third way', would have been a difficult, problematic enterprise, fraught with great economic and political problems, and certain to sharpen very greatly their differences with conservative forces at home and abroad.

The profoundly conservative implications of the acceptance of American leadership were also hidden by the evocation of an alleged Soviet threat, and the need it supposedly created for the 'free world' to join in defence of freedom, democracy, and so on. No sooner had the war ended than the United States and its allies introduced the fateful theme of Soviet aggression and expansionism into political life, where, with varying degrees of intensity, it has remained ever since.[7] Now that the Nazi threat had been eliminated, at such terrible cost, a new menace, no less awful, was casting its shadow, and its reality, upon the 'free world'. This claim, which assumed the status of a self-evident truth by dint of endless repetition over more than forty years, is, I suggested earlier, an intrinsic part of the ideological class struggle waged by all forces everywhere whose prime purpose is the prevention of radical change. It was extremely effective propaganda: but nothing more than propaganda.

Stalin had clearly indicated, from the time when it became obvious that Germany would be defeated, that he wanted regimes in Eastern Europe which would be 'friendly' to the USSR. In a famous exchange between Stalin and Churchill in Moscow in October 1944, Churchill, without any warrant, had agreed with Stalin on 'percentages' reflecting 'degrees of predominance' in Romania (90 per cent for the Russians), Bulgaria (75 per cent), Hungary and Yugoslavia (50 per cent). In return, Stalin had readily agreed to 90 per cent for Britain (in co-operation with the United States) in Greece.[8] At the Yalta Conference in February 1945, on the other hand, it was agreed that the provisional governments installed in liberated and formerly enemy countries in Eastern Europe would organize elections as soon as feasible.[9] Given the whole history of Eastern Europe, free elections were unlikely in most of the countries concerned—most notably, in Poland—to assure Stalin of the 'friendly' governments he wanted, since only governments in which Communists had a major place could be guaranteed to fit the requirement. The manner in which Stalin did ensure Communist predominance and Soviet control provided the Western allies with necessary ammunition, not only to protest against what was being done in Poland and elsewhere in the region, but also to proclaim, on the basis of what was happening there, that *Western* Europe, and indeed the whole world, faced similar treatment at the hands of an insatiable expansionist power.

It may safely be assumed that had Soviet control not involved a social revolution 'from above' in Eastern Europe and the dreaded spread of 'communism', the Western allies would have worried very little about free elections or even Soviet hegemony over the countries in question. But it did; and it is this which was always and everywhere the key issue.

As for the Soviet Union itself, the record very strongly suggests that the paramount concern of Soviet leaders always was what they conceived to be the 'national security' of their country. Already in the twenties, even before Stalin's assumption of supreme power, world revolution had ceased to be a serious expectation or concern for the Soviet (and other Communist) leaders. As E. H. Carr has noted:

Faith in imminent revolution in Europe foundered in the German *débâcle* of 1923. Events in China in 1927 showed up the limitations on the aid which Comintern could or would render to revolution in a semi-colonial country. Henceforth world revolution became an article in a creed ritualistically recited on solemn public occasions, but no longer an item of living faith or a call to action.[10]

The failures to which Carr refers may well be laid at the door of the Comintern itself; but he is undoubtedly right in his interpretation of how world revolution had come to be viewed in Moscow, and was ever more emphatically viewed by Stalin. 'Socialism in one country' did imply that the Soviet Union would, for all practical purposes, show very little interest in, let alone enthusiasm for, socialism anywhere else. Soon after Hitler came to power in Germany, Stalin said that 'we never had any orientation towards Germany, nor have we any orientation towards Poland and France. Our orientation in the past and our orientation at present is towards the USSR and only towards the USSR.'[11] It was this 'orientation' which dictated Stalin's actions in the following years, and which led him at the end of the war to insist on effective predominance in Eastern Europe, in East Germany, and, when the Cold War grew more intense, in Czechoslovakia.[12] Until 1947, this predominance had seemed fairly secure under coalition regimes in which the Communists had a preponderant place, but where political life was not by any means under their total control. With the aggravation of the Cold War, in which the proclamation of the Truman Doctrine in March 1947 was a major element, the coalition regimes were soon replaced by Stalinist ones, with all the murderous connotations which the term possesses. The same process occurred in Czechoslovakia with the *coup* of February 1948; and it was also Stalinism which was imprinted on the regime that came into being in East Germany in 1949, following the creation of the German Federal Republic in West Germany under the sponsorship of the United States and its allies.

Anti-Communist accounts of these events take it as an article of faith that exclusive control was always what the Communists wanted, and that the 'People's Democracies' were a merely intermediate step in their assumption of such control. But this, on the evidence, is by no means to be taken for granted; and a distinction needs to be made between a strong Communist presence in the governments of the countries concerned, and exclusive control. Such a Communist presence was inevitable in the post-war years; but it may not have been inevitable that it should assume Stalinist forms. That it did may reasonably be attributed to the Cold War, and to the narrowing, from the Soviet perspective, of the alternatives available to the Soviet leaders: in that perspective, and given the exacerbation of the Cold War, these regimes would either be wholly and unquestionably committed to the Soviet Union, by virtue of exclusive Communist control backed by Soviet arms, or they would be vulnerable to American penetration and potential predominance. The Stalinization of these regimes was above all due to what Stalin conceived to be required by Soviet 'national security'.

It may well be said that 'national security' is a very convenient alibi for aggression and expansionism, since the term is sufficiently elastic to encompass the whole world. But a judgement on this must be based on the record; and the record suggests that the Soviet Union has in fact interpreted the notion of 'national security' in quite narrow terms, to cover some of the countries on its borders, notably, those which had been given a Communist regime. Even this is too broad, since Stalin, faced with Yugoslavia's 'defection' from the 'socialist camp' in 1948, confined himself to ineffective attempts at the 'destabilization' of the Tito regime and then accepted its independent survival.[13] Similarly with regard to Finland, a strongly anti-Communist account notes that 'the defeat of Finnish communism was . . . turned into a rout in the elections of June 1948', when the Communists were systematically excluded from positions of power, without any Soviet reaction. 'All of this', the same account also notes, 'took place with no help from the West, in a nation with an 800-mile common border with the USSR and with Soviet troops stationed in a base just a short day's march from Helsinki.'[14] The Soviet Union had of course learnt in the war of 1939–40 that Finland was a hard nut to crack; but the caution Stalin displayed in the post-war years in relation to Finland, as in the case of Yugoslavia, confirms the very selective invocation by the Soviet Union, then and later, of the notion of 'national security'.

It is entirely possible to condemn Soviet intervention in Hungary in 1956, in Czechoslovakia in 1968, or in Afghanistan in 1979 and after, but also to insist that it *was* 'national security' considerations, however misguided, which caused these interventions, rather than an insatiable appetite for aggression and expansion.

Much additional evidence is not difficult to find which shows well enough how little Stalin was interested in multiplying Communist regimes which might have assured him of predominance. Thus he was explicitly content to leave the Greek Communists and the Greek Resistance in general to their fate at the hands of the British Army at the end of 1944, and then at the hands of Greek reactionaries, former collaborators with the German occupiers, and other such people thereafter.[15] Thus too did Stalin recommend to both Tito and Mao Tse-tung at the end of the war that they should enter into coalition with their conservative enemies, a piece of advice which would have sealed the fate of the revolution in both countries. Thus again did Stalin discount any notion of revolution in Western Europe, notably in France and Italy, and support the entry of Communists as minority partners in bourgeois governments.[16] Far from pursuing 'adventurist' and interventionist policies, Stalin, at the time when he was accused of nursing grand imperialist designs on a global scale, was in fact following a very cautious course in the international sphere. Even the most dangerous Soviet move of the immediate post-war years, the Berlin blockade of 1948, was handled by Stalin with the clear determination not to push matters to a point of no return.

The same caution characterized Soviet behaviour in relation to the Korean war and the Vietnam war, about which more will be said presently; or in relation to the Middle East; or in reaction to American interventionism in many parts of the world which could be said to be of 'strategic' importance to the Soviet Union. There have been some other occasions than the Berlin blockade when Soviet leaders have acted rashly in the field of international relations in the post-war years: the installation of Soviet missiles in Cuba in 1962 was one notable instance. It is, however, worth noting in this connection that the United States has managed since World War II to impose a remarkable set of double standards in regard to its own actions and those of the Soviet Union. As Roy Medvedev has remarked,

in supplying missiles and bombers to Cuba the Soviet Union was not contravening international law . . . The USA had not sought permission from the Soviet Union when she established military bases on the territory of Japan, West Germany, Iran, Turkey, Italy, Norway and many other countries. Some of these bases were close to the borders of the USSR; furthermore, they were equipped with facilities for launching missiles with nuclear warheads.[17]

However, what is, so to speak, sauce for the eagle is not sauce for the bear; and it has been taken for granted that the Soviet Union is not entitled to behave in international politics as the United States chooses to do. Occasions such as the Soviet installation of missiles in Cuba have been rare. Had they been more frequent, the world would have been much closer to nuclear war than has actually been the case—or would even have been precipitated into such a war.

As for Soviet intervention in Hungary, Czechoslovakia, and Afghanistan, these actions, whatever other label they merit, cannot be described as reckless; they were undertaken in the full knowledge that, however violent the verbal reaction of the United States and its allies might be, they would be understood as limited actions undertaken to maintain Soviet control over what the Soviet leaders took to be, and what the Western powers tacitly acknowledged to be, their sphere of influence.

On the other hand, any major challenge to the status quo anywhere in the capitalist world was automatically proclaimed, and probably believed by many if not most American policy-makers, to be yet another manifestation of Soviet expansionism; or at the very least, to threaten the extension of Soviet power in areas which the United States deemed to be of importance to its 'national security'—and, as noted earlier, there were few areas of the world which could not be so described.

These have been constant themes of American propaganda—and of Western propaganda in general—since the early days of the Cold War. In 1951, two years after the victory of the Chinese Communists, Dean Rusk, then Assistant Secretary of State under Truman, and later to be Secretary of State under Johnson, was expressing a widely held view when he said that Mao Tse-tung's regime was 'a colonial Russian government—a Slavic [sic] Man-chukuo on a large scale—it is not the government of China. It does not pass the first test. It is not Chinese.'[18] Thirty-six years and many such pronouncements later, President Reagan was telling the American Newspaper Publishers Association that ending US aid to the *contras* in Nicaragua would be a major victory for the Soviet Union: 'If we cut off the freedom fighters, we will give the Soviets a free hand in Central America, handing them one of their greatest foreign policy victories since World War Two.'[19]

The notion that revolutionary movements anywhere in the world are a proof of Soviet expansionist designs is an absurd and dangerous fantasy, or a mere propaganda ploy, designed to legitimate the status quo. Plainly, these movements are in-digenously generated by intolerable conditions, extreme exploit-ation, murderous tyranny, and the will to achieve national independence and social progress. Nor, for the most part, has it even been Communist parties which have led these movements and struggles. With few exceptions, such as in Vietnam and the Philippines, Communists have only played a subsidiary role— usually a moderating role.

As for the notion that revolution necessarily means the extension of Soviet power and influence, the irony is that it is precisely American hostility and pressure which push revolutionary movements and regimes closer to the Soviet Union. The point will be taken up further presently, but it may be noted here that a crucial purpose of movements of revolution and radical reform is to gain independence from foreign domination and control; and the notion that such movements are eager to welcome dependence on the Soviet Union or any other form of dependence is nonsensical.

However, it is by no means a fantasy that the Soviet Union *is* an important factor in all struggles for national independence and social change in the capitalist world, and particularly in the 'third world'; and that, as such, it is a nuisance and an embarrassment to the United States and its allies.

There is, for instance, the fact that the Soviet Union (and other Communist states) has extended help to revolutionary movements and regimes (as well as to regimes which are anything but revolutionary); and this help has often been critical for their very survival. It is very likely, to take an obvious example, that the Cuban regime would have been throttled by American action had it not been for the help which it was able to obtain from the Soviet Union; and Cuban military help, in turn, was critical for the survival of the new Angolan regime, in struggle with counter-revolutionary forces helped by South Africa and the United States. Similarly, it is not certain that the Nicaraguan regime could have survived without the help it received from the Soviet Union.

The help which the Soviet Union has extended to revolutionary movements has been selective, cautious, and even parsimonious. Even so, help has been given, both to movements and to regimes; and it has assumed considerable dimensions in the economic, technical, and military assistance which has been provided to many regimes in the 'third world'. In 1981, the Soviet Union had some 16,000 military specialists stationed in thirty-four 'less developed' countries, together with nearly 2,000 from Eastern

Europe, and a 39,000-strong Cuban contingent in Africa.[20] Similarly, 'by 1981, the total Soviet and East European contingent of economic personnel had reached the unprecedented number of 96,000 operating in 75 countries.'[21]

There is no evidence so far to suggest that the vast changes initiated by Mr Gorbachev are likely to include any drastic reduction in such aid. It is possible that, in the pursuit of 'peaceful co-existence' with the United States, the Soviet Union might be even more cautious and selective than in the past in the help it extends to movements of national liberation and revolutionary regimes. But it is unlikely that the Soviet leaders would wish to forego altogether an international role which, even though costly, holds out the promise of long-term advantage in economic and political relations.

Here too, it might be argued that all such Soviet help betokens expansionist purposes. It would, however, seem to make more sense to see it as a wish to gain friends and influence people in a world dominated by a coalition of more or less unfriendly states under American leadership.

All the more does it seem reasonable to interpret Soviet help in this way in that such help is not used to foster revolutionary movements, or to induce non-revolutionary regimes to turn themselves into Communist ones. In fact, Soviet help has often been extended to regimes in which Communists and other left activists suffered bitter persecution; and there have been notable occasions where massive economic and military help did not prevent countries from turning away from the Soviet Union and towards the United States: Egypt in 1962 is a case in point.

Soviet help nevertheless does make more difficult and problematic the global conservative enterprise in which the United States and its allies have been engaged since the end of World War II; and this has been a factor in the making of the Cold War. The label, however, is rather misleading, for it conceals the true nature of the conflicts which have dominated the post-war decades. Contrary to appearances, the fundamental source of conflict has not been the rivalry between the USSR and the United States, but rather the war which the United States has waged against all the forces of national independence, reform, and revolution in the world.[22] The Soviet Union only comes into the picture because the conflicts which occur across the globe, though quite autonomous, have been claimed by the United States to be Soviet-inspired, or at least to be dangerously encouraged by the Soviet Union.

The United States has been involved in these conflicts, not because of the mental aberrations of its leaders and policy-makers, or by mistake or misunderstanding, but in pursuit of quite specific material, political, and military interests. In a sense, it was inevitable that it should be so, and that the United States should have assumed the leading role in the global struggle against major disturbances of the status quo by forces of change. That role was conferred upon it by virtue of its emergence from World War II unscathed, wealthier and more powerful than ever, by far the strongest and richest country in the world, and the one best able to take on the burdens of leadership of the capitalist world; and the weakness of the Left in the United States itself, soon to be greatly aggravated by harassment and persecution, removed what might have been an obstacle to the pursuit of the struggle against nationalist strivings for independence, radical reform, and revolution across the world.

The Soviet Union was another potential obstacle, of an altogether different dimension. What was therefore required was to 'deter' it from intervening in class struggles anywhere in the world on behalf of forces intent on destabilizing the status quo. The general belief among policy-makers, in the United States and in the countries allied to it, was that such 'deterrence' could only be achieved by the threat that strong Soviet interventionism would lead to military conflict.

It is here, in the belief that the Soviet Union must be prevented by the fear of war from giving more active and resolute help to movements and regimes which the United States and its allies were themselves determined to oppose, that must be sought the prime source of the nuclear arms race. At the core, that race should be understood as having its origins in the counter-revolutionary crusade that began in earnest at the end of World War II, and in the concern to stop the Soviet Union from doing very much to oppose that crusade.

Of course, the arms race has also been fuelled from many other sources; and it has so greatly prospered because it has served so many powerful interests. It is a form of 'military Keynesianism' of great value to American and other corporations engaged in the defence industry. It employs vast numbers of people. It is self-perpetuating, in so far as the Soviet drive to keep pace with American military power strengthens the case for further and greater endeavours, with the constant (and mostly spurious) assertion of Soviet superiority in one or other part of the military arsenal. The arms race has also extended the domain of the military in the United States, and the military has an obvious interest in the maintenance of a large—in fact the largest possible—defence establishment. The arms race is very useful for conservative political purposes, for it places its critics on the defensive: not to support it to the full is to show a serious lack of patriotism, a dangerous naïvety, a fatal propensity to appeasement, and so on. It also has the great advantage of placing enormously heavy burdens on the Soviet economy, which it can very ill afford. Finally, it is quite possible that the threat of military escalation may have served to 'deter' the Soviet Union from intervening more actively in the struggles which have occurred in the 'third world'. But whether so or not, it is this purpose that 'deterrence' has been intended to serve, rather than the prevention of a Soviet attack on the West, which rational policy-makers have never seriously believed to be in the least likely.

It is very tempting to describe the arms race as 'insane'; and there is a profound sense in which it is indeed insane. It involves a fantastic waste of resources in a world a large part of whose inhabitants are hungry and deprived of the most elementary requirements of civilized life, from clean, potable water to rudimentary health services; and there is always the risk that an episode involving the 'super-powers' might escalate into the ultimate insanity of nuclear war.

There is an important sense, however, in which the arms race and nuclear stock-piling are not at all 'insane': on the contrary, they are propelled by quite rational purposes: namely, the service, in the ways indicated, of the economic, military, political, and ideological purposes of power elites. *Within the class framework in which it must be set*, the arms race is not insane. It is *outside* this framework, beyond the 'rationality' demanded by class interests, that the arms race must be seen as wholly irrational, and as manifesting in particularly acute ways the anti-human forms which the defence of class interests on a global scale nowadays requires.

Power-holders and policy-makers in the United States and elsewhere have ever since 1945 believed that the world they seek to defend is threatened by the forces of reform and revolution; and it is their response to that threat which must now be considered.

II

An essential preliminary point is that this response is for the most part *supplementary to internal class struggles*. It is usually in order to help indigenous conservative forces to repel challenge from below that intervention has occurred. Such intervention, in other words, must be seen as part of the class struggle from above which is waged by local dominant classes. The contribution which that intervention has made, however, has often been decisive in tilting the balance of class forces to the advantage of the Right.

We may first note a general and very potent means of intervention, namely, economic pressure exercised upon governments, particularly reforming governments. One such source of pressure is constituted by the presence of powerful foreign corporations in a given country. These corporations may play an important part in the economic life of the country, especially in weak and dependent economies; and the more substantial their implantation, the greater is their influence bound to be on the government of the country in which they are installed. That influence is naturally directed to the curbing of any economic or social policy judged to be detrimental to foreign business.

Another, even more important source of economic pressure is that exercised by the United States and other major capitalist powers either directly, or by way of such international financial institutions as the International Monetary Fund or the World Bank, both extremely responsive, to put it mildly, to the wishes of the United States.

Ever since World War II, all countries in the capitalist world have been enmeshed in a tight web of constraints, largely woven by virtue of American predominance, and intended to achieve two main purposes: the first, in the name of free trade, was to ensure that all markets in the capitalist world would be accessible to American firms and products. The second aim was to make as difficult as possible, and preferably impossible, the deviation of any capitalist country from economic and financial policies approved by the United States, its main allies and partners, and the international financial institutions. The intention was to prevent any government from embarking on measures of regulation and reform unacceptable to capitalist interests at home and abroad.

These aims met with a very large measure of success. Most capitalist governments had in any case no wish to depart from economic and financial orthodoxy; and in return for their good conduct, they could count on economic aid if required—and military aid as well. As for the governments which did seek reform, they soon found that they would either have to retreat in the face of international pressure, or that they would have to go a lot further on the path of reform. In most cases, they chose retreat.

Two cases in point, concerning very different countries, are Britain and Jamaica, at roughly the same time. When the Labour Government in Britain found itself in financial difficulties in 1976 and decided to seek a loan from the IMF, that institution, in the words of the then Senior Policy Adviser to Harold Wilson, the Prime Minister, 'refused to give any more loans without a further dose of expenditure cuts as evidence of self-discipline'.[23] It is significant that this pressure was by no means unwelcome to many people in the inner circle of government in Britain. As the same Senior Policy Adviser also notes, 'the IMF crisis provided a first opportunity for some (although not all) people in the Treasury and in the Bank of England to take the opportunity to try to change the whole economic stance which had characterised all British governments since the Second World War.'[24]

In other words, external pressure, much of it from the IMF, served to move further to the Right a Labour Government that was also subject to internal pressure. No doubt the people in the IMF who were applying pressure would reject as intolerably crude and as woefully misconceived any notion that they were moved by 'ideological' considerations of Right or Left. This, however, may be taken as mere (and typical) 'false consciousness', to which economic and financial experts, bankers, and such are very prone. The IMF has throughout its existence been deeply 'ideological', in so far as it has faithfully worshipped at the shrine of the market, and has accordingly insisted that governments seeking financial assistance must adopt deflationary policies, reduce their social expenditure (but never their expenditure on arms), impose wage reductions in the public sector, drastically reduce the public sector, encourage foreign investment, abolish social subsidies, and generally pursue policies which offer satisfaction to conservative interests at home and abroad.

The impact of this philosophy on the outcome of internal class struggle is well illustrated by the case of Jamaica. Its reformist government, under the leadership of Michael Manley, had been elected in 1972. Its reforming endeavours produced a sharp exacerbation of conflict in the following years, with a good deal of encouragement of the opposition by the CIA. This encouragement became more pronounced before the elections of 1976, the government's home and foreign policies having by then long been judged by Washington to be dangerously radical. The government nevertheless won the elections, but found itself in the throes of a major economic and financial crisis. It then sought help from the IMF, and was only able to obtain some small measure of help by agreeing to implement a drastic 'austerity' programme which produced a catastrophic decline in living standards for the mass of the population. In March 1980, Manley broke off further negotiations with the IMF and announced an 'Alternative Self-reliant Economic Path'. By then, however, the government had lost the popular support which had kept it in office for eight years, and it was swept out of office in October 1980 by a landslide victory for the conservative opposition. Whether Manley could have avoided such an outcome by pursuing different policies, and by not going to the IMF, is a moot point: but there can at least be no doubt that the IMF played a major role in this outcome.[25]

External economic and financial pressure—particularly on reforming governments—constitutes a permanent part of class struggle; and given the ever-greater integration of the world into a 'global economy', such pressure must be expected to be even greater in the future than in the past. This will be discussed further in the last chapter; for the moment, we need to consider other forms of pressure and intervention exercised by the United States, alone or in conjunction with its allies, since the end of World War II. My purpose is not to retrace in any detail the history of such interventionism, for which there exists a vast literature, most of it American, but rather to illustrate some of the more salient and significant aspects of interventionism, and to show how closely it has been woven into the pattern of internal class struggle.

Interventionism has sought to deal with several different types of situation. First, in countries with well-implanted capitalist-democratic regimes, it has been designed to help conservative and pro-American forces (and also pro-American social democratic parties, trade unions, and other organizations) against their opponents on the Left, and to help them win elections, increase their influence, and generally combat people and parties committed to policies and positions which the United States found objectionable. This kind of interventionism mainly took the form of financial help to governments and appropriate organizations. In the immediate post-war years, it was Western Europe which was the main recipient of such help; but plenty of money was available wherever else it was thought it might do some good.

Secondly, interventionism in the form of economic or military aid has occurred in support of right-wing dictatorships all over the world: however foul such regimes might be, they have the cardinal virtue of being fiercely anti-communist and reliably pro-American.

Thirdly, there have been situations where a government came to office whose reforming inclinations, purposes, and policies the United States found abhorrent on economic, political, or strategic grounds, or all three. The aim in such cases has been to help the government's local conservative opponents to get rid of it, by the application of economic, political, and ideological pressure, or, if this did not work, by military means.

Fourthly, there have been occasions when a revolutionary government has come to power by force of arms, as in Cuba and Nicaragua. These cases have been particularly obnoxious in the eyes of American policy-makers, since Cuba and Nicaragua are in a region which has always been viewed by the United States as its own 'backyard', and traditionally subject to its hegemony. Interventionism against revolutionary regimes takes the form of aid to their opponents at home, the fomenting of opposition and civil war, and anything else that can be done—by way of economic, political, ideological, and military means—to weaken, cripple, and, it may be hoped, destroy these regimes.

Finally, intervention in two cases has taken the form of full-scale war against Communist regimes, first in Korea and then in Vietnam; and the Korean war also led to direct military conflict with Communist China.[26]

In the first of these situations, the problem for the United States at the end of World War II was, as noted earlier, that the Left, including the Communists, had come out of the war greatly strengthened in numbers and influence. What was therefore required was to help the local conservative forces (and anti-communist social democrats as well) to contain, neutralize, and defeat the Communists and other dangerous radicals.

These conservative and social democratic forces could in any case be relied on to do their utmost to achieve this goal; and the post-war years did indeed witness massive anti-communist and anti-Soviet campaigns in all West-European countries. But these efforts were very usefully supplemented by considerable American help. One notable feature of that help was the attention devoted to intellectuals, academics, and other 'opinion-formers'. As one chronicler of CIA activities has written,

For some twenty years, the Agency used dozens of American foundations, charitable trusts and the like, including a few of its own creation, as conduits for payment to all manner of organizations in the United States and abroad, many of which, in turn, funded other groups . . . The ultimate beneficiaries of this flow of cash were political parties, magazines, news agencies, journalists' unions, other unions and labour organizations, student and youth groups, lawyers' associations, and any other enterprises already committed to the 'Free World'.[27]

One major organization of this type was the Congress for Cultural Freedom, founded in 1950, whose announced purpose was to 'defend freedom and democracy against the new tyranny sweeping the world'. The CCF, William Blum notes, 'was soon reaching out in all directions with seminars, conferences and a wide programme of political and cultural activities in Western Europe as well as India, Australia, Japan, Africa and elsewhere'.[28]

Philip Agee, himself a former agent of the CIA, also makes the point that the Agency was not primarily engaged in gathering intelligence information against the Soviet Union, but in using all possible means of struggle against the Left, Communist and non-Communist, everywhere in the world: 'Their targets in most countries', he notes, 'remain largely the same: governments, political parties, the military, police, secret services, trade unions, youth and student organisations, cultural and professional societies, and the public information media.'[29] Trade unions were an obvious and natural target for these endeavours. To splinter the trade union movements and cut off Communists and their organizations from other trade unionists was clearly of great importance; and the United States could count in this task on the full support of American trade union leaders, and also on British ones, not to speak of the British Labour Government itself. A World Federation of Trade Unions (WFTU), bringing together trade union federations, East and West, Communist and non-Communist, had been established in 1945. It was inconceivable that such an organization could survive in the fevered climate of the Cold War. Nor did it. In 1949, non-Communist trade union leaders met in London and, under American inspiration and guidance, established the International Confederation of Free Trade Unions (ICFTU). The ICFTU was of course bitterly anti-communist. It established regional organizations for Europe, the Far East, Africa, and the Western Hemisphere. According to Philip Agee, writing in the seventies, 'support and guidance by the Agency was, and still is, exercised on the three levels, ICFTU, regional and national centres . . . On the national level, particularly in underdeveloped countries, CIA field stations engage in operations to support and guide national labour centres.'[30]

By far the most spectacular American intervention in the class struggles of Western Europe in the early post-war years occurred in Italy, on the occasion of the general election that was to be held in April 1948. For that election, the Communist Party and the Socialist Party, then led by Pietro Nenni, had formed a Popular Democratic Front, and it seemed possible that the Front might win a majority. To prevent this, the United States, by way of public and private agencies, mounted an extraordinary propaganda campaign, combining cajolery, warning, and threat, to persuade Italian voters that a victory of the Left would have utterly catastrophic consequences for them and their country. The main burden of the electoral campaign was carried by the Christian Democrats, strongly helped by the Church. But it can hardly be doubted that the American contribution, with all the resources of money and skill it was able to command, was of great importance. In the end, the campaign was crowned with great success: the Christian Democrats won a decisive victory and established a commanding position which endured for the following three decades.[31] Nor did American support for pro-American forces wane after the election: 'the CIA itself admits', Mr Blum writes, 'that between 1948 and 1968, it paid a total of $65,150,000 to the Christian Democrats and other parties, to labour groups, and to a wide variety of organisations in Italy.'[32] The same concern, by no means confined to the United States, to protect Italy from Communist influence in government was also at work in the seventies. In July 1976, the German Social Democratic Chancellor Helmut Schmidt thus told reporters in Washington that Germany, Britain, the United States, and France had agreed that they would not provide economic aid to Italy if members of the Communist Party were included in the Italian Cabinet then in the process of formation.[33] The danger was averted, but seemed to recur in 1977, and the then National Security Adviser to President Carter, Zbigniew Brzezinski, duly recalls in his Memoirs how successful was the 'firm stand' which the United States took against any such Communist inclusion in an Italian government.[34]

Much of the ideological and political struggle has been waged by official American agencies, such as the CIA, and by various 'front' organizations covertly financed by the United States; and there are also open propaganda agencies of the American government, such as the United States Information Agency or the Voice of America. But a great deal is also done in this realm by a host of private organizations, from the AFL-CIO to major corporations, and from academic foundations to churches of various denominations. These organizations have made it their business (in more senses than one) to help export anti-communism from the United States to foreign parts, and to support local conservative forces in many countries in their struggles against the Left.

Nor of course should the pervasive impact of American

cinema and television be ignored in this connection, from the anti-communist hate propaganda of the *Rambo* type to more sophisticated portrayals of the blessings of American capitalism. It is also notable in this respect that even the most sharply critical portrayals of the American way of life seldom if ever step outside a 'liberal' framework, and simply ignore or dismiss radical alternatives to the status quo.

In many cases, conservative political propaganda—for this is ultimately what is involved—is not the declared purpose of these organizations: but this nevertheless constitutes one of their most important activities.[35] On the other hand, a vast array of organizations, notably in the United States, but elsewhere as well, with sonorous names like the World Anti-Communist League of General Singlaub, of Irangate fame, are specifically engaged in a crusade to save the world from 'communism', meaning in effect to save capitalism, anywhere in the world, and the social order which capitalism sustains, however oppressive, from challenge and erosion or upheaval. These private organizations have vast resources, and excellent links with various security and military services. Nor are many of them only engaged in ideological and political work; they are also involved in the financing and support of the military endeavours of counter-revolutionary 'freedom fighters' in many parts of the world.

By comparison with the immense anti-communist endeavours deployed by official and non-official agencies of the advanced capitalist world, the Soviet Union's own endeavours seem rather puny. Its own propaganda activities do not begin to match those of the United States and its allies. It used to be able to rely on whatever Communist parties in all parts of the world could achieve by way of defence of its actions; and it could also rely on a measure of support from people who were not members of Communist parties but who were sympathetic to the Soviet Union. But this resource has long ceased to be reliable or particularly effective; and there is in fact nothing to compare in scale and resources with the support upon which the United States can count for the defence of its own purposes.

The point again needs to be made, however, that the successes which were achieved by the anti-communist and anti-Soviet campaigns of the immediate post-war years, so soon after the Soviet Union had come to enjoy an extraordinary degree of popularity because of the decisive contribution which it made to the allied victory, were not only due to the intensity and skill of these campaigns; their success and effectiveness also owed much to the repulsive image which the Soviet Union, in the full flood of Stalinist repression, presented to the world, and also to the Soviet treatment of all opposition in the countries which the Soviet Union controlled, with the infamous trials and executions that formed an intrinsic part of the Stalinist method of government, and with the rigid orthodoxy in which Stalinism sought to imprison all manifestations of life and thought. This, the enemies of the Left gleefully proclaimed, was the only possible alternative to capitalist democracy; and the Left, if allowed to do so, would impose it everywhere it held sway.

The repressive image presented by the Soviet Union also made more plausible what was in fact an enormous *non sequitur*: namely, that because the Soviet Union was repressive and 'totalitarian', it must also be aggressive and expansionist. The linkage between repressiveness and expansionism, which was entirely spurious, had many uses: one of the most important of them was to convince the population of advanced capitalist countries that the immense expenditures that were devoted to military purposes were imperatively required to meet an urgent threat; and such episodes as the Korean and Vietnam wars, and Soviet interventions in Hungary, Czechoslovakia, and Afghanistan also very usefully served to legitimate the arms race.

Greece was one country in Europe, outside the Soviet orbit, where restoration of the old order, at the end of World War II, posed problems demanding rather more than merely political and ideological struggles. In Greece, it was Britain which initially assumed responsibility for the task. This required that the Greek liberation forces (largely but not exclusively under Communist control) should be crushed. This was no small matter, given the fact, as James Petras notes, that 'under the German occupation the Communist-led EAM/ELAS Resistance movement had rivalled the strength and penetration even of the Yugoslav partisans, covering the country with a dense network of military and civil counter institutions that organised some two and a half million men, women and children.'[36]

Armed conflict between the Greek liberation forces and British troops raged in Athens between December 1944 and January 1945, and only ended when ELAS (the People's Liberation Army) agreed to hand in its arms in return for the promise that EAM (a coalition of five left-wing, republican parties, in which the Greek Communist Party was the dominant element) would be able to participate in political life. The Greek Right, however, had no intention of allowing any such thing, and proceeded to launch a major campaign of repression against the Left; 'the Communist estimate of about 80,000 arrests at the end of 1945', Gabriel and Joyce Kolko note, 'and well over 1,000 assassinations is probably quite close to the mark.'[37] 'In the ensuing confrontation and bitterness', L. S. Wittner also notes, 'the civil war might have resumed immediately had not the KKE acted as a brake on leftwing militance.'[38] The KKE (the Greek Communist Party) was deeply divided between militants and parliamentarians;[39] but armed struggle did resume and lasted until the government forces, with the support of Britain and the United States, finally crushed the Left. Thus was a traditional ruling class, remarkable for its ferociously reactionary character, deeply tainted by collaboration with the Germans, and also by its earlier support for dictatorship, enabled to reassert its domination by virtue of the decisive and indispensable help given to it, first by Britain under both the Churchill Coalition and then by the Labour Government, and from 1947 onwards by the United States. In compliance with his wartime agreement with Churchill, Stalin stood by and was perfectly content to see the Greek resistance crushed.

From the time of the proclamation of the Truman Doctrine in March 1947, Greece was for all practical purposes an American protectorate, with the American ambassador as the most powerful person in the country. In 1964, elections brought the liberal George Papandreou to office with an outright majority. He was manœuvred out of office by the exercise of the royal prerogative the following year, but seemed again likely to win an election in 1967. A military *coup* in April 1967 removed the threat. The leader of the *coup* was George Papadopoulos, who had collaborated with the Nazis and who had also been a CIA agent for the previous fifteen years. At the very least, the *coup* could not have taken place had the United States opposed it.[40]

Greece at the end of World War II was an early example of the second type of interventionism, which has been repeated throughout the world since 1945, and which is designed to maintain in power reactionary and repressive regimes. In many cases, support by the United States is the only thing that keeps in power oligarchies whose only political purpose is to block any attempt at transforming the abominable conditions in which the vast majority of their populations are steeped, with malnutrition, disease, horrendous levels of infant mortality, premature adult death, extreme exploitation, and ruthless repression as the common lot.[41] Such conditions bring forth opposition: American support makes it possible to deal with that opposition by way of imprisonment, torture, terror, and death.

The point is not that the United States actually prefers authoritarian regimes to constitutional and 'democratic' ones. In fact, support for authoritarian and repressive regimes raises some problems at home and also abroad. The trouble is, however, that regimes in which democratic forms are permitted to function risk turning leftwards and bringing the opposition to office, with all the dangers this opens up of policies which are not acceptable to the United States.

There have been cases in the recent past where military dictatorships have had to give way to civilian and constitutional regimes, as in Argentina and Brazil. These regimes are welcome in American eyes, in so far as the people who run them are themselves exceedingly 'moderate' people, who have no intention whatever of pursuing radical policies. So long as they remain in power and pursue conservative policies, all, from the American point of view, is well.

Similarly, there have been cases recently—Haiti under Duvalier and the Philippines under Marcos—where authoritarian regimes of very long standing, supported by the United States over the years, have finally been swept away by an irresistible wave of popular anger. The problem this posed to local power elites and the United States was to make sure that the successor regimes should be able to contain and neutralize the revolutionary upsurge, to prevent the wrong people (i.e. radical reformers) from gaining power, and to avert any serious challenge to the existing structures of property and privilege, and to American economic and strategic interests. The problem was successfully solved in both Haiti (where the new regime bears a striking resemblance to the old) and in the Philippines. Such worries as the United States might have had that Mrs Aquino would seriously embark on radical policies of reform and seek to make peace with the Communist insurgents were soon put to rest.[42] Provided the regime continues on its conservative path, there is, from the point of view of the American Administration, much to be said for the constitutional government of Corazón Aquino compared to the dictatorship of Ferdinand Marcos.

The third type of interventionism occurs where governments newly come to power do show a strong disposition to undertake economic and social reform, notably land reform, to allow political space to the Left, including Communists, and also to assert some independence from the United States in the international arena, which may include better relations with Communist and non-aligned countries. However legitimate in electoral terms such governments might be, their purposes have proved quite un-acceptable to the United States; and American sentiments are fully shared by local economic, political, and military interests threatened by the moves which the new government seeks to make. This combination of local opposition and American hostility has commonly spelt disaster for reforming governments in the 'third world'.

An early example of what happens in such cases, which involved Britain as well as the United States, was that of Iran in 1953. In March 1951, the Iranian Parliament had passed a bill for the nationalization of the British-owned Anglo-Iranian Oil Company. At the end of April, the man who had led the parliamentary movement for nationalization, Mohammed Mossadegh, was elec-ted Prime Minister. Britain then sought, unsuccessfully, to undo Mossadegh by an economic blockade, boycott, and the freezing of Iranian assets. By the summer of 1953, however, it was the Eisenhower Administration, with John Foster Dulles as its Secretary of State, which took command, having decided that Mossadegh must go because of the (purely fictitious) danger that he would turn Iran (or allow Iran to be turned) into a Soviet 'satellite'.[43] A CIA-sponsored *coup* was duly arranged and oc-curred in August 1953: a key figure in the *coup*, in that he gave it some appearance of legitimacy, was the Shah, who had previously been deprived of much of his power. The *coup* gave him back all the power he could have wanted; and, with full

American support, he ran an extremely autocratic and repressive regime for the following twenty-five years. A very satisfactory settlement for the oil companies was reached over the oil question within a year of the *coup*; and as William Blum observes,

the Shah literally placed his country at the disposal of US military and intelligence operations . . . electronic listening and radar posts were set up near the Soviet border; American aircraft used Iran as a base to launch surveillance flights over the Soviet Union; espionage agents were infiltrated across the border; various American installations dotted the Iranian landscape.[44]

The same kind of satisfactory result was achieved in Guatemala in 1954. In 1950, elections had given the presidency of the country to a moderate reformer, Jacobo Arbenz, with 65 per cent of the vote. Arbenz not only legalized the Communist Party—which was bad enough—but also allowed Communists to work in junior government posts and in the state service, which was unforgivable in American eyes.[45] Moreover, Arbenz pushed forward with modest measures of agrarian reform (in a country where 2 per cent of the population owned 72 per cent of farmland); and he even went as far as expropriating 234,000 acres of land which the (American) United Fruit Company was not cultivating, and for which it was offered $1 million in compensation, against the $16 million which it demanded. In Washington, the Administration took Guatemala to be well on the way to a Communist take-over (the Communists had four seats in the legislature). Arbenz, it may be noted, 'had supported Washington in the United Nations on major issues including those that required choosing sides in the Cold War'.[46] This did him no good at all, and painstaking preparations were made for his overthrow. This involved a protracted campaign of misinformation about the imminent danger of 'communism' overwhelming Guatemala, covert military operations, including air attacks, the bribing of army officers, and finally the actual ousting of Arbenz, who fled the country. The *coup* could not have succeeded without the eager co-operation of the military. But neither is it very likely that the military could have overthrown Arbenz without the United States. Here again, foreign intervention was decisive in the outcome of internal struggles. With the *coup*, the old order, together with American hegemony, was secure. What it brought to the mass of the people was an exceptionally repressive regime and the familiar catalogue of summary executions, torture, death squads, and continued exploitation, uninhibited by tiresome constraints.[47]

The same pattern was repeated in other countries in the following years, notably in Brazil, where a mildly reforming President, Joao Goulart, was overthrown in 1964, and in the Dominican Republic, where another reforming nationalist, Juan Bosch, met the same fate in 1965.[48] But the most dramatic instance of this form of interventionism was the overthrow of Salvador Allende in Chile in September 1973. Here too, indigenous conservative forces, faced with the challenge of unacceptable reform, were given precious, and, most likely, decisive help by the United States in their struggle.

American help to these forces had begun to be provided long before the *coup*, and long even before Allende's election to the Presidency in 1970. The United States had in fact registered considerable alarm when Allende came within 3 per cent of winning the presidency in 1958; and from the early sixties onwards, it had launched a major anti-communist campaign— though Allende was not in any sense a Communist, nor was there any Communist 'threat' in the country. It had also funded the Christian Democratic Party and other anti-left parties; and this effort, which assumed enormous and frenzied dimensions in the presidential election of 1964, bore fruit with the election of the Christian Democrat Eduardo Frei, who obtained 56 per cent of the vote against Allende's 39 per cent.[49] A similar effort was mounted in the presidential campaign of 1970, with the attitude of the Nixon Administration well expressed in the often-quoted remark of Henry Kissinger in June 1970 (Kissinger was then Nixon's National Security Adviser): 'I don't see why we need to stand by and watch a country go Communist due to the irresponsibility of its own people.'[50]

This time, however, Allende, benefiting from a split in the conservative ranks, obtained a plurality of the votes (36 per cent) in the election held on 4 September 1970. It appeared likely that, in accordance with precedent in such circumstances, the Chilean Congress would vote Allende into office when it met on 24 October. Dire warnings of economic disaster and other horrors to come in the event of this happening were issued in the intervening period;[51] and discussions were held with some Chilean

military men about the possibility of promoting a *coup*. This came
to nothing, but the Commander-in-Chief of the Chilean Army,
the constitutionalist general René Schneider, was assassinated on
22 October.

Nevertheless, Allende was duly elected. From then until the
coup in 1973, everything that the United States could do to 'make
the economy scream', in Richard Nixon's expressive phrase, was
done. This was made all the easier by Chile's economic dependence
on the United States. As Petras and Morley observe, 'U.S. and
foreign corporations controlled all the most dynamic and critical
areas of the economy by the end of 1970 . . . Furthermore, U.S.
corporations controlled 80 per cent of the production of Chile's
only important foreign exchange earner—copper.'[52]

In those three years, the United States made sure that Chile
would be starved of the public and private loans and credits it
needed, which had the desired result of increasing the economic
difficulties which Allende in any case faced. On the other hand,
military assistance to Chile was increased in 1972 and 1973, and
so was the training of Chilean military personnel in the United
States and Panama.

Yet despite all the economic dislocation, the frenzied propaganda, the sabotage and subversion which confronted it, the
Allende coalition won 43.4 per cent of the votes in the Congressional elections of March 1973, compared with 36.2 per cent
in 1970. In June 1973, local elections also showed strong popular
support for the coalition. It was precisely this which persuaded
the military that the time had come to move; and they knew that
they could count on American support. The *coup* occurred on 11
September. Allende himself was killed, and there followed the
slaughter of the Left which is usual on such occasions. The
military dictatorship headed by Pinochet which has been in power
since then has had no good cause to complain of American lack
of support.

Interventionism assumes even more pronounced and violent forms
in the case of explicitly revolutionary regimes; and this is so even
though these regimes have not come into being under Communist
leadership, and have absolutely no allegiance to the Soviet Union.
As noted, American hostility was particularly marked in the case
of Cuba and Nicaragua, and was soon translated into policies and

actions designed to destabilize and destroy their regimes. It might have been otherwise if they had desisted, after the victory of their revolutions, from any action objectionable to the United States. Their insistence on the implementation of radical change turned the United States into their implacable enemy.

In the case of some revolutionary regimes, the United States has been able to rely on internal counter-revolutionary forces sufficiently strong to engage in what amounts to civil war. Angola and Mozambique are cases in point. So, in a rather different setting, is Afghanistan, where a weak regime, installed and supported by the Soviet Union, faced considerable internal armed resistance. In such cases, interventionism mainly takes the form of military assistance. The United States is seldom alone in these endeavours. In one part of the globe or another, it has been able to count on help from such countries as Britain, South Africa, Saudi Arabia, Pakistan, and so on; and Israel has often played an exceptionally useful role in the furtherance of American purposes in various parts of the world.

However, in the cases which have been of the greatest immediate concern to the United States, namely, Cuba and Nicaragua, interventionism has been complicated by the inability of counter-revolutionary forces to mount any serious form of armed struggle inside either country. Only in Grenada did a split in the revolutionary leadership, and the killing of Maurice Bishop, open the way to a successful American invasion. On the other hand, the attempt to create a counter-revolutionary base in Cuba foundered miserably at the Bay of Pigs in 1961; and the Reagan Administration has not done much better in Nicaragua. The will is there; but it meets with major political obstacles in the United States itself.

This leaves two other courses of action open. One of them is the arming of counter-revolutionary exiles and mercenaries to undertake hit-and-run raids and incursions for the purpose of destroying power stations and bridges, military installations and government offices, hospitals and schools; burning or poisoning crops; and killing government officials, teachers, social workers, and others identified as supporters of the government. This was extensively done in the early years of the Cuban revolution, and has been extensively done in Nicaragua. Such exercises cannot bring down the government, but they help maintain a constant state of alert and insecurity; and there was for a long time a lingering hope that it might yet be possible to establish a 'liberated zone' in Nicaragua, which would provide the basis for further operations.

The second course, which supplements the first, is for the United States itself to undertake various military operations in a strategy of 'Low Intensity Warfare', which involves the mining of harbours, the bombing of economic and military targets, and other such limited and covert operations, together with boycott, blockade, and all possible support for opposition inside and outside the country.

Even if such policies and actions do not achieve their ultimate objective, they do nevertheless have some distinct advantages. One is that they greatly increase the economic difficulties which the government in any case has to grapple with, not least because it is compelled to devote a large amount of desperately scarce resources to defence purposes. Moreover, economic difficulties, dislocations, shortages, and breakdowns may, it is hoped, spread discontent and disaffection, and increase opposition. The government might then be driven to adopt more drastic measures of repression and curtail civic and political rights. This makes it possible for the United States and its allies to claim that the regime is totalitarian as well as incompetent.

Economic difficulties and military attacks also lead revolutionary regimes to seek help from the sources most likely to give it: namely, the Soviet Union and other Communist states. The closer the relations of the revolutionary regime with the Soviet Union then become, the more is the United States able to claim that its fears of just such an eventuality were justified: its own actions, which brought about these closer relations with the Soviet Union, are then given retrospective legitimation, and provide a warrant for further intervention. Cuba is a classic example. Even though the notion that it is a Soviet 'satellite' is unjustified, it is reasonable to assume that, had it not been for American policies and actions to destabilize and destroy the regime, Cuba would have remained a lot more 'non-aligned' than it has been for many years.

Also, the closeness of the relations with the Soviet Union which revolutionary regimes are driven to seek by American hostility and intervention is taken to demonstrate yet again how relentless is the Soviet drive to extend its influence and control wherever in the world an opening to do so occurs: the lesson to be drawn is obviously that the United States and its allies must therefore remain ready to oppose at every turn developments anywhere in the world which favour the designs of an aggressive and expansionist power.

There have been two occasions since 1945 when American interventionism escalated into full-scale war: the first was in Korea from 1950 to 1953; the second was in Vietnam from the early sixties to 1975. The pattern and purpose of intervention was in both cases similar to that elsewhere: the difference lay in its immeasurably larger scale.

Korea had been artificially divided at the end of World War II between a Communist North and a South whose regime, under the leadership of Syngman Rhee, was dominated by the familiar combination of military men, ex-collaborators with the Japanese, large landlords, and so on. South Korea was an exceedingly repressive police state which by 1949 confronted a vast opposition movement; much of this was in the form of a guerrilla movement which, it was claimed by the North, was 90,000 strong. There was constant skirmishing between the North and the South in the border areas of the 38th Parallel which divided the two parts of the country, and there were repeated threats by Syngman Rhee to reunify Korea by force of arms.[53] In June 1950, North Korea, which had itself been calling for the peaceful reunification of the country, sent its troops across the 38th Parallel. The expectation of the North Korean leaders was that this would produce a general uprising, lead to the collapse of the Rhee regime, and bring about the unification of the country under a Communist regime.

Instead, the North Korean action produced American military intervention, in the name of the United Nations, and with the participation of forces from a number of other countries, notably Britain, Australia, and Turkey. North Korean troops were pushed back beyond the 38th Parallel, and the United States then made the momentous decision to move on and undertake what amounted in effect to the elimination of the Communist regime in the North and the reunification of the country under its own auspices. The American advance to the Chinese border brought China into the conflict and turned the episode into a major international conflict: it might well have assumed even more dramatic dimensions had it not been for the extreme Soviet caution which has already been noted.

In the case of Vietnam, the conflict had its origins in the determination of France to regain control of Indo-China at the end of World War II. This required the crushing of the Communist-led liberation movements which had fought the Japanese occupation of Indo-China in the war years.[54] In Vietnam, as in Korea, the country was artificially divided between the North, with a Communist regime, and the South, with a puppet regime installed by the French. The war, with vast American help to France,[55] lasted until the decisive French defeat at Dien Bien Phu in April 1954. The Geneva peace conference which followed provided for free elections within two years to reunify the country. The elections were never held because neither the South Vietnamese regime nor the American administration wanted them. As in South Korea, the government of South Vietnam proceeded to make war on its opponents; and armed resistance, under the leadership of a National Liberation Front, predominantly non-Communist, began in earnest in 1959. By then, the United States was fully involved in the internal struggle, and its intervention on behalf of the regime steadily escalated: 'in 1962, the United States Army flew 50,000 sorties, strafing, bombing, and blistering entire areas with napalm fire bombs.'[56] 1962 was also the year in which millions of Vietnamese began to be herded into 'strategic hamlets', in effect fortified villages designed to prevent contact between the villagers and the NLF. By 1965, the United States was fighting on the ground, and pursuing a relentless bombing campaign both of South and North Vietnam, which was itself now committing limited forces to the struggle. It was not until 1975 that the war finally came to an end, with the entry of Communist forces into Saigon and the reunification of Vietnam under Communist control.

In both Korea and Vietnam, American intervention was marked by an extraordinary—and virtually unchallenged—deployment of air power. Both Korea and Vietnam were mercilessly bombed, with TNT and napalm, and, in the case of Vietnam, with huge quantities of chemical defoliants. Intervention in these essentially local conflicts entailed the death of millions of people, and devastation on a staggering scale.

In the second half of the twentieth century, local conflicts which threatened the status quo have automatically attracted one form of intervention or another by the United States, alone or with the support and help of allies; and governments newly come to power—however constitutional and legitimate their assumption of office may have been—whose purpose was national independence and reform—have had to reckon with unremitting opposition from the same sources. Such governments have never had to deal with their local conservative opponents alone; as important, and often more important, have been the external forces which have sought to curb the zeal of reforming governments, or, if this could not be done, to get rid of them.

Interventionism has had not only a tremendous impact on the countries in which it has occurred; it has had also a major impact on the countries which have practised it, most notably, on the United States.

Interventionism has its own imperative logic. It must, wherever possible, rely on those indigenous forces which are themselves most strongly opposed to radical change. In most of the countries of the 'third world', this means reliance on movements representing tainted, corrupt, and discredited forces, or on viciously tyrannical regimes. Interventionism on behalf of the status quo means support for and complicity with extreme repression, death squads, torture, and massacre; and it means this, however much those responsible for intervention may seek to distance themselves from the perpetrators of the crimes associated with the defence of the status quo.

Interventionism, given the nature of the American political system, also requires that the men in charge of repressive governments, and leaders of counter-revolutionary movements, should be portrayed not only as 'friends of America', which they by necessity are, but also as defenders of democracy, freedom, and independence, which is sinister nonsense. This is one part of the massive enterprise of 'disinformation', dissimulation, and plain lying which is also inevitably associated with interventionism.

Similarly, such interventionism requires a sustained assault on the consciousness of the American people, designed to elicit popular support for the enterprises in which their leaders wish to engage. This assault, conducted by government officials from the President downwards, and by a communications industry which overwhelmingly supports the government in this realm, has had a profoundly adverse effect on the American political culture and on American political life in general. It has so narrowed political debate as to marginalize genuine alternatives to the politics of interventionism; and it has enabled demagogues and charlatans of the Right to foster, for the population at large, a comic-strip view of the world, in which a virulent chauvinism is allied to strident hate propaganda.

Much that is done by way of intervention requires secrecy, covert action, the bypassing and subversion of democratic forms and procedures, the evasion of any undesirable constraints and controls, and a constant struggle to enhance and extend executive power. A scandal such as Irangate is 'structurally' inscribed in the politics of interventionism; and it is only one of the many results of a politics which mocks the claims made on behalf of capitalist democracy in America.

Yet despite all the immense energies and resources which, for four decades and more, have gone into the assault on the hearts and minds of the American people, the results have not been nearly as successful as the intensity and the deafening volume of the propaganda might suggest. The 'Vietnam syndrome', so greatly deplored by conservatives in the United States (and elsewhere), long antedated Vietnam, which means that vast numbers of people stubbornly refused to surrender to the ideological and political pressures directed at them.

The reasons for this are undoubtedly very mixed; but whatever they may be, opposition to American interventionism has been a permanent factor in the equation. It has not been nearly strong enough to prevent interventionism altogether; but it has in all likelihood helped to curb to some degree at least the zeal with which interventionism has been pursued.

The pressure for intervention, I have suggested, is not produced by the 'Soviet threat', but by the will to contain and defeat radical reform and revolution. That will is certain to be severely tested in the years to come, as more and more countries, particularly in the 'third world', seek to rid themselves of oligarchies which paralyse their development. From this point of view, the confrontation between the advocates and practitioners of interventionism, and those people in the United States who oppose them, will long endure and will remain one of the most momentous struggles to be waged anywhere in the world, both for the United States and for the rest of the world as well.

7

The Future of Class Struggle

I

What, in the perspective of the previous chapters, is the future of class struggle in advanced capitalist societies likely to be? This is much the same as asking what the future of politics in these countries is likely to be; and a—necessarily tentative and speculative—answer to the question must first of all specify the context in which class relations and class struggle will be set in the relevant future.

The accent, on the Left perhaps even more than on the Right, is on the furious pace of change which marks the present epoch— on the fantastic technological advances which are occurring in every field; on the radical recomposition of the working class; on the decline of the traditional parties of the Left; the emergence of new social movements; the cultural revolution which they reflect and enhance; the crisis of socialism; the momentous changes in train in the Soviet Union and in other Communist regimes; the ending of the Cold War; and so on. What follows from this, it is insistently proclaimed on the Left, is the urgent need to abandon notions which labour movements have fondly nurtured for a hundred years and more, to discard utopian fantasies, to come to terms with new and compelling realities.

The fact of rapid change is not in question. What is very much in question, however, is the claim that the changes have fundamentally transformed the character of advanced capitalist societies, and that this in turn requires an equally fundamental transformation of the socialist agenda. For notwithstanding a torrent of propaganda to the contrary, advanced capitalist societies are now and will remain highly structured and hierarchical class societies. The precise composition of the different classes will no doubt undergo further and considerable modifications, but the social structure itself, with the patterns of domination and exploitation that have been discussed here, may be expected to endure for a long time to come. It is not the case, as is so often asserted or implied, that these societies, for all the great changes that are occurring in them, are in the grip of an immense and irresistible 'levelling' revolution which is blurring and obliterating class divisions and inequalities. Consumption patterns are some-what less class-specific than they were in the past; and the trend may become even more pronounced in time to come. But the substance of life experience for everyone in these societies remains utterly shaped by the fact of class and class inequality.

In regard to the distribution of power in advanced capitalist societies, there is indeed very good reason to believe that it will become even more unequal than it is now, with a small number of people in the corporate world exercising effective power over ever-larger conglomerates of economic resources; and there is equally good reason to believe that this concentration of economic power will be paralleled in the political realm, both because economic power spills over into political life, and also because of the further concentration of power in the state. However strident the rhetoric of democracy and popular sovereignty may be, and despite the 'populist' overtones which politics must now incorporate, the trend is towards the ever-greater appropriation of power at the top. This power is not now and is unlikely to become 'absolute', but the fact that it is variously constrained, and is likely to remain constrained by such limited checks as may be imposed upon it, should not occlude how formidable is its accumulation in formally democratic systems.

The persistence of the present social structure in the coming years also means that the working class, as defined in Chapter 2, will continue to constitute the vast majority of the population of advanced capitalist countries. The crucial question, in relation to class struggle, is how the working class will act, what demands it will make, what purposes it will seek to serve.

There are, in effect, two fundamentally different answers to this question.

The first is that such struggles as will continue to occur between workers on the one hand, and private or public employers and the state on the other, will be sporadic, limited, and specific, and well contained and routinized within a tight web of legal and political constraints. Strikes will be concerned with wages, hours, and conditions, and will have no larger purposes; and they will only constitute one instance of conflict in these societies, of no particular significance or impact as compared with the pressures exercised by other interests and groups in new social movements— black people, other ethnic minorities, gays and lesbians, feminists, young people, environmentalists, peace campaigners, animal rights campaigners, and so on. Any notion that organized labour represented anything more than one among a plurality of 'special interests' would thus have been laid to rest.

In this perspective, trade unions would mainly organize a relatively small section of the working class—notably white, male, skilled workers—and would only be concerned with 'economic' demands, with no larger purpose than the defence of the immediate interests of their members, not only against private or public employers and the state, but also against other unions and workers. Also, the unions would be vulnerable to serious penalties if they chose to display undue militancy. But most unions, under the firm leadership of business-oriented officials, would not want to engage in any such display, and would, on the contrary, be vigilantly and unequivocally opposed to left activists in their union. The order of the day would be co-operation with employers and war on trouble-makers.

Such a projection of industrial relations would amount to an 'Americanization' of industrial life, which would also find replication in the world of politics. Unlike the United States, other advanced capitalist countries would no doubt continue to have labour and social democratic parties, capable of eliciting mass electoral support and even of achieving office, in coalition or alone; and there would also be some variations between countries in relation to social provision, the regulation of capitalist enterprise, state intervention in economic life, and other such matters. But in so far as the 'socialist' label continued to be attached to labour and social democratic parties (and it might well come to be discarded), it would mean very little—no more, in fact, than that these parties were rather more inclined to moderate social reform and state intervention than their conservative counterparts, but with no thought of anything more radical than that. For all practical purposes, the notion of a fundamental challenge to the capitalist system would have been decisively and irrevocably marginalized. The thought of such a challenge would no doubt continue to inspire some small peripheral groups of people, and might even occasionally inform the rhetoric of social democratic leaders: for instance, on the occasion of party conferences; but it would have ceased to be a serious political project, with any real influence on political life.

People who believe this to be the shape of things to come do not claim that the demise of socialism would necessarily be synonymous with the achievement of complete social pacification. Conflict, they would readily grant, would continue to occur here and there, and might even on occasion assume acute forms. But no such conflict would constitute a threat to the social order itself, not least because those engaged in conflict would themselves have no thought or wish for radical and comprehensive change. In essence, they would be seeking remedy for specific grievances and problems, and nothing more. Not only would such conflicts not pose a threat to the social order: they would in fact be quite 'functional', a means of assuaging anger below and preventing over-complacency above.

An exception to this would be terrorism, as practised by small, even tiny, groups of people situated at the extremes of the political spectrum. This would be a problem and a nuisance; but it too would be a marginal phenomenon, quite incapable of destabilizing a securely legitimated system, based upon an underlying consensus about the fundamentals of the social order. At the core of that consensus would be the acceptance as given and beyond serious question of the private ownership and control of the main means of economic activity, however much disagreement there might be about the scale and scope of the state's activity in the economic realm (and even this would not create major disagreements).

The alternative scenario is based on the notion that advanced capitalism will inevitably generate further and more acute class struggle from below, not only over immediate and specific grievances and demands, but also over larger aspirations involving the achievement of deep, 'structural' transformations in the social system in the direction of socialism.

This alternative scenario does not involve a revolutionary upheaval or an insurrectionary explosion leading to the coming to power of a revolutionary government, on the pattern of the Bolshevik revolution of 1917. There is clearly no very good reason to believe that any such revolutionary upheaval is at all likely in any relevant future in advanced capitalist countries. Even social movements as 'destabilizing' as the 'May events' in France in 1968 did not suggest such an outcome, given the fact that the only political force remotely capable of providing the leadership required for such an enterprise, the Communist Party, was, as noted in Chapter 3, firmly opposed to it, in the belief that any talk of 'revolution' in the prevailing circumstances was suicidal adventurism. Communist parties in capitalist-democratic systems are more than ever committed to electoral, parliamentary, and constitutional courses, and are in any case in crisis; and other organizations on the Left committed to more revolutionary strategies are puny and barely visible on the political scene.

However, this absence of revolutionary alternatives (using 'revolutionary' in the strong sense) does not in the least preclude the persistence and exacerbation of class struggle and pressure from below: the forms which this struggle takes and the outcome it may have are separate questions, to be discussed presently. All that is at issue at the moment is whether heightened class struggle is likely in advanced capitalist societies. It is this which the alternative scenario affirms, and which prevailing currents of thought are at pains to deny.

Such denial, it is worth noting, is a recurrent theme of conservative (and often of social democratic) thought and rhetoric. In every generation, diverse voices from such quarters insistently proclaim that the very notion of class struggle is obsolete, part of a world that has irrevocably vanished, and that the manifestations of it which still occur are the work of ill-intentioned people wholly out of tune with the times. What they mean, of course, is that class struggle *from below* is obsolete. What they ignore is that even if it were true that class struggle from below was disappearing, class struggle *from above* would endure, and would indeed be given greater strength and scope, precisely because of reduced pressure from below. However, announcements of the imminent demise of class struggle from below have again and again proved false; and there are strong reasons for saying that this will remain the case for a long time to come. These reasons have to do with the nature of contemporary capitalism itself, and with the responses from below which it cannot help producing.

II

To begin with, there is the fundamental fact, underlying all others, that the dynamic of capitalism remains as much as it ever was the achievement, for any given firm, of the maximum surplus which the given historical, social, economic, political, and 'conjunctural' circumstances make possible; and that any other consideration, such as social cost or the cost to individual workers, cannot be allowed to interfere in any serious way with this supreme and compelling goal. This, as Marx noted in the Preface to *Capital*, is not a matter of greed on the part of individual capitalists (though greed may well be a spur); it is rather a matter of the imperative requirements of a system of which the individual capitalist, whether owner or controller or both, is the prisoner as well as the beneficiary.

The trouble with the pursuit of the highest possible profit for the firm, however, is precisely that those engaged upon it cannot afford to take much account of individual and social cost, and that the notion of the public good is of no relevance to it, and must indeed be taken as an unwelcome distraction. As noted in an earlier chapter, an enormous effort is deployed by business and the vast public relations industry which speaks for it to persuade the population at large that the pursuit of private profit and the achievement of the public good are congruent, not to say synonymous. This contemporary version of the 'invisible hand', however fervently expressed and believed, is a matter of dogma not reason, and is constantly belied by experience.

This is not to say that capitalist affirmations of a sense of social responsibility and concern for the public good are mere verbiage. Contemporary capitalism in capitalist-democratic regimes cannot afford to seem altogeter oblivious to considerations other than the maximization of profit, and may well point to welfare schemes, support for educational projects, patronage of the arts, and so forth, as tangible demonstrations of its public spirit. The point is not that business is necessarily and in all cases indifferent to the welfare of its employees, to the pollution it causes, to the impact of its policies on workers, communities, regions, and countries. It is rather that the sway of accountants is infinitely more weighty and compelling than that of the conscience of individual entrepreneurs or public relations advisers. Given the

nature of capitalism and the dynamic which drives it, it *cannot* be
expected to be seriously concerned with the public consequences of
private enterprise: it is idle to blame it for not possessing virtues
which its nature precludes. This is why it has always had to be
checked and resisted, either by pressure from below, or by the
constraints which the state itself is compelled to impose upon its
activities. Left to itself, as business has always wished to be left,
it constitutes and cannot but constitute a menace to its employees,
and the public, and indeed to itself.

This contradiction between what is good for the private firm
and what is good for everybody else is constantly growing, because
of the ever-greater degree of 'objective socialization' of the
productive process, and the ever-greater interdependence of all
human activity, not only on a national but on a global scale.

Marx, it may be recalled, believed that this contradiction was
bound to have explosive consequences:

The centralisation of the means of production and the socialization of
labour reach a point at which they become incompatible with their
capitalist integument. This integument is burst asunder. The knell of
capitalist private property sounds. The expropriators are expropriated.[1]

In fact, the experience of a hundred years and more has shown
that, whereas the contradiction between objective socialization on
the one hand and the dynamic of private appropriation on the
other is real enough, the revolutionary consequences which Marx
and others after him derived from it do not necessarily follow,
and have not in fact followed in any advanced capitalist country.
Marx also said, in the same vein, that, with the development of
capitalism, 'the mas of misery, oppression, slavery, degradation
and exploitation grows'.[2] The fact that this, for the working class
of these countries, has not come to pass is of course one of the
main reasons for the falsification of the prediction which Marx
also made that 'with this [growing mass of misery] there also
grows the revolt of the working class.'[3]

Nevertheless, the contradiction persists and grows, and manifests itself in a multitude of different ways—in the relations of
production, and also in all relations of life beyond it. At its root
lie the twin and related plagues of capitalism: the fact that it is
inherently and inescapably a system of domination and exploitation; and the fact that it is unable to make rational and

humane use of the immense productive resources it has itself brought into being. It is these characteristics which renew from generation to generation the search for radical alternatives, and which ensure that the search will in one way or another be continued so long as capitalism itself endures. The forms which this search assumes—meaning the ways in which struggle and pressure are manifested—is clearly a crucial question, whose answer depends on many different factors; but whatever the answer to it may be at any particular time and for any particular country, the fundamental fact remains that it is capitalism itself, not the idle dreams of disaffected individuals, which provides the basis for a permanent striving towards radical alternatives.

It is naturally the working class which most acutely experiences, and which will continue to experience, the reality of capitalism, at work and beyond; but that reality also greatly affects the petty bourgeoisie. In other words, it is the vast majority of the population of advanced capitalist countries which is and will remain profoundly and negatively affected by the failures and inadequacies of capitalism. Nor, for that matter, are people in the higher layers of the structure immune from the moral, political, and psychological miasma which the system generates.

A sharp distinction is commonly made between the most deprived part of the working class—the 'underclass'—and what is glibly described as the 'affluent' majority. But, to stress a point that was made in an earlier chapter, it is *the whole working class* which is subjected to domination and exploitation, even if its different parts experience domination and exploitation at different levels of intensity, and are differently disadvantaged. Nor is the subordinate and disadvantaged condition of the working class negated by the fact that most of it now has access to household durables, colour television, microwave ovens, and so on; that workers and their families are now able to take holidays abroad; that many workers have cars; that home ownership by workers has grown dramatically since World War II; or even that many workers now own some shares in newly-privatized (or other) corporations.

All this is commonly taken to mean that an ever more 'affluent' working class is being transformed out of all recognition, effectively 'de-classed', and consequently immunized against radical ideas.

But we have already noted that the notion of 'affluence' is an apologetic obfuscation, which serves to hide the real condition of the working class, and that life for the vast majority remains cramped, insecure, alienating; and the political orientations of the working class are therefore unlikely to be nearly as conservative as is so often proclaimed.

Despite all the talk of 'post-industrial society', work will remain of crucial importance in shaping the life circumstances of the vast majority of people; and for members of the working class, it will remain a profoundly oppressive and stultifying process as well as an exploitative one, steeped in hierarchical and authoritarian relations, and marked by virtual or actual exclusion from responsibility and power. No doubt workers in the upper layers of the working class may be able to carve out a place for themselves in the productive process which enables them to deploy some degree of initiative and control. But for the vast majority, work, within the compass of the relations of production dictated by capitalism, will remain a cramping, constraining, and impoverishing expenditure of time and energy.

Even so, work is better than unemployment; but members of the working class will also remain the people most directly exposed to the fear and the fact of unemployment, and to the scourge of insecurity; with the prospect, for older workers, of remaining unemployed for the rest of their lives. After the post-war decades of boom and near full employment, mass unemployment has now returned as a permanent threat for all workers and as a grinding reality for millions upon millions of them in the advanced capitalist world, with all the misery and despair which it engenders. Full employment, which had in World War II, when the co-operation of the working class was essential, been proclaimed to be a fundamental right, is now derided and dismissed as a dangerous condition—which, from the point of view of employers and the capitalist state, is no doubt quite true.

Beyond the world of work, it is also the working class which will be—as it is now—most negatively affected by the multiple inadequacies of social and collective services. The level of such services, as was also noted in earlier chapters, varies from country to country; but public provision in the realm of health, education, transport, housing, the environment, leisure, social benefits, and pensions will continue to be generally poor, short of funds and resources, bureaucratically administered, and grudgingly, reluctantly dispensed. Here too, the promise of the post-war decades has been dissipated in a cold climate in which welfare, social services, and collective provision are natural targets of attack and erosion. Some workers, alongside members of the petty bourgeoisie, are able to imitate those members of the bourgeoisie who resort to private provision in such realms as health and pensions; and they are encouraged to do so by the state of public provision and by massive advertising. But the vast majority of the population cannot hope to cover essential needs by private provision. For that majority, inadequate and impoverished collective services mean a marked deterioration in what constitutes the standard of living, even though personal disposable income may rise; and the worse off people are, the more marked is the deterioration. Higher wages cannot make up for inadequate services in regard to the health of families, the education of children, the care of elderly parents, transport needs, and all else by way of collective provision on which the condition of life of much the largest part of the population depends, and will continue to depend. J. K. Galbraith's *The Affluent Society*, published in 1957, linked the notion of 'private affluence' to that of 'public squalor'; and even though the notion of 'affluence', as applied to the working class, was an ideological deformation of reality, and has remained a deformation of it, the notion of 'public squalor' was perfectly accurate as a characterization of the welfare and public provision which most states in the advanced capitalist world are willing to make. There is only one exception to this: provision is ample in favour of the apparatus of coercion and surveillance, and may confidently be expected to remain ample— indeed, to grow.

Gramsci once said that 'the crisis consists in the fact that the old is dying and the new cannot be born.' More important, however, was what he thought followed from this: 'In this interregnum,' he went on, 'a great variety of morbid symptoms appear.' The 'interregnum' is still with us, and will endure for some time to come.

III

This being the case, why should it be thought that all that is wrong with the system is at all likely to produce, not only local struggles for immediate, limited, specific, and largely 'economistic' alleviation and reform, but substantial popular support and pressure for far-reaching and radical alternatives?

The answer to this question is deeply rooted in the agenda of reform which the nature of capitalism itself drives labour movements to adopt. In a long-term perspective, they find themselves compelled to place two crucial items on that agenda. One concerns the economic structures of capitalism; the other relates to the political structures of the system. The two words which encapsulate what is fundamentally at issue are 'socialization' and 'democratization', both constituting of course the twin and interrelated foundations of socialist democracy.

Throughout their history, labour movements have been driven by dire necessity to demand the control, regulation, curbing, and direction of the industrial, financial, and commercial activities of capitalism. Whereas capitalist entrepreneurs of every sort quite naturally seek 'freedom' to do as they wish with the resources they own and control, organized labour just as naturally has invoked external intervention (largely by the state) to reduce or eliminate the individual and social cost which untrammelled capitalist activity implies. How much control labour movements and social democratic parties should seek over the activities of capital has in fact often been one of the main issues of contention between Left and Right in these movements and parties, with the former seeking more such control (and going beyond it to demand outright nationalization), and the latter usually resisting it with great vigour.

This issue will not go away. On the contrary, the very development of contemporary capitalism, and the objective socialization which accompanies it, forces on to the political agenda the question of the enormous power enjoyed by a small number of people over resources, notably in the strategic heights of the economy, whose disposal is of crucial importance to the whole of society. But as labour movements are driven to seek the control, regulation, and direction of the strategic heights of the economy, so do they also discover that this cannot be effective unless the firms which own and control the resources in question are brought into the public domain. In other words, the socialization of the strategic heights of the economy is and will continue to be a demand produced by the nature and dynamic of capitalism itself. Far from being obsolete and 'irrelevant', and therefore doomed to relegation in the museum of antique and long-discarded goals, the demand for socialization is more 'modern' than it ever was, because of the growing gap between what giant firms under capitalist control do (and do not do), and what parties and movements of the Left find socially desirable.

This, it should be added, is not to ignore the many problems which the socialization of a substantial part of economic life is bound to pose. It is clearly necessary to keep in mind the warning which Wlodzimierz Brus, drawing on the experience of Communist regimes, issues on this score;

In certain situations, the relations of dominance and subordination based on public ownership can be far more relentless than those which are based on private ownership in the generally accepted sense, since (1) the state, gathering in one centre disposition over all—or almost all—the places and conditions of work, has in its hands an instrument of *economic coercion* the scale of which cannot be equalled by individual capitalists or corporations; (2) the state can directly link economic coercion with *political coercion*, in particular in a totalitarian system which actually liquidates political rights, the right of assembly and freedom of speech.[4]

Brus is not here arguing against public ownership: he is in favour of it. What he is saying is that public ownership without democratic forms and a democratic political system makes easier an oppressive statist domination of society.

In a different perspective, it is clear that the internationalization of capital poses critical problems for any nationalizing project of a substantial kind;[5] and so too is there now virtual unanimity among the socialist proponents of such a project that the kind of nationalization measures undertaken by social democratic governments since World War II have very little to do with the construction of an alternative, socialist-inspired social order.

But when all this, and more, has been fully taken into account, as it must be, the fact remains that the control over economic life which labour movements and socialist parties have always asserted to be one of their main purposes cannot be achieved unless the power of capital is broken by way of a process of socialization involving different forms of social ownership. It is such a process which capitalism itself places upon the political agenda, however much the leaders of social democratic parties seek to remove it from the agenda.

The other major item which the nature and evolution of contemporary capitalism places upon the agenda of labour movements and parties of the Left is the defence of democratic forms, and their radical extension in all walks of life.

The capitalist-democratic systems of advanced capitalism define democracy in exceedingly narrow terms, mainly as the right to choose and therefore to change office-holders by the exercise of the vote; and these are also systems formally dedicated to the defence of civic, political, and 'human' rights. But the democracy of which they boast is fundamentally vitiated by the context of inequality in which it operates; and the rights to which they are constitutionally committed are similarly undermined by that context. As was noted in earlier chapters, a good deal of class struggle from above is concerned with the attempt to limit and constrain the scope, substance, and efficacy of democratic forms. In a system of domination and exploitation, such as capitalism, those who run it are naturally and inevitably wary of those forms and of the rights which go with them, and are always inclined to seek their limitation—and, where necessary, their abrogation.

No less naturally, labour movements, for their part, are driven to seek the enlargement of democratic forms, not only because democratization is an ideal to be realized, but because democratic forms are a 'functional' necessity if the majority of the population is to be defended against the dominant forces in society, and the state which is allied to them; and so they are driven to seek the introduction of democratic forms in areas where democracy, from the point of view of dominant classes, is very unwelcome, for instance, in the process of production itself.

In this realm too, social democratic governments have, in practice, been very reluctant, to put it mildly, to upset existing arrangements, and have generally been content to administer the bourgeois state more or less as they found it. In this field even more than in others, their capacity for innovation, or their will for innovation, has been very limited. Communist parties in capitalist-democratic regimes, for their part, have, at least since World War II, often put forward programmes of democratization; but their whole tradition has made it very difficult for them to emancipate themselves from a stilted view of what democratization entails. Nor have their own internal practices been such as to strengthen their democratic credentials.

As for revolutionary groups and parties further to the left, they have tended to spurn any notion of the democratization of the bourgeois state, and have insisted that it must on the contrary be 'smashed'. As one of the theorists of the Socialist Workers' Party in Britain has recently stated, a 'strategic focus' on measures of democratization 'could only reinforce the deep-seated parliamentary cretinism of the British left, and encourage their resistance to the fundamental truth of classical Marxism . . . that the path to socialism lies through the revolutionary destruction of the state, not its reform'.[6] One of the not inconsiderable problems which have always beset such formulations is that they fail to suggest what, in terms that could carry conviction, would replace the 'smashed' bourgeois state. Reference to the dictatorship of the proletariat, or to workers' councils, cannot supply an adequate answer to that question.

Still, however poorly the Left has tackled the question of alternatives to capitalist democracy, this cannot but remain a crucial item on the agenda of labour movements, simply because the concentration of power which marks contemporary capitalism, and the erosion of democratic forms which it entails, do make it a problem which imperatively demands to be dealt with.

This, however, is not to say that, even though they *need* to be tackled, the tasks associated with socialization and democratization soon *will* be tackled: what societies need to be done may remain undone for a very long time, even at the high cost of the 'morbidity' noted earlier. I have already referred to the unwillingness of social democratic leaderships to embark on radical enterprises. That unwillingness feeds upon the fact that there is clearly no popular clamour for the socialization of the strategic heights of the economy, or for the democratization of the social and political order. This is often spoken of as if it was a new phenomenon, linked to the 'affluent' society, the new consumerism, 'popular capitalism', 'post-industrialism', and so forth. But the whole history of labour movements for a hundred and fifty years and more in all advanced capitalist countries shows well enough that no such clamour can be expected to burst forth, ready-made, from the working class at large, as distinct from a minority of class-conscious activists drawn from the ranks of the working class and also from other classes.

The question is rather whether radical demands, which by definition entail profound changes in traditional structures, are certain to be rejected in time to come by the overwhelming majority of the working class, not to speak of the petty bourgeoisie.

The current fashion is to argue very strongly that the answer is without the slightest doubt that this is precisely the shape of things to come, and that for parties of the Left to adopt radical and transformative programmes is now, and will ever more definitely prove to be, a certain recipe for political irrelevance, electoral disaster, and permanent conservative rule. Whatever 'fundamentalists' may advocate, it is said with great emphasis, the working class itself has very firmly and unequivocally rejected the ancient nostrums that form part of the baggage of an unreconstructed Left, and will continue to do so, ever more emphatically.

But a point that has been made in earlier chapters must again be recalled in this connection. This is that a crucial distinction needs to be drawn with regard to the programmes and proposals in question. It is undoubtedly futile to expect any large measure of popular support for programmes whose central premiss is that a clean sweep must be made of everything to do with the existing social and political order, so that it may be replaced by a totally new social order whose shape and character tend to be only very loosely and vaguely sketched out. Such a perspective may well be the only realistic one available in countries with tyrannical regimes, and in conditions of under-development, extreme poverty, and imperialist subjugation: even there, however, it must be noted that it is a perspective which only appeals to a minority. In the conditions of advanced capitalism, and in the framework of capitalist democracy, such a project can only have appeal to a tiny minority, notwithstanding the crying inadequacies and injustices of these regimes; and in so far as radical change in capitalist-democratic conditions imperatively requires a very large measure of strong popular support, the project is doomed to remain of very marginal political significance. Nor even, it may be added, is it very likely that it would gain much greater support in conditions of great economic or some other form of crisis. The political repercussions of any serious tear in the social fabric would certainly be considerable; but it may be doubted whether they would, in these countries, produce the kind of 'revolutionary situation' of the 1917 type in Russia which many revolutionary groups take as their model. The Bolshevik seizure of power in 1917 was the product of a coming together of many different circumstances which have been repeated nowhere else. All revolutions which have occurred since 1917 have been of a very different type, and owed their success to conditions and circumstances that were specific to them, and which were crucially different from the conditions prevailing (and which will, most likely, continue to prevail) in advanced capitalist countries.

Communist regimes, with the exception of Czechoslovakia and the German Democratic Republic, came to power in countries at a relatively low level of economic development—in some cases, for instance, China, Vietnam, Laos, and Cambodia, at a desperately low level of economic development. This meant, among other things, that contrary to Marx's 'model' of socialist transformation, the revolution was not the ultimate inheritor of industrialization and economic growth, but a means to its achievement; and it also meant that the overwhelming majority of the population, even in countries like Russia, where a substantial measure of industrialization had occurred in the decades preceding the revolution, was made up of peasants. Even that small part of the population which was made up of industrial workers was of very recent origin, with a very limited experience of industrial life, working-class organization, and political involvement.

The political experience of most of these countries, previous to the installation of Communist regimes, consisted in varying forms of very strong executive power, with very weak or non-existent representative traditions and an equally weak civic life. Only Czechoslovakia and East Germany (which became the German Democratic Republic in 1949) could be said to have had any real experience of capitalist democracy for any extended period of time (namely, between 1918 and 1939). Hungary and the territories which became Yugoslavia after World War I had also had some limited representative experience as part of the Austro-Hungarian Empire; but the fact remains that European states which became Communist regimes had all previously had strong, near-authoritarian or actually authoritarian regimes, with very weak civil societies, in which not only the state but dominant classes had enjoyed great power to dominate and exploit largely peasant populations.

As for China, North Korea, Laos, Cambodia, and Cuba, they had previously been colonial, semi-colonial, or dependent countries, subject to oppressive external or indigenous rule, or both. As such they too lacked anything resembling a strong civic life or the experience of democratic forms.

In addition to all this, the new regimes all came to power in conditions of war or civil war or both, foreign intervention, huge losses of life, and appalling material destruction—all of it superimposed upon conditions of great poverty further aggravated by boycott and blockade.

A radically transformative project in advanced capitalist countries, such as is encompassed by the notions of socialization and democratization, is inscribed in a very different context, and has therefore to be conceived in rather different terms. It has to be conceived as a development of what already exists, in economic, social, and political terms.

Fundamental change, in this sense, cannot mean the total negation of all that has gone before, but a radical, qualitative improvement upon it. There are many reasons why this must be so. One of them is that the Left, in advanced capitalist countries, does not have to confront the infinitely arduous and painful task of economic development: it has the inestimable advantage of a context shaped by two hundred years and more of such development—the legacy of the toil of past generations to present and future ones. Another such reason is that the Left is located in a political framework which includes democratic forms, however inadequate and limited and vulnerable they may be; and that framework also includes strong democratic currents of thought— the collective memory of past struggles and strivings for such forms.

That framework is not to be taken for granted. But even if capitalist democracy was to be replaced by an authoritarian regime of the Right in one or other advanced capitalist country, resistance to it would have to be based on an appeal for the restoration (*and* the radical extension) of the democratic forms which had been extinguished.

What this means is that a revolutionary project, in this economic, social, political, and cultural framework, has to have a strong 'reformist' dimension, in so far as it requires pressure and struggle within the existing institutional system, at local, regional, and national level, as well as outside it; and also that pressure and struggle have to include limited objectives (as well as long-term ones), and piecemeal reforms. Warnings against the dangers of absorption into the system are in this respect well taken; but these dangers, it is arguable, are not greater than the dangers of permanent marginalization and impotence.

In this perspective, the question is, then, whether transformative programmes involving 'reformist' struggles *within a revolutionary project* are certain to be rejected (as is so often proclaimed) by the constituencies whose support is a condition of advance.

As was noted earlier, the record does not tell us so. Elections in advanced capitalist countries have in fact repeatedly been won on the basis of programmes which did precisely have a strong transformative thrust, and whose language was indeed emphatic about the intention to construct a new social order; and these elections were won only because a large part of the working class and the petty bourgeoisie, and members of the bourgeoisie as well, voted for the parties that were pledged to these purposes. By no means all those who voted for these parties were committed to radical change; but the fact remains that electoral legitimation by way of popular majorities—sometimes huge popular majorities—has been elicited on the basis of programmes that did promise radical change.

It is true that the eighties have witnessed a marked reflux of working-class parties in a number of (but by no means all) advanced capitalist countries. The Labour Party in Britain has endured three successive electoral defeats since 1979 at the hands of a Conservative Party under exceptionally reactionary leadership, and is clearly in rather poor shape. Other far more successful social democratic parties, like the Socialist Party in France, have in recent years moved sharply to the right and their leaders have made quite explicit their lack of radical ambitions. It is also in this decade that the French Communist Party has suffered a very notable loss of popular support; and other Communist parties in Europe have to one degree or another experienced decline and crisis. Nor has this been compensated by gains for other parties and groupings on the Left: the trend has, with few exceptions, been towards gains for the Right.

In their haste to pronounce the obsequies of socialism, many commentators, not least on the social democratic Left, have interpreted this loss of support by the traditional parties of the Left and the gains registered by conservative parties as evidence of a profound ideological and political shift in the working class (and of course beyond) towards conservatism, again due to the changes occurring in the societies of advanced capitalism.

This, however, seems an exceedingly facile reading of recent political trends. For there is in fact very little serious evidence of any profound ideological shift having occurred in any of the countries where conservative forces have registered electoral successes; and it is worth recalling in this connection that even such notable conservative electoral successes as the victories of Mrs Thatcher in Britain have been obtained with the support of one third of those eligible to vote, and the support of some 40 per cent of votes cast, most of the rest being cast in favour of opposition parties. This hardly seems to warrant the notion of a massive conversion to 'Thatcherism', all the more so since a large part of the votes cast for the Conservative Party in these elections came of course from traditional Conservative voters. An even smaller percentage of votes was cast in 1980 and 1984 for Ronald Reagan, which also throws a bleak light on the attractions of 'Reaganism', as distinct from the popularity which Reagan himself managed to elicit.

Nevertheless, the loss of support for the main parties of the Left has, at least in some advanced capitalist countries, been real enough. But the reasons for this are not to be found in any profound ideological shift in the working class, but in two other, closely related, political phenomena. One of them has to do with the performance of social democratic parties in office. As was noted in previous chapters, social democratic governments, faced with great economic problems and crises, have always retreated in the direction of policies detrimental to the working class, and have as a result produced immense disappointment and anger among people who had hitherto been willing to support them; and Communist parties, like the French Communist Party, which have been associated with these retreats have suffered from them as well. The same may be said of the setbacks which have been suffered in recent years by the Italian Communist Party: although not part of a government coalition, it was, from 1976 onwards, one of the main elements of support for governments that were pursuing orthodox economic policies, and it may be taken to have paid the price in electoral and political terms for that support, or for its lack of firm opposition.

The failures registered by parties of the Left in government do not produce great ideological shifts in the working class. They merely produce disillusionment and cynicism, and a greater availability to the frantic propaganda directed at the working class by conservative forces. All the more is this effective when these forces, unlike their opponents, appear assured, united, and confident. The remarkable thing is not that a substantial part of the working class responds—as it has always done—to these appeals, but that a large part of it does not, and remains, in electoral terms, faithful to the parties of the Left.

The other reason for the relative decline of these parties is, relatedly, that they have been beset by internal division, and have often given an appearance of uncertainty and vacillation, which was actually an accurate reflection of their condition. Social democratic parties have always been divided between a Right, a Centre, and a Left. But what is significant about recent decades in this respect is that while the Right and the Centre have remained in quite secure control of the apparatus of these parties, they have been unable to affirm a sufficient degree of hegemony over them so as to subdue Left activists. The concessions that social democratic leaderships have consequently had to make to the Left have meant little in practice; but they have helped to enhance an impression of incoherence, indecision, and disunity which has been of great advantage to conservative parties.

As for Communist parties, they too have greatly suffered from deep-seated crises of orientation and identity, with a constant vacillation between a lingering revolutionary vocation on the one hand, and social democratic propensities on the other. These parties too have conveyed a strong impression of hesitation and incoherence, allied to considerable political opportunism; and their own divisions, though often prevented from coming to the surface by the principle of 'democratic centralism', have also added to their difficulties.[7]

It is to such factors, relating to the condition and performance of these traditional parties of the Left, rather than to vast ideological and political shifts in popular opinion towards 'neo-conservatism', that their loss of support must largely be attributed. The root of the problem, which is of historic proportions, lies not in the working class, nor in 'the electorate', but in these political agencies themselves, and notably in the main political formations of the Left in advanced capitalist countries—namely, social democratic parties.

The failings of these parties do not necessarily prevent them from winning elections, largely because of the discredit and unpopularity which comes to attach to conservative governments. But these electoral victories herald no significant challenge to the power structure and no advance in the direction of socialist change. Challenge and advance will not occur until what may be called the *crisis of agencies* has been overcome—until, that is, mass parties of the Left are able and willing to speak and act as parties committed to the advancement of 'reformist' policies and struggles *within the perspective of a fundamental transformation of the social order*.

It is of course impossible to say how this crisis of agencies will be resolved, and its resolution will in any case assume different forms in different countries. According to the first scenario presented at the beginning of this chapter, parties adopting this radical role are doomed to failure and impotence. I have suggested, on the contrary, that the contradictions and failings of capitalism, allied to the campaigns and struggles in which these parties would by definition be engaged, are capable of disproving that scenario.

Moreover, there are some other factors which help to reinforce this perspective. There is, for instance, the likelihood that some at least of the divisions which have separated and weakened different parts of the socialist Left in the past will increasingly come to be dissipated. No doubt, the Left will continue to include social democrats of the 'moderate' sort at one end of the Left spectrum, and revolutionaries committed to revolution-as-insurrection at the other end. It is, however, reasonable to expect that a growing number of socialists, and new generations of socialists free from the weight of the past, will want to reject these alternatives, and will find common ground, unity in diversity, common orientations and strategies.

Another—and very large—factor is constituted by the changes in the Soviet Union which have been generated by Mikhail

Gorbachev. If these changes are allowed to continue and to be extended, they are bound to have an immensely beneficial effect on the fortunes of the socialist Left in advanced capitalist countries. As was noted in previous chapters, the repressive features of the Soviet regime have been of enormous value to conservative forces in their struggle against the Left; and so too has the psychosis engendered by the Cold War ever since the end of World War II. A Soviet regime reconstructed in truly democratic directions would deprive conservative forces everywhere of an immensely precious asset; and together with Soviet initiatives in such areas as arms limitation, it would also make much more difficult the task of presenting the Soviet Union as an aggressive and expansionist power, representing a fearsome threat to the rest of the world. The Soviet threat would then be of a very different order, and this time quite real—namely, the threat presented to conservative forces everywhere by the existence of a regime which, for the first time in history, could lay claim to being a plausible version of socialist democracy.

In any case, it may be expected that a government of the Left will in due course be elected in one or other country of the advanced capitalist world on a programme of radical reform, and will be determined to implement the policies on which it had been elected. The question this raises is what the election of such a government, bent as it would be on the fundamental transformation of the social order in socialist directions, would be likely to mean for class struggle, from above and from below.

IV

It must be assumed that the period preceding the election of a government of the Left unequivocally pledged to radical change would be one of acute economic, financial, political, and moral crisis, with a majority of people giving clear indications that they wanted such change, and with conservative forces equally determined to resist it. Nor would that determination only be caused by deep hostility to the policies which the Left was proposing to adopt at home. In many ways, the hostility would probably be even more pronounced in regard to the defence and foreign policies that were being proposed. For a programme of radical change would hardly be worthy of the name if it did not include a drastic reorientation of policy in these fields in the direction of 'non-alignment', but including strong support for liberation movements and progressive regimes across the world.

The notion cannot be discounted that, faced with the danger of a truly radical government coming to power, members of the power elite in the state and the corporate sector would seriously consider serving the 'national interest' and saving the country by a pre-emptive *coup*. That such a *coup* would occur was at one time more or less taken for granted by the revolutionary Left: a socialist government, it was thought, would simply not be allowed to come to power. But even though such an eventuality cannot be discounted, it seems rather unlikely—if only because failure would give an enormous boost to the very forces which prospective *coup*-makers would be seeking to defeat; and also because the people concerned would rely on defeating the purposes of the government in other and more effective ways. It is worth recalling in this connection that it was only three years after Salvador Allende's assumption of the presidency in Chile, and after it appeared that he could not be dislodged in other ways, that his overthrow was engineered.

Of the absolute determination of conservative forces to defeat such a government, by whatever means available, there need, however, be no doubt at all. All the more is this certain to be the case where, as in Britain, major conservative gains have been registered in the previous years, with all the confidence—indeed arrogance—which continued success engenders. From the end of World War II until the early seventies, and coinciding with the years of boom, it was widely believed, by conservatives as well as the Left, that the advances which had been achieved by organized labour and the working class in various fields such as trade union rights, welfare legislation, the curbing of managerial prerogatives, the regulation of capitalist enterprise, and the extension of collective services were all but irreversible. But to the surprise and delight of many conservatives, the eighties have in fact shown that these advances *were* reversible, and that it was indeed possible to regain terrain which had long been thought to be irremediably lost.

In these circumstances, the attempt by a government of the Left even to regain the terrain conquered by the Right—let alone to advance beyond it—would be viewed as an intolerable presumption. Concessions which conservative forces deemed at one time, however reluctantly, to be acceptable would, at a different point and in a different context, be taken to be an outrageous and 'extreme' challenge, or would at least be virulently proclaimed to be such. The very successes and advances of the Right change the terms in which reforms and concessions are perceived; and the determination to resist is further strengthened by the prevailing crisis-laden economic climate.

What follows in such circumstances is not at all mysterious. Quite simply, conservative forces seek then to deploy every available weapon in their arsenal to defeat the government, on lines which have been made familiar by the destabilization to which many governments throughout the world have been subjected, and which were discussed in Chapter 6. There is only one qualification that this requires: namely, that the *effectiveness* of this deployment must to a large extent depend upon the strength and determination of the Left, in government and in the country. More will be said about this in a moment.

But it must in any case be reckoned that the government will be mercilessly attacked and abused by the majority of the press and other media, and that its every weakness and mistake will be fully exploited and denounced. A multitude of organizations, political and 'non-political', must be expected to attack, deplore, regret the government's policies and actions; and some, with the best intentions, will plead with the government to desist from courses which foster disunity and strife. Large sections of industrial, financial, and commercial corporate power will deem it their patriotic duty not to co-operate with the government, and some will actively seek to counter its purposes. People in the upper reaches of the state system will similarly seek to stay the hand of ministers and to prevent the implementation of measures which they will take to be the product of dogma, ignorance, or malice. Of course, all such forces of opposition will be confident of the support of their counterparts abroad, and of the efforts of foreign governments to bring the government to its senses, or to bring it to its knees.

All this, it should be noted, is a 'normal' part of class struggle when the power and position of dominant classes come under serious challenge; and it occurs largely within the existing constitutional framework, with the qualification that some people on the Right, belonging to proto-fascist groups, may be expected to engage in violent enterprises, such as the fire-bombing of meeting-places of the Left, the beating-up of left activists, and the occasional murder of an activist or a public figure. Nor are activities of this sort likely to be undertaken by private individuals only: in conditions of acute class tension and conflict, some members at least of the coercive and surveillance branches of the state will also be moved by reactionary sentiments to use any means available to destroy 'the enemy within'.

Faced with such challenges, a government committed to radical change would have one of two clear options: it could either capitulate, and try to mask its capitulation with some cosmetic measures of innocuous reform; or it could decide to proceed with its programme. The first of these scenarios has been commonly followed by social democratic governments, and is of no great interest in the present context. The second is a different matter altogether and raises many crucial and difficult questions.

One of the most important of these concerns the character of the state, given the central role which it would inevitably have to play in the enterprise.

It may, to begin with, be taken for granted that the whole process of transformation would be doomed from the start if the leading personnel in the state were not wholly committed to its success. Mrs Thatcher, from her own perspective, asked the right question about senior appointments in all areas of the state: 'Is he one of us?' This is precisely the question that a government bent on radical change would need to ask in relation to all parts of the state apparatus, the only qualification being in the form of the question—namely, 'Is he or she one of us?' The renewal of the senior personnel of the state which is implied would be a far more difficult task for a government of the Left than of the Right, not least because of the far greater resistance which it would encounter, and also because of the far greater disruptions which it would cause in the conduct of the state's business, but it is nevertheless an essential task: it is not realistic to believe that the project can be advanced if people in key positions in the state apparatus—most of whom could be expected to be ranged in a spectrum encompassing bitter hostility at one end and lack of enthusiasm at the other—were not replaced with people who believed wholeheartedly in it, and who were willing to bend all their energies and intelligence to its success.

Secondly, there can be no doubt that the state would have to be possessed of very considerable power, so as to be able to advance its purposes effectively, and also to defend itself against its enemies. What this means is that the government would have to possess the power which the capitalist state, even in capitalist-democratic regimes, has always and 'naturally' arrogated to itself in conditions of crisis, not to speak of its wartime powers: it is a typical class logic which denies to a government committed to radical change the powers which all capitalist governments have assumed to prevent radical change and to defend the status quo.[8]

On the other hand, there is nothing pleasing, from a socialist point of view, in the prospect of a strong capitalist state being succeeded by a strong non-capitalist state. The purpose embedded at the heart of the socialist project is not to inflate state power, but on the contrary to reduce it, and to restore to society many of the powers and prerogatives appropriated by the state in class societies. To hope that this process of reappropriation may be completed at once is illusory; but to defer its beginning, and more than its beginning, to an indefinite future, and meanwhile to invest the state with a plenitude of power, is a dangerous perversion of the socialist project, however well wrapped up this may be in a democratic and revolutionary rhetoric.

The only way in which this dilemma may be resolved is in the considerable extension of democratic power in society itself, in a process of democratization in all spheres of life where power and authority are exercised; and the process would be advanced by activists in a multitude of organizations, working in support of the state, but independently of it. As noted in Chapter 2, what would be involved is the forging of a new partnership, replicating the partnership of the capitalist state with corporate power, but now involving the state on the one hand and popular or social power on the other. As in the case of the partnership between the state and corporate power, the new partnership would be close, but it would leave a great deal of autonomy and independence to each of the partners, and it would undoubtedly involve disagreement, tension, and even conflict, notwithstanding a fundamental unity of purpose. On this basis, it is reasonable to hope that the opposition between state power and popular power would be resolved, or at least greatly attenuated.

This notion of partnership *assumes* a high degree of popular support for the government in power. The assumption follows from the point of departure of this discussion: namely, that a government pledged to radical change in a capitalist-democratic regime had come to power on the basis of such support. This means that the problem would not be the generation of popular support but its maintenance, and its extension, in conditions which are certain to be very difficult.

Two factors are bound to be critical in this connection. The first has to do with the calibre, resilience, integrity, and clarity of purpose of the activists constituting the forward elements of popular power; and much of this would clearly depend on the kind of movement that had been built up over the years preceding the government's accession to power. The second factor relates to the calibre, resilience, and determination of the government itself. That government, it may also be assumed, would in all likelihood be a coalition of different forces; and their degree of unity, and their capacity to maintain a high degree of unity in the face of great difficulties, would be of crucial importance. In this perspective, a point raised in the discussion of new social movements in Chapter 4 needs to be recalled. This is that a coalition in these circumstances needs a core, a solid centre; and this would have to be provided by the representatives of a socialist party able to exercise a major influence in the coalition, without any presumption of a privileged position.

It has often been said in recent years that the ever-greater integration of capitalism on a world scale has made radical change in a single country impossible. Any such attempt would not only have to confront the opposition of internal conservative forces, but of an international capitalist 'community' as well, whose members would be determined to see a dangerous 'experiment' brought to an end, and who would dispose of formidable resources for the purpose. In any case, it is said, there would be no need for any great capitalist conspiracy to be set in train: the operation of the financial markets, and the flight of capital from an 'unreliable' country whose government, in the traditional phrase, had lost the confidence of business on a world scale, would be sufficient to bring the government to heel, or to destroy it.

What is supposed to follow from this scenario, in terms of the purposes of the Left, is not clearly spelled out; but if what does follow from it is that only a synchronized international attempt at radical change is likely to succeed, it is as well to acknowledge that radical change is out of the question for a very long time to come (maybe for ever), since synchronized international revolutions may be taken to belong to the realm of fantasy. What really follows from the scenario is that only marginal reform, such as would not incur the implacable opposition of combined internal and external capitalist forces, is possible and 'realistic'.

In fact, the prospect of achieving radical change in any given advanced capitalist country is not nearly as bleak and hopeless as is made out.

There is of course no doubt, as has repeatedly been stressed here, that a government of the Left bent on such change and clearly seeking to implement it would find itself confronted, immediately on taking office, with severe problems of all kinds, including, pre-eminently, financial problems; and it could only hope to surmount financial problems if it adopted drastic measures, worked out well in advance of the assumption of office, to protect the currency and the economy from the destabilizing operations of financial markets and hostile governments and institutions. What this means, in this realm as in all others, is that a government bent on radical change would need to move very fast and very far in radical directions: the inescapable choice confronting it would be radicalization or retreat.

On the assumption that the government's resolve remained unshaken, there would be other factors which would work in its favour. Whilst the hostility of other capitalist powers, and of international institutions like the International Monetary Fund and the World Bank, may be taken for granted, these forces do not constitute a monolithic bloc with a single mind and strategy. On the contrary, they are made up of diverse entities, each of which has particular interests; and the divisions this creates over strategy and tactics, and even ends, could be played upon and used to advantage by a determined and single-minded government.

Nor is any advanced capitalist country in the position of vulnerability which afflicts weaker countries of the 'third world'. Again, though it is absurd to expect a synchronized international movement to bring about radical governments in a number of countries, it is not absurd to think that a radical government, confronted with national and international capitalist hostility, would attract a great deal of support from labour and socialist forces in other countries, and from progressive forces in general, and that this support would find translation into pressure upon governments at least to desist from hostile policies and actions. All the more would this be likely to be the case if close ties had previously been forged between labour and socialist movements in different countries. In addition, the international capitalist 'community' would have to take into account the fact that an independent radical government, faced with implacable international opposition, would seek an alleviation of its problems by closer co-operation with the Soviet Union and other Communist regimes, and with some 'non-aligned' countries as well; and this too would strengthen the hand of the government.

None of this is intended to minimize the problems which the internationalization of capital would pose to a government intent upon the radical transformation of the social order: it is, however, intended to suggest that these problems are not insuperable, *provided* that the government has the will to overcome them. Will alone is not enough: but it is the absolutely indispensable point of departure.

V

Just as capitalist democracy has many institutional and other variants, so too would socialist democracy assume different forms in different countries. But some of its main features would be common to them all. Three such features may be singled out as primary.

As already suggested earlier, the notion of socialist democracy must be taken to be the merest rhetoric if it does not include, as a crucial, determinant feature, the dissolution of the private and gigantic concentrations of economic power which are typical of advanced capitalism. 'Radical change' in this connection means the transfer into the public domain, under one form or other of social ownership, of the strategic heights of the economy, and of some of its lesser heights as well. A 'mixed economy' would nevertheless continue to exist, but it would be a 'mixed economy' in which the 'mix' would be the reverse of the one prevailing in all advanced capitalist countries: instead of the public sector being relatively small and marginal, and a junior partner to the private sector, it would be predominant. There is no question, in other words, of 'nationalizing' shopkeepers, petty traders, independent artisans, small-scale private enterprise. The nature of the 'mix' is bound to vary from country to country and from one period to another. The crucial point is that the maximization of private profit for the firm would cease to be the main dynamic of economic activity. Socialist democracy does not require a command economy of the kind which the Soviet Union—the country of origin of such economies—is now, alongside other Communist regimes, giving up; but neither can it be based on a system of production and distribution which is not, in some strategic areas, determined or influenced by planning mechanisms at central level. These mechanisms need to involve the greatest possible degree of democratic, grassroots 'input', and the fullest degree of accountability; indeed, the efficient functioning of these mechanisms requires the spread of democratic procedures and habits in this and all other parts of society's life.

Secondly, radical change must be taken to involve a drastic diminution in the vast inequalities of every sort which are an intrinsic part of a capitalist social order. The goal is not perfect equality, which is an absurd notion, but a striving for a rough equality, which is a very different thing.

Egalitarianism has many different facets. One of them is the disappearance of the huge disparities in wealth and income which now prevail. No more than public ownership is this sufficient to turn an atomized and competitive society into a community of co-operation and fellowship. But no such community is conceivable in which great hierarchies of wealth and income exist and enable a privileged minority to live lives totally different from those of the vast majority.

The disappearance of these huge disparities would be decisively advanced by the disappearance of the private ownership of large concentrations of capital and property; and also by the fact that the salaries paid to the controllers and managers of large public enterprises would be subject to public scrutiny, with the scales of remuneration a matter of public agreement. Also, democratic accountability and control would mean that the hidden subsidies and perks which accrue to people in positions of power would similarly be subject to public scrutiny, and would as a result be severely constrained. In any case, the moral and political climate of such a society would itself create its own constraints.

It need hardly be said that egalitarianism entails the most vigorous struggle against all forms of discrimination, whether based on gender, race, ethnic identity, religion, sexual preference, or whatever. Here too, it is idle to pretend that all traces of such discrimination could be ended from one day to the next, by decree or injunction: but it can be strenuously fought, both at state and grassroots levels, and thereby relentlessly forced into retreat until it is no more than a rare and furtive occurrence.

The third fundamental feature which socialist democracy would possess is the partnership between state power and popular power to which I have already referred. This notion of partnership clearly implies the continued existence of the state, not only to cope with the immediate problems and crises confronting the government, but for the relevant future as well. The day may come when the state, in Engels's phrase, will wither away and disappear. If so, this will only happen in a far distant future whose character cannot now be foretold. But the building and consolidation of socialist democracy will long require a state to carry out essential tasks which the state alone can accomplish: for instance, the decisions which must ultimately be made about priorities regarding the allocation of scarce and essential resources; the adjudication of a diversity of competing claims in societies where division and conflict, though greatly attenuated, would continue to occur; the ultimate guarantee of civic, political, and social rights which give much of its force to the notion of socialist pluralism; and so on.

The state would perform its tasks in a democratic context, in co-operation with society, and under its surveillance. But just as society would check state power, so too would the state, democratically invested with the capacity to do so, constitute a check on the power of popular institutions and agencies. It is on the basis of such a partnership between state power and popular power that there might begin to be built, 'in place of the old bourgeois society, with its classes and class antagonisms', 'an association, in which the free development of each is the condition for the free development of all'.[9]

It is extremely improbable that the issues discussed in this chapter will soon be put to the test: the conditions do not at present exist—and will not exist for some time to come in any advanced capitalist country—for the coming to power of the kind of government that would seek to bring about a radical transformation of the existing social order. But as I have sought to argue, it is quite realistic to think that these conditions will come into being within the next ten, twenty, or thirty years—a long time in the life of an individual, but a mere moment in historical time. In this perspective, class struggle for the creation of democratic, egalitarian, co-operative, and classless societies, far from coming to an end, has barely begun.

Notes

Chapter 1

1. K. Marx and F. Engels, *Collected Works* (London, 1983), xxix. 62.
2. Some parts of this chapter draw heavily on my essay 'Class Analysis', in A. Giddens and J. Turner, eds., *Social Theory Today* (Oxford, 1987).
3. Marx and Engels, *Selected Correspondence* (London, 1956), p. 379.
4. F. Engels, Preface to the third German edition of K. Marx, *The Eighteenth Brumaire of Louis Bonaparte*, in K. Marx and F. Engels, *Selected Works* (Moscow, 1950), i. 223.
5. For a notable instance of this 'post-Marxist' critique of class analysis, see E. Laclau and C. Mouffe, *Hegemony and Socialist Strategy: Towards a Radical Democratic Politics* (London, 1985). For a vigorous rebuttal of the trend, see E. Meiksins Wood, *The Retreat from Class: A New 'True' Socialism* (London, 1986).
6. K. Marx and F. Engels, *Manifesto of the Communist Party*, in K. Marx and F. Engels, *Collected Works* (London, 1976), vi. 482.
7. K. Marx, *Capital* (London, 1976), i. 344.
8. See e.g. *Marx's Critique of the Gotha Programme*, in Marx and Engels, *Selected Works*, i. 20-1.
9. G. de Ste Croix, *The Class Struggle in the Ancient Greek World* (London, 1981), p. 57. Emphasis in text.
10. L. A. and C. Tilly, *Class Conflict and Collective Action* (London, 1981), p. 17.
11. P. Anderson, *Lineages of the Absolutist State* (London, 1974), p. 403. Emphasis in text.
12. S. Pollard, *The Genesis of Modern Management* (London, 1965), p. 186.
13. R. Hilton, 'Feudalism in Europe: Problems for Historical Materialism', in *New Left Review*, 147 (Sept.-Oct. 1984), 88. Similarly, Michael Mann notes in relation to the early medieval economy that 'no monopolistic power organisation existed in the local economy. Formidable as were the powers of the Lord, they were restrained by the fact that even the serf could find support from the village community and from customary law' (M. Mann, *The Sources of Social Power* (Cambridge, 1986), i. 395).

14. Marx, *Capital*, i. 277.

15. S. Bowles and H. Gintis, 'The Marxian Theory of Value, and Heterogeneous Labour: A Critique and Reformulation', in *Cambridge Journal of Economics*, i (1977), 277.

16. Z. Bauman, *Memories of Class* (London, 1982), p. 94.

17. Stalinist industrialization provides a good example of the point. See e.g. D. Filtzer, *Soviet Workers and Stalinist Industrialization* (London, 1982).

18. For an interesting analysis of one such case of 'intra-class' conflict, see M. Zeitlin, *The Civil Wars in Chile (or The Bourgeois Revolutions that Never Were)* (Princeton, 1984).

19. K. Marx and F. Engels, *The Holy Family*, in *Collected Works* (London, 1975), iv. 37. Emphasis in text.

20. K. Marx, General Rules of the International Working Men's Association, in Marx and Engels, *Collected Works* (London, 1985), xx. 14.

Chapter 2

1. C. W. Mills, *The Power Elite* (New York, 1956), p. 126.

2. Ibid., p. 4. My emphasis.

3. Ibid., p. 9.

4. K. Marx, *Capital* (London, 1976), i. 450.

5. On 'elite pluralism', see e.g. P. Bachrach, *The Theory of Democratic Elitism: A Critique* (London, 1969). 'Countervailing power' was first formulated by J. K. Galbraith in *American Capitalism: The Theory of Countervailing Power* (London and New York, 1951), one of the early essays in a vast apologetic literature.

6. For some data on the distribution of income and wealth in advanced capitalist countries, see the Note at the end of this chapter.

7. F. Morin, *La Structure financière du capitalisme français* (Paris, 1975), p. 65.

8. M. Useem, *The Inner Circle: Large Corporations and the Rise of Political Activity in the US and the UK* (New York, 1984), p. 30.

9. Ibid., p. 29.

10. Ibid., p. 30. The same author also notes that 'a study of the remuneration of the top executives of fifty large American manufacturing enterprises during the early 1960s reveals that their after-tax incomes from stock-based compensation schemes, capital gains and stock dividends were six times as large as their salaries' (ibid., p. 30).

11. R. Barnet, *Global Reach* (New York, 1970).

12. 'So-called' because the one thing that multi-national corporations

are not is 'multi-national', in terms of ownership and control. In those terms, they are mostly American, or British, or Japanese, or of some other nationality; it is mainly their field of operations which is 'multi-national'.

13. K. Marx, 'Moralising Criticism and Critical Morality' (1847), in K. Marx and F. Engels, *Collected Works* (1976), vi. 318.

14. Ibid., p. 318.

15. R. Miliband, 'State Power and Class Interests', in *New Left Review*, 138 (Mar.–Apr. 1985), 65; and 'State Power and Capitalist Democracy', in S. Resnick and R. Wolff, eds., *Rethinking Marxism* (New York, 1985).

16. D. Vogel, 'Why Businessmen Distrust their State: The Political Consciousness of American Business Executives', in *British Journal of Political Science*, viii. 1 (Jan. 1978), 54.

17. Ibid., p. 24.

18. For Britain, see e.g. A. Giddens and P. Stanworth, 'Elites and Privilege', in P. Abrams, ed., *Work, Urbanism and Inequality* (London, 1978). For France, Jane Marceau, *Class and Status in France: Economic Change and Social Immobility* (Oxford and New York, 1977); for the United States, G. W. Domhoff, *The Powers that Be: Processes of Ruling-Class Domination in America* (New York, 1978).

19. F. G. Castles, *The Social Democratic Image of Society* (London, 1978), p. 96.

20. The Meidner Plan in Sweden, adopted in diluted form by the trade union movement and the Social Democratic Party in the late seventies, did envisage the achievement of just such predominance, though over a very long period of time. The Plan, as Jonas Pontusson notes, proposed that 'firms above a certain size . . . should be required to issue new stocks corresponding to twenty per cent of their annual profits, and that these stocks should be owned by funds representing wage-earners as a collective group' (J. Pontusson, 'Radicalization and Retreat in Swedish Social Democracy', in *New Left Review*, 165 (Sept.–Oct. 1987), 13). The legislation which was introduced by the Social Democratic Government in 1983 represented a further and drastic dilution of the Plan, and was explicitly not intended to challenge, in however long a perspective, the overwhelming preponderance of the private sector.

21. For the most notable attempt in the recent past to establish a highly restrictive definition of the working class, see N. Poulantzas, *Classes in Contemporary Capitalism* (London, 1975). For a detailed critique, see E. O. Wright, *Class, Crisis and the State* (London, 1978), ch. 2.

22. Marx, *Capital*, i. 644.

23. K. Marx, *Theories of Surplus Value* (London, 1963), pt. i, p. 157.

24. Ibid., p. 158. See also Marx, *Capital*, i. 1038 ff.

25. L. Harris and B. Fine, *Rereading Capital* (London, 1979), p. 53.

26. Marx, *Capital*, i. 644.

27. Marx, *Capital* (London, 1981), iii. 407.

28. K. Marx, *The Eighteenth Brumaire of Louis Bonaparte*, in K. Marx and F. Engels, *Collected Works*, xi (London, 1979), 187.

29. E. P. Thompson, *The Making of the English Working Class* (London, 1963), pp. 9–10.

30. E. P. Thompson, *The Poverty of Theory* (London, 1978), pp. 288–9.

31. P. Anderson, *Arguments within English Marxism* (London, 1980), p. 40. See also G. A. Cohen, *Karl Marx's Theory of History: A Defence* (London, 1978), pp. 73 ff.

32. Thompson, *The Making of the English Working Class*, pp. 9–10.

33. Preface to *A Contribution to the Critique of Political Economy*, in *Selected Works*, i. 329.

34. Perhaps the most ambitious attempt ever made to analyse this complex totality in relation to a single individual is Jean-Paul Sartre's work on Gustave Flaubert, *L'Idiot de la famille* (Paris, 1971–2).

35. R. Skidelsky, 'The Decline of Keynesian Politics', in C. Crouch, ed., *State and Economy in Contemporary Capitalism* (London, 1979), p. 79.

36. Ibid.

37. A. Gorz, *Farewell to the Working Class: An Essay on Post-industrial Socialism* (London, 1982), p. 28. It is of some minor interest that in its original French version the book is entitled *Adieux au prolétariat: Au delà du socialisme*. The 'beyond socialism' of the French sub-title was presumably thought to be inappropriate for the English-speaking reader.

38. D. Bell, *The Coming of Post-industrial Society* (New York, 1973), p. 125.

39. F. Parkin, 'Social Stratification', in T. B. Bottomore and R. Nisbet, eds., *A History of Sociological Analysis* (London, 1979), p. 607.

40. P. Adler, 'Technology and US', in *Socialist Review*, 85 (1986), 89. Note also his remark that 'for the period that has been studied most adequately, the post-World War II years, the verdict is unambiguous: *not one* of the systematic, nationwide studies for the US shows a deskilling trend in either individual or average job requirements; most show a clear up-grading both for the labor force as a whole *and* for most occupations taken individually' (ibid., p. 81; emphasis in text).

41. J. Zeitlin, 'Shop Floor Bargaining and the State: A contradictory Relationship', in S. Tolliday and J. Zeitlin, *Shop Floor Bargaining*

and the State (Cambridge, 1985), p. 14. Note similarly Michael Burawoy's observation: 'There are few work contexts . . . in which labourers do not construct "games", with respect to technology and to one another. Even on the assembly line workers manage to secure spaces for themselves in which to introduce uncertainty and to exercise a minimal control' (M. Burawoy, *The Politics of Production* (London, 1985), p. 37).

42. E. Mandel, 'Marx, the Present Crisis and the Future of Labour', in *The Socialist Register 1985/6* (London, 1986), p. 437.

43. Ibid., p. 438. Emphasis in text.

44. D. Noble, 'Social Choice in Machine Design: The Case of Automatically Controlled Machine Tools', in A. Zimbalist, ed., *Case Studies in the Labour Process* (New York, 1979), p. 19.

45. D. Clawson, *Bureaucracy and the Labor Process* (New York, 1980), p. 51.

46. A. Gorz, *Adieux au prolétariat* (Paris, 1980), p. 187. The chapter in which this passage occurs is omitted from the English translation.

47. A. J. Mayer, 'The Lower Middle Class as Historical Problem', in *Journal of Modern History*, xlvii. 3 (Sept. 1975), 43.

48. See e.g. *The Communist Manifesto*, in *Collected Works*, vi. 494.

49. J. M. Wiener, 'Marxism and the Lower Middle Class: A Reply to Arno Mayer', in *Journal of Modern History*, xlviii. 4 (Dec. 1976), 666.

50. See e.g. V. I. Lenin, *'Left-Wing' Communism: An Infantile Disorder*, in *Selected Works* (1969), p. 158. In the same vein, see also L. Trotsky, *The Struggle Against Fascism in Germany* (London, 1971), p. 284.

51. F. Bechhofer, B. Elliott, M. Rushforth, R. Bland, 'The Petits Bourgeois in the Class Structure: The Case of the Small Shopkeepers', in F. Parkin, ed., *Social Analysis of Class Structure* (London, 1974), pp. 115-16.

52. S. Hellman, 'The PCI's Alliance Strategy and the Case of the Middle Classes', in D. L. M. Blackmer and S. Tarrow, eds., *Communism in France and Italy* (Princeton, 1975).

53. A. F. Shorrocks, 'UK Wealth Distribution: Current Evidence and Future Prospects', in E. N. Wolff, ed., *International Comparisons of the Distribution of Household Wealth* (Oxford, 1987), p. 35. My emphasis.

Chapter 3

1. For the classical statement of the revolutionary position on the issue of social reform, see Rosa Luxemburg, 'Reform or Revolution', in M.-A. Waters, ed., *Rosa Luxemburg Speaks* (New York, 1970).

2. H. Gruber, *International Communism in the Era of Lenin* (New York, 1972), pp. 241–6.

3. Ibid., p. 243. A story circulating at the same time, no doubt apocryphal but well in line with the spirit of the document, was that Lenin was asked what would happen if the German Independent Socialist Party, which included some leading 'reformists', were to accept the Twenty-one Conditions and apply for membership. 'Then we'll think of a twenty-second condition', Lenin was supposed to have said.

4. The phrase occurs in Lenin's polemic, *The Proletarian Revolution and the Renegade Kautsky*, in *Selected Works*, (London, 1969). See also *The State and Revolution* and *'Left-wing' Communism: An Infantile Disorder* (ibid.). It may be noted, however, that Lenin had a much more qualified attitude to bourgeois democracy before 1914 and World War I. See e.g. some of his remarks in *Two Tactics of Social Democracy in the Democratic Revolution* (ibid.). Even then, he was emphatic about the limitations of bourgeois democracy; but it was with the war, and with what he believed to be bourgeois democracy's degeneration into a 'bloody morass of bureaucratic-military institutions which subordinate everything to themselves, and suppress everything', as he put it in *The State and Revolution*, that his attacks upon it assumed a much more unqualified and virulent character than before.

5. The 'Third Period' was thus called to distinguish it from two preceding periods: a first period of revolutionary upheaval in the immediate post-war years; and a second period of capitalist consolidation which was now declared to have come to an end.

6. E. H. Carr, *The Twilight of Comintern, 1930–1935* (London, 1982), p. 51.

7. The bitterness which Communists felt towards social democrats was greatly enhanced by such episodes as the killing by the police of eighteen Communists in a demonstration in a suburb of Hamburg in July 1932, a district whose police-president was a Social Democrat (Carr, *Twilight*, p. 61).

8. D. Desanti, *L'Internationale Communiste* (Paris, 1970), p. 170.

9. J. V. Stalin, *Works* (1953), x. 53–4. 'The principle of the defence of the USSR', E. H. Carr also notes, 'was formally inscribed in the programme of the Comintern at its sixth Congress in 1928' (*Twilight*, p. 151).

10. R. Hyman, *Strikes* (London, 1984), pp. 39, 41. Another author goes further and suggests that 'conflict arising from the use of unofficial work place union power is, in effect, the specific, concrete form that the class struggle in industry has generally taken in Britain,

re-emerging at least from the mid-1950s onwards' (D. Strinati, *Capitalism, the State and Industrial Relations* (London, 1982), p. 73).

11. J. Barkan, *Visions of Emancipation: The Italian Workers' Movement since 1945* (New York, 1984), p. 68. Note also the following: 'The first working class conflicts, in the spring of 1968, broke out spontaneously, completely beyond the control of the trade unions' (M. Barbagli and P. Corbetta, 'The Italian Communist Party and the Social Movements, 1968-1976', in M. Zeitlin, ed., *Political Power and Social Theory*, iii (Greenwich, Conn., 1982), 78).

12. See e.g. D. A. Hibbs, 'On the Political Economy of Long-run Trends in Strike Activity', in *British Journal of Political Science*, viii. 2 (Apr. 1978), 154.

13. See e.g. H. Wilensky, *The Welfare State and Equality* (Berkeley, 1975); F. G. Castles, *The Social Democratic Image of Society* (London, 1978); D. Cameron, 'Social Democracy, Corporatism and Labour Quiescence: The Representation of Economic Interest in Advanced Capitalist Society', paper presented at Stanford University Conference on Representation and the State, October 1982, in T. B. Edsall, *The New Politics of Inequality* (New York, 1984), pp. 146-7; P. Flora and A. J. Heidenheimer, eds., *The Development of Welfare States in Europe and North America* (New Brunswick, NJ, 1979); and C. Hewitt, 'The Effect of Political Democracy and Social Democracy on Equality in Industrial Societies: A Cross-national Comparison', in *American Sociological Review*, xlii. 3 (June 1977).

14. F. F. Piven and R. A. Cloward, *The New Class War: Reagan's Attack on the Welfare State and its Consequences* (New York, 1980), pp. 116-18.

15. Edsall, *New Politics*, p. 162.

16. For some interesting considerations on this topic, see S. Tarrow, 'Party Activists in Public Office: Comparisons at the Local Level in Italy and France', in D. L. M. Blackmer and S. Tarrow, eds., *Communism in France and Italy* (Princeton, 1975), pp. 143-72. In the same volume, see also A. Stern, 'Political Legitimacy in Local Politics: The Communist Party in North-eastern Italy', pp. 221-58, and P. Lange, 'The PCI at the Local Level: A Study of Strategic Performance', pp. 259-304.

17. For one of the most elaborate defences of this thesis, see A. Przeworski, *Capitalism and Social Democracy* (Cambridge, 1985).

18. R. Keohane, 'The World Political Economy and the Crisis of Embedded Liberalism', in J. H. Goldthorpe, ed., *Order and Conflict in Contemporary Capitalism* (Oxford, 1984), pp. 22, 23.

19. R. Hamilton, *Who Voted for Hitler?* (Princeton, 1982), p. 281.

20. A. Rabinbach, *The Crisis of Austrian Socialism: From Red Vienna to Civil War, 1927-1934* (Chicago, 1983), p. 22.

21. Rabinbach, *Crisis of Austrian Socialism*, p. 91, quoting from O. Bauer, *Austrian Democracy Under Fire* (London, 1934), p. 43. February 1934 in the quotation refers to the occasion when the workers *were* crushed in blood.

22. D. Beetham, *Marxism in the Face of Fascism* (London, 1983), pp. 47–8.

23. Jagan, it may be added, won two further general elections, under a new constitution in each case, in 1957 and 1961, and again became Prime Minister. It was not until yet another general election, in 1964, that, having failed to win an absolute majority of seats, he was finally forced out of office, under the auspices of another Labour Government in London, and replaced by the much more amenable Forbes Burnham.

24. G. Lavau, 'The PCF, the State and the Revolution: An Analysis of Party Policies, Communications and Popular Culture', in Blackmer and Tarrow, *Communism in France and Italy*, p. 114. Emphasis in text. In the same vein, Dimitrov, speaking at the Seventh Congress of the Comintern in 1935, advocated Popular Fronts and the formation of Popular Front governments; but he also issued the following warning: 'We say openly to the masses: this government *cannot* lead you to *definitive salvation*. It is not capable of beating the domination of the exploiters—and therefore cannot definitively eliminate the danger of a fascist counter-revolution. It is therefore necessary to *prepare for the socialist revolution*! Soviet power alone and uniquely can lead to salvation!' (G. Vacca, 'The "Euro-communist" Perspective: The Contribution of the Italian Communist Party', in R. Kindersley, ed., *In Search of Eurocommunism* (London, 1981), p. 129. Emphasis in text.)

25. Lavau, 'The PCF, the State and the Revolution', p. 114. Note, however, that another essay in the same volume refers to a statement by Maurice Thorez, the General Secretary of the Party, in 1936, which, in urging a merger with the Socialist Party, speaks of the goal as being 'the violent overthrow of the power of the bourgeoisie and . . . installation of the dictatorship of the proletariat through the means of soviets . . . organized on the model of the Great Party of Lenin and Stalin' (R. Tiersky, 'Alliance Politics and Revolutionary Pretensions', in Blackmer and Tarrow, *Communism in France and Italy*, p. 426).

26. Vacca, 'The "Euro-communist" Perspective', p. 129.

27. G. Lefranc, *Histoire du Front populaire* (2nd edn., Paris, 1974), pp. 164–5.

28. P. Spriano, *Stalin and the European Communists* (London, 1985), p. 113.

29. C. de Gaulle, *Mémoires de guerre*, iii (Paris, 1959), 276.

30. In Spring 1946, the head of the Cochin Chinese delegation in Paris said that Thorez, then Vice-Premier in de Gaulle's Government, had 'affirmed to me that the Communist Party under no circumstances wished to be considered as the eventual liquidator of the French position in Indochina and that he ardently wished to see the French flag fly over all corners of the French Union' (A. J. Rieber, *Stalin and the French Communist Party, 1941-1947* (New York, 1962), p. 324). This fits in with the PCF's commitment to the idea of a French Union encompassing former colonial dependencies. For a well-documented appraisal of the PCF's colonial policies, written from a Trotskyist perspective, see J. Monata, *La Politique du Parti communiste français dans la question coloniale* (Paris, 1971).

31. See e.g. R. W. Johnson, *The French Communist Party and the Students* (London, 1972); D. Singer, *Prelude to Revolution: France in May 1968* (London, 1970); and, for a Communist view, R. Andrieu, *Les Communistes et la Révolution* (Paris, 1968).

32. See Chapter 6.

33. In Portugal, where a 'revolutionary situation' appeared to exist in April 1984 as a result of the officers' *coup* and the toppling of the dictatorship, the Portuguese Communist Party played a strongly moderating role in the crucial first period of the revolution. When the Party later adopted more militant policies, the political climate had become unfavourable. See e.g. L. Graham and L. D. Wheeler, eds., *In Search of Modern Portugal: The Revolution and its Consequences* (Madison, Wisc., 1983), and P. Mailer, *Portugal: The Impossible Revolution* (London, 1977).

34. D. L. M. Blackmer, 'Introduction', in Blackmer and Tarrow, *Communism in France and Italy*, p. 5.

35. C. Seton-Watson, 'The PCI's Taste of Power', in Kindersley, *In Search of Eurocommunism*, p. 148.

36. Ibid., p. 148.

37. V. I. Lenin, *What is to be Done?*, in *Collected Works*, v (Moscow, 1961), 383.

38. Ibid., p. 40, from *Neue Zeit*, xx. 1. 3 (1901-2), 79.

39. Ibid., p. 40.

40. F. Parkin, *Class Inequality and Political Order: Social Stratification in Capitalist and Communist Societies* (London, 1971), p. 82. Emphasis in text.

41. For an interesting account of the struggle to disseminate Marxism in Britain in the years following the Bolshevik Revolution, see S. MacIntyre, *A Proletarian Science: Marxism in Britain, 1917-1933* (Cambridge, 1980).

42. Note in this connection, in relation to the PCI, that 'the central unit in charge of the National Party School had only held three national conferences in the thirty years between 1945 and 1975. It then held two conferences in 1976–1977. The last of these focused entirely on the problems facing the party in the wake of its electoral victories and organizational expansion' (S. Hellman, 'Italian Communism in Crisis', in *The Socialist Register, 1988* (London, 1988), p. 264.

Chapter 4

1. Movements based on the 'moral majority' in the United States and proto-fascist movements such as the National Front in France are also, in a sense, 'new social movements', in so far as they function outside the existing party system. But the label has generally been applied to movements located at one point or another on the left spectrum, and is used here in this sense.

   Nationalist movements engaged in armed struggle, as in Northern Ireland or the Basque country, tend to see themselves as on the Left, and as engaged in a class as well as a national struggle. But they are not generally taken to be part of new social movements, and are not discussed in this chapter.

2. The question also arises of the status of crime in this connection. Free from any political or public connotation or purpose, crime, e.g. robbery, rape, or murder, is clearly not part of class struggle, even though crime and the response to it cannot be understood outside their class context. There are, however, many forms of activity which constitute alleged or real infractions of the law, and which are an intrinsic part of class struggle, such as alleged offences committed on the picket-line or a vast range of political activities which the state has 'criminalized'. As noted, armed struggle may also be part of class struggle, and often has been.

3. Such destabilization was also the aim of small terrorist groups with revolutionary ambitions, such as the Red Brigades in Italy, the Baader-Meinhof Group in the Federal German Republic, and other such groups in various advanced capitalist countries. These groups have certainly had an impact, though in the opposite direction to what they wanted, since their activities have mainly served to legitimate the reinforcement of the police and military apparatus of the state.

4. Many feminists insist on other significant differences in the women's movement, e.g. between black and other feminists, lesbians and others, etc. Note also the emergence of 'conservative feminism' in recent years, as represented in the writings of Betty Friedan, *The*

Second Stage (New York, 1981). Jean Bethke Elsthain, *Public Man, Private Woman: Women in Social and Political Thought* (Princeton, 1981), and Germaine Greer, *Sex and Destiny: The Politics of Human Fertility* (New York, 1984). On this current, see J. Stacey, 'Are Feminists Afraid to Leave Home? The Challenge of Conservative Pro-Family Feminism', in J. Mitchell and A. Oakley, eds., *What is Feminism?* (London, 1986).

5. For a virulent (but not very convincing) rejection of any such view, and of the very notion of 'bourgeois women', see C. Delphy, *Close to Home: A Materialist Analysis of Women's Oppression* (London, 1984).

6. F. Parkin, *Class Inequality and Political Order* (London, 1971), p. 15. Emphasis in text.

7. R. McDonough and R. Harrison, 'Patriarchy and Relations of Production', in A. Kuhn and A. Wolpe, eds., *Feminism and Materialism* (London, 1978), p. 36. My emphasis.

8. Z. Eisenstein, 'Reform and/or Revolution: Towards a Unified Women's Movement', in L. Sargent, ed., *Women and Revolution: A Discussion of the Unhappy Marriage of Marxism and Feminism* (Boston, 1981), p. 341).

9. A. M. Jaggar and P. S. Rothenberg, eds., *Feminist Frameworks* (New York, 1984), p. xiv.

10. V. Burstyn, 'Masculine Dominance and the State', in *The Socialist Register, 1983* (London, 1983), p. 46.

11. G. Lerner, *The Creation of Patriarchy* (New York, 1986), p. 89. 'From its inception in slavery,' she also notes, 'class dominance took different forms for enslaved men and women: men were primarily exploited as workers; women were always exploited as workers, as providers of sexual services, and as reproducers' (ibid., p. 214).

12. The term 'black' does not of course encompass the differences in the patterns of oppression and exploitation of different communities, for instance, of Caribbean as compared to Indian or Pakistani men and women.

13. 'The almost complete unanimity with which trade unions virulently opposed the entry of women into their craft [in the nineteenth century in Britain] was part and parcel of a general attempt to limit potentially ruinous competition from labour willing to work at reduced rates . . . It is quite clear that when unions were unable to exclude women, a rapid depression of wages and general degradation of work resulted' (J. Brenner and M. Ramas, 'Rethinking Women's Oppression', in *New Left Review*, 144 (Mar.–Apr. 1984), 45).

14. E. Wilson and A. Weir, 'The British Women's Movement', in *New Left Review*, 148 (Nov.–Dec. 1984), 87.

Chapter 5

1. See below, pp. 162 ff.
2. M. Davis, *Prisoners of the American Dream* (London, 1985), p. 109. See also e.g. R. M. Pfeffer, *Working for Capitalism* (New York, 1979).
3. J. Halliday, *A Political History of Japanese Capitalism* (New York, 1975), p. 228. A comparative study of British and Japanese factories by Ronald Dore takes a much more favourable view of Japanese industrial relations, but notes (in relation to Hitachi) that 'plausible stories are told of co-operation between union and management in keeping communists out of the company, giving them punitive out-postings, or if they show signs of repentance, giving them jobs on condition that they do not meddle in union affairs' (R. Dore, *British Factory, Japanese Factory: The Origins of National Diversity in Industrial Relations* (London, 1973), p. 172). Such 'stories' are not likely to be peculiar to Hitachi; and 'communist' is a conveniently elastic label.
4. Such attempts go back a long way. 'In the years before 1914 German big business had laid increasing stress on indirect techniques of integration and discipline which had enabled it to avoid direct confrontation with labour. Through company pension funds, bonuses, works' magazines, anniversary celebrations, lectures and other welfare benefits, employers had tried to generate employee loyalty and, dependence and in this way reduce the opportunities for trade union influence' (J. Kocka, *Facing Total War: German Society 1914–1918* (Leamington Spa, 1984), p. 71).
5. M. Burawoy, *The Politics of Production* (London, 1985), p. 150. Emphasis in text.
6. R. Hyman, 'Occupational Structure, Collective Organisation and Industrial Militancy', in C. Crouch and A. Pizzorno, eds., *The Resurgence of Class Conflict in Europe since 1968* (London, 1978), p. 58.
7. Thus the Royal Commission on Trade Unions and Employers' Associations noted in 1968 that shop stewards 'may be striving to bring some order into a chaotic situation, and management may rely heavily on their efforts to do so . . . quite commonly they are supporters of order exercising a restraining influence on their members in conditions which produce disorder' (Royal Commission on Trade Unions and Employers' Associations, 1965–8, Cmd. 3623, para. 110, p. 28).
8. Davis, *American Dream*, p. 116.
9. In 1962, 'there were 60,000 full-time, salaried union officials in the United States (one for every 300 workers), as contrasted to 4,000 in

Britain (one for 2,000) or 900 in Sweden (one for 1,700)' (ibid., p. 116).

10. Ibid., p. 139. CETA stands for Comprehensive Employment and Training Act. See also K. Moody, 'Reagan, the Business Agenda and the Collapse of Labour', in *The Socialist Register, 1987, Conservatism in Britain and America: Rhetoric and Reality* (London, 1987).

11. One of its provisions bans the closed shop altogether, another effectively bans Communists from union office.

12. Lord Wedderburn, *The Worker and the Law* (3rd edn., London, 1986), p. 69.

13. Ibid., p. 70.

14. See e.g. H. Beynon, ed., *Digging Deeper* (London, 1985), B. Fine and R. Millar, eds., *Policing the Miner's Strike* (London, 1985), and J. Coulter, S. Miller, and M. Walker, *State of Siege* (London, 1984).

15. See e.g. K. Jeffery and P. Hennessy, *States of Emergency: British Governments and Strike-breaking since 1919* (London, 1983).

16. See R. Miliband, 'Activism and Capitalist Democracy', in C. Harlow, ed., *Public Law and Politics* (London, 1986).

17. Such aspirations, however, long antedate World War II. Thus Keith Middlemas notes, in relation to Britain, that, on the basis of the experience of World War I, 'a sufficient number of union and employers' leaders had accepted the need for formal collaboration with the state'. But, he adds, 'the claims of governing institutions to a share of state power and enhanced status rested on *their acceptance of fundamental national aims and their abandonment in practice (though not on the public platform) of the ideology of class conflict* (K. Middlemas, *Politics in Industrial Society: The Experience of the British System since 1911* (London, 1979), pp. 20, 21; emphasis added).

18. For an excellent 'theorization' of corporatism, see L. Panitch, *Working Class Politics in Crisis: Essays on Labour and the State* (London, 1986), chs. 5, 6, 7.

19. P. Schmitter, 'Still the Century of Corporatism?', in P. Schmitter and G. Lehmbruch, eds., *Trends Towards Corporatist Intermediation* (London, 1979), pp. 107–8.

20. D. R. Cameron, 'Social Democracy, Corporatism, Labour Quiescence and the Representation of Economic Interest in Advanced Capitalist Society', in J. H. Goldthorpe, ed., *Order and Conflict in Contemporary Capitalism* (Oxford, 1984), p. 146.

21. *The Economist*, 7 Mar. 1987, p. 19.

22. R. J. Flanagan, D. W. Soskice, and L. Ulman, *Unionism, Economic Stabilization, and Incomes Policies: European Experience* (Washington, 1983), p. 1. Emphasis added.

23. Panitch, 'The Development of Corporatism in Liberal Democracies', in *Working Class Politics in Crisis*, p. 137.

24. J. H. Goldthorpe, 'The End of Convergence: Corporatist and Dualist Tendencies in Modern Western Societies', in Goldthorpe, *Order and Conflict*, p. 339.

25. Flanagan *et al.*, *Unionism, Economic Stabilization, and Incomes Policies*, p. 3.

26. M. Kalecki, 'Political Aspects of Full Employment', in *Selected Essays on the Dynamics of the Capitalist Economy, 1933–1970* (Cambridge, 1971), p. 140.

27. D. A. Hibbs, jun., 'Political Parties and Macro-economic Policy', in *American Political Science Review*, lxxi. 4 (Dec. 1977), 1487.

28. For a useful discussion of the issue, see G. Therborn, *Why Some People Are More Unemployed than Others* (London, 1986).

29. Note Ian Gough's remark that 'the very term the welfare state reveals the ideological nature of most writing about it' (*The Political Economy of the Welfare State* (London, 1979), p. 3); also J. Krieger: 'There is no welfare state, only a set of welfare provisions' (*Reagan, Thatcher and the Politics of Decline* (Cambridge, 1986), p. 200).

30. See Chapter 6.

31. For surveys of the different aspects of the Reagan and Thatcher regimes, see e.g. *The Socialist Register, 1987*.

32. F. F. Piven and R. A. Cloward, *The New Class War* (New York, 1980), p. 8.

33. See e.g. J. L. Palmer and I. V. Sawhill, *The Reagan Record: An Assessment of America's Changing Priorities* (Cambridge, Mass., 1984), ch. 6.

34. D. Hall, *The Cuts Machine: The Politics of Public Expenditure* (London, 1983), p. 9.

35. J. Westergaard and H. Resler, *Class in a Capitalist Society: A Study of Contemporary Britain* (London, 1975), p. 59.

36. J. Cohen and J. Rogers, ' "Reaganism" After Reagan', in *The Socialist Register, 1988, Problems of Socialist Renewal: East and West* (London, 1988), pp. 400–1. Emphasis in text.

37. Ibid., p. 395.

38. J. Rentoul, *The Rich Get Richer: The Growth of Inequality in Britain in the 1980s* (London, 1987), p. 49.

39. L. C. Thurow, 'The Dishonest Economy', in *The New York Review of Books*, 21 Nov. 1985. In France tax evasion in 1985 was estimated to amount to 44 billion francs for VAT, 15 billion francs for company taxation, and 58 billion francs for income tax (J.-P. Jean, 'Le Libéralisme authoritaire', in *Le Monde diplomatique*, Oct. 1987, p. 16 n. 11.). The first two figures refer exclusively to business, the

third may be taken to refer predominantly to higher-income groups.

40. In 1983, fraud investigators of the Department of Health and Social Security, aided by the Thames Valley police, engaged in an 'Operation Sting' in Oxford and rounded up 283 claimants. Charges were made against 179 of them; and whereas the operation was claimed to have uncovered a £15 million fraud, the resulting prosecutions concerned amounts totalling £20,000. The operation itself cost £180,000. (M. Loney, 'A War on Poverty or on the Poor?', in A. and C. Walker, eds., *The Growing Divide: A Social Audit, 1979–1987* (London, 1987), p. 13.)

41. Quoted by J. Blum, *The End of the Old Regime in Rural Europe* (Princeton, 1978), p. 5. Note also Marx: 'The advance of capitalist production develops a working class which by education, tradition and habit looks upon the requirements of that mode of production as self-evident natural laws' (*Capital* (London, 1976), i. 899).

42. B. Brecht, 'The Other Germany', in *Gesammelte Werke*, xx (Frankfurt, 1967), 283–9, quoted in B. Frankel, *Beyond the State?: Dominant Theories and Socialist Strategies* (London, 1983), p. 2.

43. A. Bevan, *In Place of Fear* (London, 1952), p. 6.

44. E. J. Hobsbawm, 'Mass-Producing Traditions: Europe, 1870–1914', in E. J. Hobsbawm and T. Ranger, eds., *The Invention of Tradition* (Cambridge, 1983), p. 267.

45. Ibid., p. 268.

46. For an extended analysis of the phenomenon, see *The Socialist Register, 1984, The Uses of Anti-communism* (London, 1984).

47. Piven and Cloward, *The New Class War*, p. 9.

48. See e.g. S. P. Sethi, *Advocacy Advertising and Large Corporations: Social Conflict, Big Business Image, the News Media, and Public Policy* (Lexington, Mass., 1977).

49. Edsall, *The New Politics of Inequality* (New York, 1984), p. 111. On the same lines, D. Vogel writes that 'beginning in the mid-1970s, a number of firms made extensive efforts to mobilize their "natural constituencies", meaning their stockholders and present and former employees' ('The Power of Business in America: A Reappraisal', in *British Journal of Political Science*, xiii. 1 (Jan. 1983), 33).

50. Edsall, *New Politics*, p. 109.

51. Ibid., p. 110.

52. M. Useem, *The Inner Circle: Large Corporations and the Rise of Political Activity in the US and the UK* (London, 1984), p. 87.

53. Ibid., p. 25.

54. Ibid.

55. K. Marx and F. Engels, *The German Ideology*, in *Collected Works* (London, 1976), v. 60.

56. Ibid., p. 59.
57. Marx, *Capital*, i. 97.
58. See e.g. Noam Chomsky's detailed and searing indictment of American scholars on the subject of American interventionism in Vietnam and elsewhere, in *American Power and the New Mandarins* (London, 1969), *Towards a New Cold War* (New York, 1982), and other works.
59. H. Schiller, *The Mind Managers* (Boston, 1973), p. 49.
60. For accounts of the process in Britain in recent years, see e.g. J. Margach, *The Abuse of Power: The War between Downing Street and the Media from Lloyd George to Callaghan* (London, 1978); A. May and K. Rowan, *Inside Information: British Government and the Media* (London, 1982), and M. Cockerell, P. Hennessy, and D. Walker, *Sources Close to the Prime Minister: Inside the Hidden World of the News Manipulators* (London, 1985).
61. The distinction I make between 'authoritarian' and 'fascist' regimes is based on the fact that fascist regimes are supported by well-organized and highly structured mass movements, whereas authoritarian regimes are not. Defined thus, only Mussolini's Italy and Hitler's Germany have had, properly speaking, fascist regimes. Franco in Spain was much less successful with the Falange in this respect. However, the similarities between authoritarian and fascist regimes are so marked in all other respects as to rob the distinction of much of its significance.
62. H. A. Turner, jun., *German Big Business and the Rise of Hitler* (New York, 1985).
63. See e.g. H. D. Lasswell and D. Lerner, eds., *World Revolutionary Elites* (Westport, Conn., 1966), ch. 5. One member of the Kaiser's family, Prince August Wilhelm, 'was an early party member and a very public supporter of Hitler' (R. F. Hamilton, *Who Voted for Hitler?* (Princeton, NJ, 1982), p. 413). Prince Wilhelm the Crown Prince gave his public and unqualified support to the Nazi Party after the presidential election of November 1932 (ibid.).
64. 'Those business executives who gave public expression to their alarm in that regard remained exceptions' (Turner, *German Big Business*, p. 253).
65. Ibid.
66. Turner, *German Big Business*, pp. 329 ff.
67. Ibid., p. 322.
68. Ibid., pp. 115 ff. 'Endorsement' must obviously be taken to mean that the manufacturers paid the Nazis for the endorsement of these goods.
69. Professor Richard Hamilton describes the Deutschnazionale Volkspartei as 'a conservative, nationalist, monarchist and antirepublican

party', and the Deutsche Volkspartei as '*the* party of the industrial bourgeoisie', with 'a major segment of the party' working for 'the abandonment of liberal principles, wishing to make common cause with the demagogic right' (Hamilton, *Who Voted for Hitler?*, pp. 233, 240, 245; emphasis in text).

70. Turner, *German Big Business*, p. 193.

71. Hamilton, *Who Voted for Hitler?*, p. 401.

72. Ibid., p. 401. The reference is to H. A. Turner, jun., 'Big Business and the Rise of Hitler', in *American Historical Review*, lxxv (1969-70), 66.

73. Turner, *German Big Business*, p. 348. Emphasis added.

74. Ibid., p. 338.

75. R. O. Paxton, *Vichy France: Old Guard and New Order, 1940-1944* (New York, 1982), p. xii.

76. A. Werth, *France, 1940-55* (1956), p. 23.

77. The majority of the French people also supported Pétain and the Vichy regime in 1940, and for some time thereafter. They were merely following the lead of the traditional elites, and were subjected to a massive propaganda campaign on behalf of Pétain and Vichy, with a 'cult of personality' that yielded nothing in hysterical quality to the cult of Stalin in the USSR.

78. 'Beyond the Milice wide sections of the French Establishment collaborated by no means unenthusiastically in the deportation to forced labour of millions of French workers, the murder of 90,000 French Jews (rounded up, frequently, by French police), the parallel murders of thousands of Communists, Socialists, gypsies and freemasons, and so on' (R. W. Johnson, *The Long March of the French Left* (London, 1981), p. 289 n. 4).

79. In addition to Paxton, *Vichy France*, see R. Aron and G. Elgey, *The Vichy Regime, 1940-44* (London, 1958), M. Cotta, *La Collaboration 1940-1944* (Paris, 1963), and P. Novick, *The Resistance versus Vichy* (London, 1968).

80. In exceptional circumstances, even well-implanted formations of the Left become subject to fierce repression, within a suitably strengthened but still capitalist-democratic state, e.g. in the case noted in Chapter 3 of Communists in France in the period between the outbreak of war in September 1939 and defeat in June 1940.

81. See e.g. R. J. Goldstein, *Political Repression in 19th Century Europe* (London, 1983); and by the same author, Political Repression in Modern America from 1870 to the Present (Cambridge, Mass., 1978).

82. E. W. Schrecker, *No Ivory Tower: McCarthyism and the Universities* (New York, 1986), p. 5.

83. S. I. Kutler, *The American Inquisition: Justice and Injustice in the Cold War* (New York, 1982), p. 181. The trial of the Communist leaders was also notable for the hounding and harassment of counsel for the accused, with the full support and involvement of judges and the American Bar Association, and to the enormous personal, monetary, and professional cost of the lawyers concerned.

84. For a detailed account, see F. J. Donner, *The Age of Surveillance: The Aims and Methods of America's Political Intelligence System* (New York, 1980).

85. For an excellent survey, see R. Whitaker, 'Fighting the Cold War on the Home Front: America, Britain, Australia and Canada', in *The Socialist Register, 1984*.

86. The *Guardian*, 31 Jan. 1975.

87. Ibid. It was indeed the Wilson Labour Government which had defined political activity coming within the purview of the Special Branch as 'activities which threaten the safety or wellbeing of the state and are intended to undermine or overthrow parliamentary democracy by political, industrial or violent means'.

88. W. Graf, 'Anti-communism in the Federal Republic of Germany', in *The Socialist Register, 1984*, p. 194.

89. See e.g. D. Caute, *The Great Fear: The Anti-Communist Purge under Truman and Eisenhower* (New York, 1978).

90. The system of proscription was formally abandoned in 1972.

91. Even these are not immune. Note, for instance, the belief of members of the security services in Britain in the sixties that the Wilson Government was itself a threat to 'national security', and their efforts to destabilize it. See e.g. P. Wright, *Spycatcher* (New York, 1986) and D. Leigh, *The Wilson Plot* (London, 1988).

92. H. Beynon, ed., *Digging Deeper*, p. 60.

93. C. L. Rossiter, *Constitutional Dictatorship: Crisis Government in the Modern Democracies* (2nd edn., Princeton, 1967).

94. P. Furlong, 'Political Terrorism in Italy: Responses, Reaction and Immobilism', in J. Lodge, ed., *Terrorism: A Challenge to the State* (Oxford, 1981).

Chapter 6

1. A. J. Mayer, *Politics and Diplomacy of Peacemaking: Containment and Counter-revolution at Versailles, 1918-1919* (London, 1967), p. 9. At a meeting of the British War Cabinet in November 1918, Mayer also notes, the Prime Minister, Lloyd George, 'called attention to the importance of generating public support for these policies of containment and counter-revolution' (ibid., p. 313).

2. This was the short-lived regime of Bela Kun, whose overthrow was followed by a murderous White Terror and the installation of a proto-fascist regime that lasted until 1944.
3. When the first minority Labour Government in Britain restored diplomatic relations with the Soviet Union in 1924, one of the stipulations it made was that the Soviet Union should not engage in Communist propaganda in any British colonial territory.
4. For the distinctly favourable view which many members of the dominant class in Britain, including members of the power elite, took of the Fascists and the Nazis in the inter-war years, see R. Griffiths, *Fellow Travellers of the Right* (London, 1980).
5. Professor Mayer makes the point that the Nazi–Soviet Pact of August 1939 was 'a concomitant of the prior Munich agreement' (*Policy and Diplomacy of Peacemaking*, p. 18).
6. The French Government, corroded by defeatism as regards Germany, was full of determination as regards Russia, and made much of the fact that a large French army was concentrated in the Middle East, facing Russia's Caucasian border.
7. In the General Election campaign in Britain in 1987, Mrs Thatcher was insisting that 'of course, there is and will continue to be a Soviet threat. I find it astonishing that anyone should suggest that there is not, particularly when you look at the Soviet military might' (The *Independent*, 29 May 1987).
8. W. S. Churchill, *Triumph and Tragedy* (London, 1953), pp. 225–9; and D. Yergin, *Shattered Peace: The Origins of the Cold War and the National Security State* (Boston, Mass., 1978), p. 60.
9. Hungary and Romania had been allies of Germany in the war.
10. E. H. Carr, *The Twilight of Comintern, 1930–1935* (London, 1982), p. 151.
11. J. Haslam, *The Soviet Union and the Struggle for Collective Security in Europe, 1933–1939* (London, 1984), p. 34.
12. Stalin himself made the point as follows in an interview in *Pravda* in March 1946, following Churchill's Fulton speech: 'The Germans made their invasion of the USSR through Finland, Poland, Rumania, Bulgaria and Hungary. The Germans were able to make their invasion through these countries because, at the time, governments hostile to the Soviet Union existed in these countries . . . And so what can there be surprising about the fact that the Soviet Union, anxious for its future safety, is trying to see to it that governments loyal in their attitude to the Soviet Union should exist in these countries?' (L. G. Churchward, *Contemporary Soviet Government* (London, 1975), pp. 253–4).
13. According to Roy Medvedev, 'Stalin seriously considered plans for

the invasion of Yugoslavia from Soviet Armenia, but ultimately could not bring himself to embark on such a risky venture. Instead he decided to rely on the creation of underground groups in Yugoslavia through which he could organise Tito's murder' (R. A. Medvedev, *On Stalin and Stalinism* (London, 1979), p. 145).

14. J. H. Billington, 'Finland', in C. E. Black and T. P. Thornton, eds., *Communism and Revolution: The Strategic Uses of Political Violence* (Princeton, 1965), p. 130).

15. See e.g. H. Richter, *British Intervention in Greece* (London, 1986); L. S. Wittner, *American Intervention in Greece, 1943–1949* (New York, 1982); S. G. Xydis, *Greece and the Great Powers, 1944–47: Prelude to the 'Truman Doctrine'* (Thessaloniki, 1963).

16. At the meeting between Churchill and Stalin in Moscow in October 1944, Stalin had also agreed that the Soviet Union should 'soft-pedal the Communists in Italy and not . . . stir up trouble' (Yergin, *Shattered Peace*, p. 60).

17. Medvedev, *On Stalin and Stalinism*, p. 186.

18. R. Steel, *Pax Americana* (London, 1968), p. 129.

19. *The Independent*, 4 May 1987.

20. V. V. Aspaturian, 'Eastern Europe in World Perspective', in T. Rakowska-Harmstone, ed., *Communism in Eastern Europe* (2nd edn., Manchester, 1984), p. 18.

21. Ibid., p. 39. Also, 'during the period 1955–79, nearly 120,000 students from less-developed countries were reached by . . . academic assistance programs'; and 'approximately 72,000 students from the Third World were enrolled in Soviet and East European universities at the end of 1981, with nearly one half in Eastern Europe. Africa provided the largest contingent (about 50 per cent)' (ibid.).

22. 'The so-called Cold War . . . was far less the confrontation of the United States with Russia than America's expansion into the entire world—a world the Soviet Union neither controlled nor created' (G. and J. Kolko, *The Limits of Power: The World and United States Foreign Policy, 1945–1954* (New York, 1972), p. 2).

23. B. Donoughue, *Prime Minister: The Conduct of Policy under Harold Wilson and James Callaghan* (London, 1987), p. 93.

24. Ibid., p. 94. Donoughue also writes: 'The broad policies which are now characterised as "Thatcherism", together with the now familiar language, were in fact launched, in primitive form, at Mr Callaghan from the Treasury, the Bank, and above all from the IMF and sections of the US treasury' (ibid.).

25. See e.g. W. James, 'The IMF and Democratic Socialism in Jamaica', in W. E. Brett *et al.*, *The Poverty Brokers* (1983), and F. Ambursley, 'Jamaica: The Demise of "Democratic Socialism" ', in *New Left Review*, 128 (July–Aug. 1981).

26. There is a sixth situation where intervention of a sort occurs, in the form of help to Communist regimes—e.g. Yugoslavia after 1948—which have turned against the Soviet Union; and help is also extended to some new left-wing regimes—e.g. in Africa—in the hope that they might be brought back into the capitalist fold.

27. W. Blum, *The CIA: A Forgotten History: US Global Interventions since World War II* (London, 1986), p. 116.

28. Ibid., p. 114.

29. P. Agee and L. Wolf, eds., *Dirty Work: The CIA in Western Europe* (Secaucus, NJ, 1978), p. 19.

30. P. Agee, *Inside the Company: CIA Diary* (London, 1975), p. 74.

31. For details of the American campaign, see Blum, *The CIA*, pp. 23 ff. A number of Labour MPs sent a telegram of good wishes for success in the election to Pietro Nenni. The National Executive Committee of the Labour Party summoned them to undertake individually that they would cease 'acting as a group in organized opposition to Party policy', failing which they would be expelled from the Party. The assurances were given. The 'Nenni telegram' was an important milestone in the taming of the Labour Left by the Labour leadership in the post-war years.

32. Blum, *The CIA*, p. 130. J. Barkan writes that 'during the 1950s, U.S. strategic services spent between $20 m and $30 m in each year to finance anti-communist political parties, unions, newspapers and other institutions in Italy' (*Visions of Emancipation: The Italian Workers' Movement since 1945* (New York, 1984), p. 47).

33. *The Times*, 19 July 1976; *Le Monde*, 20 July 1976.

34. Z. Brzezinski, *Power and Principle: Memoirs of the National Security Adviser, 1977-1981* (New York, 1983), pp. 311-12.

35. The Unification Church of the Reverend Moon, for instance, is not usually taken to be a 'political' organization, and certainly does not describe itself as such. But it is all the same one of the most important private organizations of the extreme Right in the world, with immense financial resources, industrial plants, fishing-fleets, publishing and printing houses, networks of newspapers in Latin and North America (notably the *Washington Times*), and powerful friends among the power elites of many countries, including President Reagan and General Pinochet. See e.g. J.-F. Boyer and A. Alem, 'L'Internationale Moon', in *Le Monde diplomatique*, Feb. 1985.

36. J. Petras, 'The Contradictions of Greek Socialism', in *New Left Review*, 163 (May-June 1987), 4.

37. Kolko, *Limits of Power*, p. 221.

38. Wittner, *American Intervention*, p. 32.

39. Kolko, *Limits of Power*, pp. 219 ff.

40. Blum, *The CIA*, pp. 246–7.

41. A case in point is Honduras, the second poorest country after Haiti in the Western Hemisphere and a base of operations of the *contras* and the United States against Nicaragua. A recent traveller there writes: 'I travelled with a priest by mule as he brought the sacraments to his scattered flock. There are no roads, no doctors, no medicines, no electricity, few schools, and much disease. The *campesinos* live in hovels, without potable water, and the children are infested with parasites that stunt their growth' (E. R. F. Sheehan, 'The Country of Nada', in *New York Review of Books*, 27 Mar. 1986, p. 11).

42. One of the guerrilla leaders engaged in the abortive peace talks with the Aquino government put the difference between the two sides as follows: 'There are liberal reactionaries, like Cory [Aquino] who define peace as an end to the fighting, but with no solution to the people's basic needs. Our definition is peace based on justice and democracy, a principled peace based on solving the poverty, powerlessness and neo-colonial domination which are the root causes of the insurgency' (J. Steele, 'Ka Vicvic Goes back to War in the Hills', The *Guardian*, 20 Feb. 1987).

43. It was the same kind of fear which, more than thirty years later, fuelled the overtures and sales of arms to the Khomeini regime in 1986, which produced the Irangate fiasco.

44. Blum, *The CIA*, p. 74.

45. In March 1950, George Kennan, then the State Department's expert on Soviet affairs, had addressed United States ambassadors in South America and had told them that under no circumstances must Communists be allowed in power: 'The final answer might be an unpleasant one, but . . . we should not hesitate before police repression by the local government. This is not shameful since the Communists are essentially traitors . . . It is better to have a strong regime in power than a liberal government if it is indulgent and relaxed and penetrated by Communists' (W. LaFeber, *Inevitable Revolutions: The United States in Central America* (New York, 1984), p. 107).

46. Ibid., p. 119.

47. On the coup in Guatemala, see also S. Schlesinger and S. Kinzer, *Bitter Fruit: The Untold Story of the American Coup in Guatemala* (New York, 1982) and R. H. Immerman, *The CIA in Guatemala: The Foreign Policy of Intervention* (Austin, Texas, 1982).

48. It was also in 1965 that there occurred one of the bloodiest episodes of the post-war years, namely, the massacre of hundreds of thousands of members of the Indonesian Communist Party and its supporters (or alleged supporters), following an abortive *coup* by generals in

which Communists were claimed to have been involved. The massacre and the annihilation of the Indonesian Communist Party (the largest in the world outside the Communist countries) was an Indonesian enterprise; but those who were responsible for it had the encouragement and support of the CIA, which had a strong presence in Indonesia. (On this, see e.g. B. May, *The Indonesian Tragedy* (London, 1978)).

49. 'At least $20 million in support of the Frei candidacy—about $8 per voter—was funneled into Chile by the United States in 1963 and 1964, much of it through the Agency for International Development (AID)' (S. M. Hersh, *Kissinger: The Price of Power* (London, 1983), p. 260). Hersh also notes that Frei received further help from American corporations via the Business Group for Latin America, organized in 1964 by David Rockefeller, chairman of Chase Manhattan Bank, and also from ITT.

50. P. E. Sigmund, *The Overthrow of Allende and the Politics of Chile, 1964-1976* (London, 1977), p. 103.

51. The United States ambassador, William Korry, for instance, warned that 'not a nut or bolt shall reach Chile under Allende. Once Allende comes to power we shall do all within our power to condemn Chile and all Chileans to utmost deprivation and poverty' (H. Sklar, ed., *Trilateralism: The Trilateral Commission and Elite Planning for World Management* (Boston, 1980), p. 29).

52. J. F. Petras and M. M. Morley, *How Allende Fell* (Nottingham, 1974), p. 11.

53. See Kolko, *Limits of Power*, pp. 574 ff.; and J. Halliday, 'Anticommunism and the Korean War', in *The Socialist Register, 1984*, pp. 135 ff.

54. The British made an important contribution in the autumn of 1945 to the restoration of French rule in Indo-China—a contribution which involved the use of recently defeated and captured Japanese troops. See J. Saville, 'Ernest Bevin and the Cold War, 1945-1950', in *The Socialist Register, 1984, pp. 77 ff.*, and G. Rosie, *The British in Vietnam: How the Twenty-Five Year War Began* (London, 1970).

55. By 1954, the United States was paying for some 80 per cent of the cost of the war: France could not have prosecuted the war for so long without this help.

56. D. Horowitz, *From Yalta to Vietnam: American Foreign Policy in the Cold War* (London, 1969), p. 153.

Chapter 7

1. K. Marx, *Capital* (London, 1976), i. 929.
2. Ibid.
3. Ibid.

Notes

4. W. Brus, *Socialist Ownership and Political Systems* (London, 1975), pp. 17–18. Emphasis in text.
5. See e.g. R. Murray, 'Ownership, Control and the Market', in *New Left Review*, 164 (July–Aug. 1987).
6. A. Callinicos, 'Exception or Symptom? The British Crisis and the World System', in *New Left Review*, 169 (May–June 1988), 102.
7. On the recent problems of the French Communist Party, see G. Ross, 'Organization and Strategy in the Decline of French Communism', in *The Socialist Register, 1988.*
8. A blatant example of this class logic is provided by the Reagan Administration's insistence that the Sandinista Government of Nicaragua, faced with an armed rebellion financed and directed by the United States, should accord the fullest democratic rights to its enemies, including rebels in the field and others openly preaching rebellion. It is not difficult to imagine how the government of the United States, or any other, faced with anything like the same threat (or even a much lesser threat) would handle the question of democratic rights for its opponents. Indeed, examples abound of ruthless response to even *imagined* threats: e.g. the mass deportation from the West Coast and internment of American citizens of Japanese origin after the entry of the United States into the war in 1941.
9. K. Marx and F. Engels, *The Manifesto of the Communist Party*, in K. Marx and F. Engels, *Collected Works* (London, 1976), vi. 506.

Bibliography

ABERCROMBIE, N. and URRY, J., *Capital, Labour and the Middle Classes* (London, 1983).

ABRAMS, P., ed., *Work, Urbanisation and Inequality* (London, 1978).

ANDERSON, P., *Passages from Antiquity to Feudalism* (London, 1975).

—— *Lineages of the Absolutist State* (London, 1975).

—— *Arguments within English Marxism* (London, 1980).

ARMSTRONG, P. GLYN, A., and HARRISON, J., *Capitalism since World War II: The Making and Breakup of the Great Boom* (London, 1984).

ASTON, T. H., and PHILPIN, C. H. E., eds., *The Brenner Debate* (Cambridge, 1985).

BACHRACH, P., *The Theory of Democratic Elitism: A Critique* (London, 1969).

BARRETT, M., *Women's Oppression Today: Problems in Marxist Feminist Analysis* (London, 1980).

BAUMAN, Z., *Socialism: The Active Utopia* (London, 1976).

—— *Memories of Class: The Pre-history and After-life of Class* (London, 1982).

BEETHAM, D., *Marxism in the Face of Fascism* (London, 1983).

BENDIX, R., and LIPSET, S. M., *Class, Status and Powers* (2nd edn., New York, 1966).

BERGER, S., ed., *Organizing Interests in Western Europe: Pluralism, Corporatism, and the Transformation of Politics* (New York, 1981).

BERTAUX, D., *Destins personnels et structure de classe: Pour une critique de l'anthroponomie politique* (Paris, 1977).

BLACKBURN, R., ed., *Revolution and Class Struggle: A Reader in Marxist Politics* (Hassocks, 1978).

BLACKMER, D. L. M. and TARROW, S., eds., *Communism in France and Italy* (Princeton, 1975).

BLUM, W., *The CIA: A Forgotten History: US Global Interventions since World War II* (London, 1986).

BOGGS, J., *Racism and the Class Struggle* (New York, 1970).

BOTTOMORE, T. B., *Classes in Modern Society* (London, 1965).

—— *Elites and Society* (London, 1966).

BRAVERMAN, H., *Labor and Monopoly Capital* (New York, 1974).

BRUNHOFF, S. DE, *The State, Capital and Economic Policy* (London, 1978).

BURAWOY, M., *The Politics of Production* (London, 1985).

CARILLO, S., *Eurocommunism and the State* (London, 1977).

CASTLES, F. G., *The Social Democratic Image of Society* (London, 1978).

CAUTE, D., *The Great Fear: The Anti-Communist Purge under Truman and Eisenhower* (London, 1978).

CHANDLER, A. D., jun., *Visible Hand: Managerial Revolution in American Business* (Cambridge, Mass., 1977).

CLAUDIN, F., *The Communist Movement from the Comintern to the Cominform* (London, 1975).

CLAWSON, D., *Bureaucracy and the Labor Process* (New York, 1980).

COHEN, G. A., *Karl Marx's Theory of History: A Defence* (London, 1978).

COTTRELL, A., *Social Classes and Marxist Theory* (London, 1984).

CROMPTON, R. and GUBBAY, J., *Economy and Class Structure* (London, 1977).

CROUCH, C., ed., *State and Economy in Contemporary Capitalism* (London, 1979).

—— and PIZZORNO, A. eds., *The Resurgence of Class Conflict in Europe since 1968* (London, 1978).

DAHRENDORF, R., *Class and Class Conflict in Industrial Society* (London, 1959).

DEUTSCHER, I., *Ironies of History* (London, 1966).

—— *Heretics and Renegades* (London, 1969).

DOMHOFF, G. W., *The Powers that Be: Processes of Ruling-Class Domination in America* (New York, 1978).

DRAPER, H., *Karl Marx's Theory of Revolution* (New York, 1977–8).

EDSALL, T. B., *The New Politics of Inequality* (New York, 1984).

EISENSTEIN, Z., ed., *Capitalist Patriarchy and the Case for Socialist Feminism* (New York, 1979).

ENGELS, F., *Introduction* to K. Marx's *The Class Struggles in France, 1848 to 1850*, in *Selected Works*, ii (Moscow, 1950).

FLORA, P. and HEIDENHEIMER, A. J., eds., *The Development of Welfare States in Europe and North America* (New Brunswick, NJ, 1980).

FRANKEL, B., *Beyond the State?: Dominant Theories and Socialist Strategies* (London, 1983).

FRÖBEL, F., et al., *The New International Division of Labour* (New York, 1980).

FRIEDMAN, A. L., *Industry and Labour: Class Struggle at Work and Monopoly Capitalism* (London, 1977).

GALLIE, D., *In Search of the New Working Class: Automation and Social Integration within the Capitalist Enterprise* (Cambridge, 1978).

GEARY, D., *European Labour Protest, 1848–1939* (London, 1981).

GERAS, N., *The Legacy of Rosa Luxemburg* (London, 1976).

GIDDENS, A., *The Class Structure of the Advanced Societies* (London, 1973).

—— *The Constitution of Society: Outline of the Theory of Structuration* (Oxford, 1984).

—— *A Contemporary Critique of Historical Materialism* i (London, 1981), ii (London, 1985).

—— and HELD, D., *Classes, Power, and Conflict* (London, 1982).

—— and MACKENZIE, G., *Social Class and the Division of Labour* (Cambridge, 1982).

—— and STANWORTH, P., *Elites and Power in British Society* (London, 1974).

GOLDSTEIN, R. J., *Political Repression in Modern America from 1870 to the Present* (Cambridge, Mass., 1978).

—— *Political Repression in 19th Century Europe* (London, 1983).

GOLDTHORPE, J. H., ed., *Order and Conflict in Contemporary Capitalism* (Oxford, 1984).

GORDON, D. M., EDWARDS, R., and REICH, M., *Segmented Work, Divided Workers: The Historical Transformation of Labor in the United States* (Cambridge, 1982).

GORZ, A., *Farewell to the Working Class: An Essay on Post-industrial Socialism* (London, 1982).

GOUGH, I., *The Political Economy of the Welfare State* (London, 1979).

GRAMSCI, A., *Selections from the Prison Notebooks* (London, 1971).

HALLIDAY, F., *The Making of the Second Cold War* (London, 1983).

HEIDENHEIMER, A., *et al.*, *Comparative Public Policy: The Politics of Social Choice in Europe and America* (New York, 1983).

HIMMELSTRAND, U., *et al.*, *Beyond Welfare Capitalism: Issues, Actors, and Forces in Societal Change* (London, 1981).

HOBSBAWM, E. J., *Labouring Men* (London, 1964).

—— *Worlds of Labour: Further Studies in the History of Labour* (London, 1984).

—— and RANGER, T., eds., *The Invention of Tradition* (Cambridge, 1983).

HUNT, A., ed., *Class and Class Structure* (London, 1977).

HYMAN, R., *Industrial Relations: A Marxist Introduction* (London, 1975).

—— *Strikes* (London, 1984).

—— and BROUGH, I., *Social Values and Industrial Relations: A Study of Fairness and Equality* (Oxford, 1975).

JEFFERY, K. and HENNESSY, P., *States of Emergency: British Governments and Strike-breaking since 1919* (London, 1983).

JOHNSON, R. W., *The Long March of the French Left* (London, 1982).

KATZNELSON, I., *City Trenches: Urban Politics and the Patterning of Class in the United States* (New York, 1981).

—— and ZOLLBERG, A., eds., *Working Class Formation: Nineteenth-Century Patterns in Western Europe and the United States* (Princeton, 1986).

KAUTSKY, K., *The Dictatorship of the Proletariat* (Ann Arbor, 1964).

—— *The Class Struggle* (New York, 1971).

KINDERSLEY, R., ed., *In Search of Eurocommunism* (London, 1981).

KOLKO, G., *The Politics of War: The World and United States Foreign Policy, 1943-1945.*
—— *Confronting the Third World: United States Foreign Policy, 1945-1980* (New York, 1988).
—— and KOLKO, J., *The Limits of Power: The World and United States Foreign Policy, 1945-1954* (New York, 1972).
KOLKO, J., *The Restructuring of the World Economy* (New York, 1988).
KORPI, W., *The Democratic Class Struggle* (London, 1983).
KUHN, A. and WOLPE, A., eds., *Feminism and Materialism* (London, 1978).
LACLAU, E., and MOUFFE, C., *Hegemony and Socialist Strategy. Towards a Radical Democratic Politics* (London, 1985).
LENIN, V. I., *Two Tactics of Social Democracy in the Democratic Revolution,* in *Selected Works* (London, 1969).
—— *The State and Revolution,* ibid.
—— *The Proletarian Revolution and the Renegade Kautsky,* ibid.
—— *'Left-Wing' Communism: An Infantile Disorder,* ibid.
LIEBICH, A., *The Future of Socialism in Europe* (Montreal, 1979).
LINDBERG, L., *et al., Stress and Contradiction in Modern Capitalism: Public Policy and the Theory of the State* (London, 1975).
LINZ, J. and STEPAN, A., eds., *The Breakdown of Democratic Regimes* (Baltimore, 1978).
LUKACS, G., *History and Class Consciousness* (London, 1967).
LUXEMBURG, R., *Rosa Luxemburg Speaks* (New York, 1970).
MANDEL, E., *Late Capitalism* (London, 1975).
MANN, M., *The Sources of Social Power,* i (London, 1986).
MARCEAU, J., *Class and Status in France: Economic Change and Social Immobility* (London and New York, 1977).
MARX, K., *The Class Struggles in France: 1848-1850,* in K. Marx and F. Engels, *Collected Works,* x (London, 1978).
—— *The Eighteenth Brumaire of Louis Bonaparte,* ibid., xi (London, 1979).
—— *The Civil War in France,* ibid.
—— *Capital* (London, 1976).
—— and ENGELS, F., *Manifesto of the Communist Party,* in K. Marx and F. Engels, *Collected Works,* vi (London, 1976).
MAYER, A. J., *Politics and Diplomacy of Peacemaking: Containment and Counter-revolution at Versailles, 1918-1919* (London, 1967).
—— *Dynamics of Counter-revolution in Europe, 1870-1956: An Analytic Framework* (New York, 1971).
MICHELS, R., *Political Parties* (London, 1915).
MILIBAND, R., *The State in Capitalist Society* (London, 1969).
—— *Marxism and Politics* (Oxford, 1977).
—— *Class Power and State Power* (London, 1985).
MILLS, C. W., *White Collar* (New York, 1951).

—— *The Power Elite* (New York, 1956).

MITCHELL, H. and STEARNS, P., *Workers and Protest: The European Labour Movement, the Working Classes and the Origins of Social Democracy, 1890–1914* (Itasca, Ill., 1971).

MITCHELL, J. and OAKLEY, A., eds., *What is Feminism?* (London, 1986).

NICHOLS, T., *Capital and Labour: Studies in the Capitalist Labour Process* (London, 1980).

—— and BEYNON, H., *Living with Capitalism: Class Relations and the Modern Factory* (London, 1977).

OFFE, C., *Contradictions of the Welfare State* (London, 1984).

PANITCH, L., *Social Democracy and Industrial Militancy: The Labour Party, the Trade Unions and Incomes Policy* (London, 1976).

—— *Working Class Politics in Crisis: Essays on Labour and the State* (London, 1986).

—— ed., *The Canadian State: Political Economy and Political Power* (Toronto, 1977).

PARKIN, F., *Class Inequality and Political Order* (London, 1971).

—— *Marxism and Class Theory: A Bourgeois Critique* (London, 1979).

—— ed., *Social Analysis of Class Structure* (London, 1974).

PARSONS, T., *Politics and Social Structure* (New York, 1969).

PAXTON, R. O., *Vichy France: Old Guard and New Order 1940–1944* (New York, 1982).

PIVEN, F. F. and CLOWARD, R. A., *Poor People's Movements: Why They Succeed, How They Fail* (New York, 1977).

—— *The New Class War: Reagan's Attack on the Welfare State and its Consequences* (New York, 1980).

Political Power and Social Theory, 1982– (Greenwich, Conn.,).

POULANTZAS, N., *Political Power and Social Classes* (London, 1973).

—— *State, Power, Socialism* (London, 1978).

—— *Classes in Contemporary Capitalism* (London, 1979).

PRZEWORSKI, A., *Capitalism and Social Democracy* (Cambridge, 1985).

RENTOUL, J., *The Rich Get Richer: The Growth of Inequality in the 1980s* (London, 1987).

ROSS, G., *Workers and Communists in France* (Berkeley, 1982).

ROSSITER, C. L., *Constitutional Dictatorship: Crisis Government in the Modern Democracies* (Princeton, 1967).

RUBINSTEIN, W. D., *Wealth and Inequality in Britain* (London, 1986).

SABEL, C. F., *Work and Politics: The Division of Labour in Industry* (Cambridge, 1982).

SARGENT, L., ed., *Women and Revolution: A Discussion of the Unhappy Marriage of Marxism and Feminism* (Boston, 1981).

SARTRE, J.-P., *Critique of Dialectical Reason* (London, 1976).

—— *L'Idiot de la famille: Gustave Flaubert de 1821–1857* (Paris, 1971–2).

SCHMITTER, P. and LEHNBRUCH, F., eds., *Trends toward Corporatist Intermediation* (London, 1979).

Socialist Register (London, 1964-).

SPRIANO, P., *Stalin and the European Communists* (London, 1985).

STE CROIX, G. DE, *The Class Struggle in the Ancient Greek World* (London, 1981).

STEPHENS, J. D., *The Transition from Capitalism to Socialism* (London, 1979).

STURMTHAL, A., *The Tragedy of European Labour* (London, 1944).

SULEIMAN, E., *Politics, Power and Bureaucracy in France* (London, 1974).

—— *Elites in French Society* (London, 1978).

THERBORN, G., *What Does the Ruling Class Do when it Rules?* (London, 1978).

THOMPSON, E. P., *The Making of the English Working Class* (London, 1963).

—— *The Poverty of Theory* (London, 1978).

TILLY, L. A. and C., *Class Conflict and Collective Action* (London, 1981).

TROTSKY, L., *The Struggle Against Fascism in Germany* (London, 1971).

TUCKER, R. C., ed., *The Marx-Engels Reader* (London, 1978).

URRY, J., *The Anatomy of Capitalist Societies: The Economy, Civil Society and the State* (London, 1981).

USEEM, M., *The Inner Circle: Large Corporations and the Rise of Political Activity in the US and the UK* (London and New York, 1984).

VOGEL, L., *Marxism and the Oppression of Women: Towards a Unitary Theory* (New Brunswick, NJ, 1983).

WAINWRIGHT, H., *Labour: A Tale of Two Parties* (London, 1987).

WALKER, A. and C., *The Growing Divide: A Social Audit, 1979–1987* (London, 1987).

WESTERGAARD, J. and RESLER, H., *Class in a Capitalist Society: A Study of Contemporary Britain* (London, 1975).

WILLIAMS, R., *Politics and Letters: Interviews with New Left Review* (London, 1979).

—— *Towards 2000* (London, 1983).

WILSON, E. and WEIR, A., *Hidden Agendas: Theory, Politics and Experience in the Women's Movement* (London, 1986).

WOLFE, A., *The Limits of Legitimacy* (New York, 1977).

WOOD, E. M., *The Retreat from Class: A New 'True' Socialism* (London, 1986).

WRIGHT, E. O., *Class, Crisis and the State* (London, 1978).

YERGIN, D., *Shattered Peace: The Origins of the Cold War and the National Security State* (Boston, 1978).

Index